BOMBER BOYS

BOMBER BOYS

MEL ROLFE

Bounty
Books

DEDICATION
To all the Bomber Boys

First published in 2004 by Grub Street Publishing

This edition published in 2015 by Bounty Books,
a division of Octopus Publishing Group Ltd
Endeavour House,
189 Shaftesbury Avenue,
London WC2H 8JY
www.octopusbooks.co.uk

An Hachette UK Company
www.hachette.co.uk

ISBN: 978-0-753728-23-9

A CIP catalogue record for this book is available from the British Library

Printed and bound by CPI Group (UK) Ltd, Croydon, CR0 4YY

CONTENTS

ACKNOWLEDGEMENTS

Many thanks to the former aircrew I interviewed for *Bomber Boys*. They endured my many questions with patience and good humour. There were others, too, whose help was invaluable in leading me to men with stories to tell, checking facts and pointing me in the direction of other sources of material. Thank you all for your assistance:

Roger Baldwin, Alan H. Bates DFM, Pete Barber, George Cash DFC, Sally Farman, Friends of Metheringham Airfield, Rob Glover, Raymond Glynne-Owen, Margery Griffiths, Hank Johnson, Victor Jordan, Kathleen Kellard, Walter Keul, Rainer Klug, Ve Lewis, Wallace McIntosh DFC and Bar, DFM, Jim Norris CGM, Gerry Payne, Des Richards, Gary Rolfe, the late John Sargeant DFM, Mark Sargeant, the late Reg Sargeant, Maisie and Leslie Sewards, Harry Shinkfield, David Steed, Bill Thomas, the late Ivor Turley, Terry Vamplew, Harry Warwick DFC, Joan Warwick, Bill Williams and David Winter.

I also thank Jessie, my darling wife, without whom my books would not have been written. The value of her encouragement is incalculable and includes: editing skills, gentle prodding when spirits flag, the ability to pounce voraciously on terrible grammar and tortured sentences – while waving her magic wand to unravel the brain-freezing complications of a new laptop computer – together with her general tenacious support which has, as usual, never wavered.

INTRODUCTION

They were mostly ordinary young men, many straight from school, with fresh and eager faces, who lived for the thrill of flying.

At a time when few twenty-year-olds had driven anything more powerful than a bicycle, or travelled in transport more swift or exotic than a bus,they were asked to fly in huge inhospitable bombers,packed with bombs,ammunition and high-octane fuel, deep into hostile territory to pulverise enemy strongholds, destroy cities, and kill other human beings.

Waiting in vast numbers was the enemy with guns and fighter aircraft, determined our bomber boys would never see another dawn.So full of life yet so close to death each time they flew off on another bombing operation.

Of approximately 125,000 aircrew who served in Bomber Command during the Second World War, over 55,500 lost their lives. Another 8,403 were wounded and 9,838, many of them injured, were prisoners of war. In addition, 2,835 men were killed at bomber operational training units from their inauguration in 1940 to 1947.

These are the stories of a few of those remarkable yet largely unsung men who helped crush Nazism and were later denied Bomber Command campaign medals by ungrateful and hypocritical governments. Survivors of a horrific war they are modest individuals, hating to be described as heroes, shrinking from a real fear of being accused by their contemporaries of shooting a line and suffering the scorn of others who know nothing about the bomber war and believe it could not happen like this. But it did.

CHAPTER ONE

RESCUE

The Dakota flew low, grinding doggedly over the endless jungle and forests of Burma, towards a hastily-constructed airstrip at an isolated position not even marked on a map. When the rugged DC3 had taken off from RAF Jessore, India, in June 1945, a small army of Siamese villagers 600 miles away was still putting the finishing touches to the makeshift runway which might just be long enough to accommodate it.

The aircraft's mission was to somewhere across Burma, beyond the great Mekong river into Siam, 300 miles behind the Japanese lines: a search which made the task of looking for a needle in a haystack a doddle.

It was dangerous, with no guarantee anyone in the Dakota would find the landing ground or come back alive. Two other Dakota crews had already failed. But if anyone could succeed it would be the pilot of the third Dakota, a big ebullient man with a degree of experience few could match, and who displayed great enthusiasm for every kind of job thrown at him.

Larry Lewis had joined the RAF in 1938 and trained as an aircraft rigger on Hawker Hinds and Hurricanes. After getting his feet off the ground he completed an operational tour of thirty-three sorties as an air gunner. Now he was a pilot and there was none better to negotiate this inhospitable terrain, much of which was uncharted wilderness of jungle, mountains and scrub, dotted with small remote villages, and Japanese strongholds.

Lewis was born on 25 October 1918 into a middle-class family in Bristol where his father, Harry, worked as a printer's representative. From an early age the boy wanted to be a pilot, but when offered the chance to train for a ground crew job on a fighter squadron he did not think it would be an end to his dreams, rather that it was the first positive step towards fulfilling them.

Even as a humble AC2 Lewis, a garrulous product of Bristol Grammar School, stood out among his peers. He was good looking, well built,6ft 1in,with dark-brown hair, twinkling hazel eyes, and a rapid way of talking, as if there was barely sufficient time to release the torrent of words stacked up inside his mind.

Rather more importantly, he had a photographic memory, which meant that during the early hectic days of the war when an aircraft needed to be repaired in a hurry, but competently, so it could be sent out in good shape to continue the fight, a job needed to be explained only once and he would do it without hesitation. He recalls:

'I was posted to Filton where 501 Squadron was converting from Hawker Hinds to Hurricanes.The rigger had control over any fabric surfaces, the hydraulics and cables. In those days the Hurricane was fabric-bodied so constantly available were a little bolt of Irish linen, a tin of dope, a brush, and needle and thread for sewing up any tears.

'The squadron moved to Middle Wallop, then France and I, only a junior member of the team, went to Manston to join a Boulton Paul Defiant servicing and refuelling unit during the evacuation of Dunkirk.

'The Luftwaffe was initially surprised to find a single-engine aircraft firing backwards from the turret but quickly learned to attack the fighter from underneath. A lot of Defiants got shot down and I saw my first casualties coming back to Manston.

'I rejoined 501 Squadron when it returned from France and immediately got immersed in the Battle of Britain. We went to Croydon, Kenley, Biggin Hill and Gravesend, which was the most exciting because it was in the Thames estuary. Huge formations of German aircraft, mostly Heinkels and Dorniers, came over the aerodrome passing up the estuary and we could see our own pilots engaged in battle. Occasionally we'd have a German pilot,who had been picked up in the south,coming to the airfield and being given a cigarette and cup of tea; looking after him before he was taken away.

'We watched vapour trails of aircraft wheeling around, heard the chatter of machine guns as dog fights took place and very often saw an aeroplane shot down. When our pilots returned, if they had been successful, they did a victory roll over the airfield.

'I observed this with great relish, but wanted to be closer to the action, although pushing an aeroplane about on the ground and strapping the pilot, Flying Officer Percy Pickup, into his cockpit was a thrill for me.

'The CO called me in one day to say the pilot's course was still pending, but they were short of bomber aircrew. Would I be interested in being an air gunner?'

He spent four weeks training at Manby, Lincolnshire, graduating as sergeant on 19 October 1940, joining 12 Squadron, which was converting from Fairey Battles to Wellington Mk IIs at Tollerton, Nottinghamshire, later moving to Binbrook.

'I just fitted into the turret, my head touching the rotating service joint. It was ferociously cold because we had no heated clothing and the only way I could keep the circulation going in my hands was by beating the back of the guns with my palms. The only entertainment available in the turret was trying to unwrap the paper from a Horlicks tablet with hands encased in several pairs of gloves. I dropped quite a few tablets while maintaining my vigil searching the sky for enemy fighters.'

Lewis completed his tour more quickly than his crewmates because he was always willing to join other crews who needed a gunner. On 24 July 1941, the squadron commander, Wing Commander Maw, told him his rear gunner was getting married and the tail turret needed occupying for the daylight raid on Brest.

Bomber Command's plan had originally been to attack two battleships, *Scharnhorst* and *Gneisenau*, holed up in Brest harbour. This was changed at the last minute when it was learned *Scharnhorst* had left for La Pallice. Fifteen Halifaxes were despatched to La Pallice, inflicting sufficient damage on the warship for it to be returned to Brest for repairs.

Maw piloted Wellington W5397 which left Binbrook at 11.30am to join another ninety-nine bombers heading for Brest.

'We came in low on the bombing run,' says Lewis. 'It was extremely dangerous and we were immediately met by blistering anti-aircraft fire from the battleship, no more than 200ft below. Wg Cdr Maw said calmly:"Hold your water chaps, we've got to take our medicine."

'Regrettably, but not surprisingly, our bombs overshot the target,then we got mixed up in a balloon barrage in the harbour and just as we got away from that we were jumped by a Messerschmitt-109. I said:"Do you mind if I keep the intercom on, it's getting a bit exciting back here?"

'We fought off three attacks,two from the beam and one from absolute dead rear. The German must have been an amateur because I could see the trails from his bullets going just under my turret. He seemed upset by the fire from the rear turret and turned away. Flying across the harbour I said to the skipper:"The natives are friendly, two fishermen are waving to us."

'We came home about fifty feet above the sea, badly shot up. Holes were all over the place, the flaps hung down and great strips of fabric fluttered past my turret which had a few bits knocked out of it.'

Shortly afterwards Maw called the gunner to his office and said:'Lewis, I would like to recommend you for a commission.'

He replied: 'That's very flattering Sir. I appreciate that very much, but I would really prefer my pilot's course.' Maw smiled and said:'We might be able to engineer both.' A few weeks later Lewis was a pilot officer and Maw had recommended him to be awarded the DFM.

Lewis's skipper was Sergeant Cab Kellaway, from Paignton, who would complete three tours, finishing with 617 Squadron A gentle fellow, but very determined,he told Lewis at a reunion fifty years later that he had been briefed to go on the Dambusters' raid but while practising low-level flying was slip-streamed by the Lancaster in front and had crashed.

'We were coned by searchlights three or four times on the tour,' says Lewis.'We always managed to get out of it,diving and corkscrewing, but the anti-aircraft fire got more fierce as additional searchlights were beamed on to us and we felt naked with all that light around. I carried a few empty beer bottles in the turret which I dropped out when we were coned. I doubt this did any good but it was my own little offensive against the Germans and made me feel better.

'Coming back across the North Sea we met Dorniers and Heinkels, having bombed England, going the other way, 300 to 400 yards from us, which was exciting. But it was not our business, nor theirs, to engage the enemy. Our job was to drop bombs and return to base. It was the night fighters' responsibility to shoot down the bombers on either side. Besides, you'd give away your position and might lose a valuable aircraft.

'We had the most crude navigational equipment. You relied on loop bearings on top of the aircraft which gave you information from two different stations in England and you hoped to plot a position. There was no radar, it was all dead reckoning navigation. You took off, flew at a certain height, hoping you had the right wind, but we got lost a couple of times, including the night of 19/20 September 1941 in bad weather after attacking Bremen.

'For some reason the loop bearings were not satisfactory, we were running out of fuel and Cab told us to put on our parachutes. We crawled across the North Sea, landing at the first available airfield, Coltishall, Norfolk, one of the engines cutting out as we touched down.

'We were attacked and knocked about by two fighters one night. They were no more than darting dark shadows and we escaped again.'

At the end of his tour Lewis collected the DFM from King George VI and was posted in early 1942 as a flight lieutenant to instruct at 12 OTU, Chipping Warden, Northamptonshire.

A week after his arrival he heard from Binbrook that his old crew had been shot down off the Dutch coast. The rear gunner who had replaced Lewis, and the copilot, were killed. The injured skipper, Flight Lieutenant Paddy Thallon, who crash-landed his aircraft on Terschelling island, had been copilot to Kellaway, who had already moved on.

Lewis rented a small house near the airfield, installed his wife, Ve, pregnant with their first child, and bought an ancient rickety Austin Seven for two pounds. It had a drop head, split windscreen, and crepe bandages wrapped tightly around threadbare tyres. He was very proud of the car and named it Timoshenko after a Russian tank commander.

'I had a few hairy moments with sprog crews, but was lecturing more than flying. Then, all of a sudden, some of us were called up to take part in the first 1,000-bomber raid in these old aircraft. I flew with Flight Lieutenant Dougie Farmer.'

The OTU operated Wellingtons which had been retired from front-line duty but were thought adequate for training novice crews. Lifting off at 11pm, they were among 1,047 aircraft which attacked Cologne on 30 May 1942.

'When we arrived at 16,000ft Cologne was a sea of fire from one end to the other. The greatest danger to us was in colliding over the target with so many bombers milling about, some skippered by sprog pilots. We saw many going down, some from flak, others from night fighters. We had near collisions too and heard anti-aircraft shells exploding all around us. Our aircraft jumped with the near misses and the smell of cordite seeped through every aperture. I had a few shots against night fighters and occasionally fired down at the searchlights, but that was no more than a token gesture, like chucking out beer bottles.

'It was an extraordinary sensation. You knew you were dropping high explosives, but there was no animosity to the people down there. You felt sad about the Germans bombing our cities and seeing the devastation and we had to do something to carry the fight. But it was more of a professional exercise to get to the right place, drop the bombs at the right time and return to base. You did not think about that bomb going off and smashing a perambulator to pieces. You hoped it would fall on a munitions factory.'

Two nights later Lewis flew with Farmer to Essen when only 956 bombers could be mustered, but bombing was said to be scattered, less successful than Cologne. Seventy-four bombers were lost on the two sorties.

'My wife and I were going along quite nicely, the family life and all that, when suddenly the pilot's course came through to my great surprise and joy.'

Posted to an initial training wing at Torquay, Lewis rented a flat near the action for himself, Ve and their baby son, Peter, and was precipitated into what he describes as 'the magical world of pilot training'.

'ITW taught you navigation with Mercator's projection, star recognition, astro-navigation, meteorology, aircraft recognition, the Morse code, and so on. All brand-new subjects, all fascinating. Less fun was putting on someone else's cold wet Mae West, to jump twenty or thirty feet off the pier into the sea and turn over a big dinghy before righting it again for the next chap and then swimming ashore.

'Afterwards, at a little pre-AFU outside Manchester, I did six hours' training in a Tiger Moth which is the best plane ever designed, wonderfully strong and a joy to fly. The instructor said: "Okay Lewis, off you go. Solo." That was the most tremendous thrill. Just one circuit but I sang, roared and shouted because of the thrill of being up in the air. I could fly.'

Lewis, a decorated flight lieutenant, with thirty-three bombing operations behind him, joined an elementary flying training course packed with AC2s in Bowden, north of Calgary, Canada, where he was invited to speak at several war bond rallies.He passed out top of his course before submitting to more advanced training at other Canadian airfields.

After returning to England for a few weeks he was posted in February 1945 to Jessore, Bengal, to start his second tour in special duties with 357 Squadron, which was equipped with Liberators,Dakotas, Lysanders and Austers. Jessore, some 85 miles north-west of Calcutta, was hardly love at first sight to Lewis.

'Jessore was awful. It was a little jungle airstrip. In our spare time we lounged about in the mess, playing a lot of darts and having a drink, mainly Carew's Indian gin, which we knew was safe. There was also Motan's Indian brandy, Motan's rum and Motan's whisky. It was all the same, with different labels,and we were lucky not to go blind drinking it.The beer was not much cop. The food was terrible. We consumed a good deal of curried pigeons which put me off curries forever. The only consolation was the bananas, tiny, not much bigger than your thumb and very sweet. You could eat ten or twelve at a sitting.I didn't catch anything serious in the Far East, although others were going down with dysentery and cholera.I think the drinking kept me healthy.

'We slept in bashas, rather primitive but substantial structures of wood, with beds made of rope and wood, covered by mosquito nets. We were a mixed-bag squadron. We had English and Burmese officers and Gurkha troops, and were given a whole host of mysterious operations to do, all very secret and exciting. They had code names like Mongoose Blue, Cutter, Otter and Squirrel. We took English or Burmese officers with a patrol of Gurkhas, who were probably going to attempt to destroy a Japanese position.We had to find tiny obscure clearings in the jungle or paddy fields, not easy in monsoon conditions. They radioed back to say whether the drop had been successful and we supplied them with food, money and ammunition.

'Sometimes the dropping zone was in a valley with mountains and jungle all around which meant a spiralling descent or sideslipping down to get to the right height, eighty feet or so, to drop supplies.'

Germany surrendered to the Allies on 4 May 1945, but fighting continued grimly against Japan in the Far East. So it was that, at 3.30am on 23 June 1945, well into the monsoon season, a Dakota lifted off in the dark from Jessore airfield with Larry Lewis at the controls.

About three weeks previously, a Liberator with a crew of ten Americans had crashed in a remote part of Siam. Radio contact had been established and the skipper reported everyone unharmed except one injured man. Siamese policemen found a piece of suitable ground, a recently-abandoned paddy field, and began organising villagers to convert it into a crude air strip. Two previous rescue attempts had failed when Dakota crews could not locate the tiny runway. All they had been given were the latitude and longitude readings. Much depended on the pinpoint dead reckoning skills of Lewis's navigator, Pilot Officer Bertie Cumber.

'We had not been warned about possible hazards or areas to avoid because our senior officers didn't know the sort of territory we would have to go over,' says Lewis. 'We knew Japanese air strips were not in the immediate vicinity of our destination so we were unlikely to meet any Zero fighters, but we might come under fire from the ground. As we were in the dark most of the way out we flew at our normal height, 5,000ft to 6,000ft, climbing over the ridge of mountains running down the spine of Burma, known as The Hump.

'To me, trying to get to a very obscure location with no other assistance than the skill of the navigator plus a bit of local knowledge from a chap who came with us, was a fascinating exercise. It was also a trip which needed intense concentration. The major difficulty was navigation because all the maps of Burma were pretty sparse with many large white patches, listing only major towns and the rivers. The weather, too, could be ferocious in the monsoon season. All these operations – dropping people and supplies – had to be done at the crack of dawn before the clouds and humid atmosphere obscured mountain tops. Gaining altitude we guessed our climbing speed and hoped we would miss the mountains.

'Once, early in the tour, I wondered whether it was possible to fly under the monsoon. I went up and down valleys, through mountains, with rain pouring down and trees on either side, landing at Meiktila. I'd done it but it was foolhardy and I didn't attempt it again.

'The Dakota was a wonderful gentlemanly aircraft,a real work horse.You could fly at very low speeds without stalling. It could use a short takeoff and landing space if necessary, didn't have any vicious characteristics and was, providing you knew what you were doing, extremely docile.

'We were lucky with the weather that day, pleasant all the way, but we had to refuel after 300 miles at Imphal which was in an area being gallantly defended by British troops and which still had a little airfield. We took off from there and came under fire from a few enemy machine guns but they didn't hit us.

'There were ten of us in the Dakota, my own crew, and a number of specialists, including a medical chap, someone who could speak the language when we got there and, very importantly, the fellow who knew the territory. He recognised the Mekong river when we flew over it and that was a good pinpoint for us.'

It was an exciting moment when, soon after dawn, they spotted the air strip which looked no bigger than a tiny footprint in the great sprawling tangled mass of vegetation surrounding it.

'It was not much more than a jungle clearing and had been marked by recognition letters and a white cross, showing the direction of the wind. I made two or three passes to check that I could get in. We could see people waving as I decided it was just long enough,800 to 900 yards, but very narrow which,with the Dakota's ninety-five foot wing span, made it a tight fit,with scrub undergrowth on either side. There were no trees in the way but hedges were growing at both ends of the runway, so we had to touch down very accurately on to the strip immediately after crossing them.

'You have to get the speed exactly right so you don't go too fast or too far. I managed to get down and quickly put the brakes on, but they were not all that effective on that sort of surface, which was like a damp field.I had about fifty yards to spare when we stopped. I swung round and taxied up to some little huts where the Americans had been kept and turned off the engines. They came tumbling out,carrying on a stretcher a chap who had injured his back.They were delighted to see us and I told them: "Please get loaded up as quickly as you can. We don't want to hang about here too long." I couldn't see the crashed Liberator and supposed they had set fire to it, the Americans didn't tell me and there was no time to talk.

'We got everybody inside and it was time to go. I had to start up the engines and this was always a tense moment. Would they start? If not I might end up as a prisoner of war, or they might have to send another aeroplane. The engines started but the aircraft began sinking into the soft spongy ground. It was getting a bit hairy, we had to get out of there fast. I got a crowd of villagers to push the aircraft on the trailing edge of the wings to get it moving a little bit. They did all right, got out of the way and we taxied as close as I could to the end of the strip and turned into position. I opened up the throttles against the brakes as much as I dared to get maximum thrust, without touching the props on the ground, let off the brakes, sprang forward and belted down the field, just clearing the hedges at the end.

'Now we had to try to get back without attracting the attention of the Japanese Air Force. We returned on a different course. It was daylight and we were at zero feet, hedge hopping all the way, dodging anything which appeared to be nefarious. We hadn't got any guns, except revolvers, but my crew kept watch and a despatcher was looking out the side door.

'We were fired at a few times. We could see some of the machine-gun nests and I spoke to one of the despatchers, Shag O'Shaughnessy, a burly bluff Irish-American, who once impressed us at a remote air strip when he advanced on a battered piano and played boogie-woogie with the fingers of an angel. "Open the door, Shag, we're being shot at. If you want a bit of fun take a few pot shots with your revolver".'

So he did. None of the Japanese machine-gun bullets came close to the Dakota. Nor, it is believed, did any of O'Shaughnessy's exuberant potting create problems for the Japanese.

'We landed at a small air strip to refuel, then on to Dum Dum airfield at Calcutta. To my great surprise there was a reception party waiting, with a few VIPs scattered about. They didn't take much notice of me. I was thanked laconically, but to them I was a bit like a bus driver, and they immediately pushed off with the Liberator crew who were very pleased to be back.'

Lewis received a DFC for this trip, which had taken eleven hours.

One of the more bizarre jobs given to Lewis was Operation Numeral, before the invasion of Rangoon when his flight commander, Squadron Leader Pat O'Brien, told him one aircraft was needed to create a diversion.

It was a secret plan devised among the highest echelons of the RAF in the Far East and had to be carried through with all the expertise and panache expected from an experienced and imaginative British officer.

'My job was to go to Rangoon when the Allied seaborne forces were coming in and drop hundreds of 'paratroops' made from sandbags. They were small, but with heads, arms and legs, and they came down on little parachutes, quite realistic seen from a distance. I had to give the impression that it was an airborne invasion. I flew in with the first batch then ducked down behind mountains and trees or into clouds and came back from different angles, pretending we were another aeroplane with more paratroops. I did that many times.'

In the back of the Dakota on 28 June Sergeant O'Shaughnessy presided calmly over great heaps of little sandmen which were pushed in a steadily impressive stream through the door. Also dropped were fireworks which exploded spectacularly, simulating gunfire, over a wide area of the jungle.

The game would, of course, have been up if the Japanese had discovered only one of the sandbag mannikins. But the plan seemed so shrewd and innovative that it went ahead, in an attempt to create a wave of confusion and panic among the fleeing enemy, and, although Lewis never heard about the success of his deception, the Japanese Army was eventually evicted from Rangoon.

At the end of the war Larry Lewis, and other officers from 357 Squadron, flew Lysanders into tiny remote jungle air strips to pay off villagers who had helped the Allied war effort. Leaving the aircraft, carrying a bag of money, Lewis mounted the waiting elephant, steered by a mahout, to ride in some style through the jungle to villages where feasts with rice wine and entertainment had been prepared, and long moving speeches were made to The Great White King Across The Water.

Larry Lewis had flown on sixty-three operations and was a squadron leader when he was demobbed. Nearly sixty years on he says: 'I was in the RAF from 1938 to 1945 and loved every minute. It took me out of a relatively humdrum environment, changing my life for ever. I made a lot of friends and, sadly, lost a great number of them. So many good chaps did not come back.'

But his proudest moment was, at the end of it all, reading in his logbook Squadron Leader O'Brien's assessment of his flying ability: 'Exceptional'.

CHAPTER TWO

DITCHING

The Lancaster, gliding down through the sky like a huge black bird searching for a perch, struck the water with a terrible, violent thud. The inside of the aircraft became blurred from the vibration and many cubic feet of the North Sea immediately poured in a freezing torrent through various apertures, the largest being the gaping hole aft of the bomb bay. This rear section broke off and began floating away as Joe 'Mac' Thompson, the mid-upper gunner, struggled to release the dinghy.

The dinghy sea switch did not work and Thompson located the emergency release cord at the top right-hand side of the fuselage. He pulled it, hand over hand until he stared at the broken end of wire.

'It's useless,' he said aghast, as rising water slopped around their feet. 'Must have been the impact.'

It was the afternoon of 12 December 1944. They had left Chedburgh, Suffolk, at 11.04am to bomb Witten. Damaged by flak the Lancaster had tottered helplessly towards England and was now sinking beneath them with the dinghy trapped inside the starboard wing. It was their first sortie together. Chances were, it would be their last.

The crew had fretted at Chedburgh the previous day when their skipper, Flight Lieutenant Harry Warwick, had flown on his first operation as second dickey with an experienced pilot. Aircrews became close, welded into a unit, during the comparatively short time they were together, relying on each other for support and comfort. When the valued leader of that unit left to be blooded with another bunch of fellows, unease often set in.

Warwick's rear gunner, Sergeant Ivor Turley, from Birmingham, later wrote: 'We'd watched his aeroplane take off that cold crisp morning. For several hours we had been headless, full of foreboding, morose, irritable, deep in thought and prayer. A whole day, it seemed, of sickness and worry. What if he didn't come back?'

The drone of the first of the returning bombers sent them hastily to the airfield, watching the Lancasters land. Then to the debriefing hut and there was the skipper, safe and well, grinning expansively.

'Hello chaps, it's not too bad.'

They had joined 218 (Gold Coast) Squadron not long before. Looking forward to that first testing op, yet dreading the uncertainty of it.

In the briefing room they learned their target was the large coking plants at Witten in the Ruhr.

Their steed was a Lancaster I, PB766 HA C-Charlie, waiting silently to take them on board as they stepped off the crew bus. Exhaustive checks were made before they went outside for a last cigarette.

Mac Thompson knelt and kissed the ground. He slapped the earth and said:

'Ta-ta love, shan't be long. Don't forget to be here when I come back.'

He rose, the others grabbed him, pushing the gunner up the ladder into the bomber. Their laughter helped diminish the tension.

Turley closed and secured the rear door, plugged into a nearby intercom point and reported:

'Okay Skip, rear door closed and locked.' Lumbering laboriously in his heavy flying gear, Turley crawled through the gap by the tailplane spar into the rear turret. He unlocked the turret, and turned it, depressing and raising the guns, making sure rotation was free. Plugging in his heated suit he repeated his checks, then found he had forgotten the Thermos flask of hot tea. The consequent irritation made him feel overwhelmingly thirsty.

The engines started in sequence, the bomber shaking and shuddering as they roared into life. The cockpit was a well-organised office.

Warwick, a fraction under six feet, well-built and charismatic, had been brought up from the age of two by his mother in Westminster, London, after the death of his father from influenza during the 1918 epidemic. He had been a Metropolitan policeman before joining up in August 1941.

Sergeant Tom Waring, from Sheffield, the flight engineer, focused on banks of dials and instruments, would assist his pilot during takeoff.

Flying Officer Alex Stott, an Oxford undergraduate from Plymouth, the navigator, hunched over a map, busy with dividers and pencil, would be the skipper's best man at his wedding the following January. Wireless operator Sergeant Joe Naisbitt, concentrating on his T1154/R1155 transmitter/receiver sets, came from Liverpool.

The bomb aimer, Flying Officer Bill Perry, from Charlton Kings, near Cheltenham, who had played rugby for Gloucestershire, tried to make himself comfortable in the nose.

The bomber moved slowly forward and Turley felt the tail end swing as Warwick lined the aeroplane up with the exit from the dispersal pen. The ground crew gave them the thumbs up as they rattled on to the perimeter track. The tail wheel jolted over ruts and holes, shaking the turret and Turley inside it:

'The briefing room came into view and with it crowds of bods watching each kite as it rolled by. They gave the V-sign to us all. My turret was facing port, guns elevated, sliding door behind me open. I was ready to roll out backwards if anything went wrong.'

Nothing did go wrong. Their takeoff was perfect, the fields and ancient thatched cottages of Suffolk falling away as they clawed into the sky. C–Charlie shook briefly and sideslipped after hitting the slipstream of another Lancaster. They circled and slowly caught up with the formation leader, Q–Queenie. C–Charlie was the second of three Lancasters, with 218 Squadron proudly leading the stream.

The bombers climbed out near Clacton-on-Sea, turned to port and continued climbing. The increasing cold seeped into the rear turret where Turley, suffering from cramp, found he could escape some of the icy draught through the open front of the turret, by squeezing back in his seat.

They crossed the French coast with Dunkirk to starboard and as the rear gunner peered at the bombers behind he saw eight black puffs of smoke. He recalls:

'They bloomed slowly into large black mushrooms. I saw another cluster of eight. This time they looked white, the sun's rays glinting off them. How pretty they looked hanging there in the clear air like ragged balloons. This then was flak.'

As they neared their bombing height of 20,000ft the navigator said they were almost at the appointed rendezvous with their fighter escort. The gunners searched the sky but could not see them. It would be comforting to be protected by the Brylcreem boys.

'My operating of the turret controls was now fully automatic. Search, search and search again. Monotonous, but our lives depended on it.

'The stream had lengthened considerably, the rear formations being reduced to dots which occasionally became distorted by the heat and slipstream from our engines. I was very cold. A draught was hitting my knees, cutting through my flying clothes. Leaning forward the icy blast coming from the clear vision panel – the gap in the perspex – struck my forehead and eyes. My forehead became icily numb. Pushing my gauntleted fingers under the flying helmet I pulled down the front of my balaclava so only my eyes were uncovered. I could no longer feel any warmth from elements in my electric suit, chills were coursing up my spine and I shivered.

'I thought my electric suit had packed up and switched the power off. Within seconds the icy cold reached every part of me. I began stiffening and hurriedly switched the suit back on. They weren't kidding when they said it was cold at 20,000ft.'

The rear gunner checked his guns, sliding the breech blocks backwards and forwards. They were okay. Depressing the guns and finding a piece of sky not occupied by aeroplanes, he fired a short burst to clear the barrels.

Their expected escort had still not been seen, then Turley spotted a column of small aircraft approaching on their port beam. No one was sure if they were friend or foe. A brown plummet of smoke swirled among the newcomers and Turley cried:

'Skip, bandits! Stand by, intercoms on.'

'Right chaps,' said Warwick, calmly. 'Watch them closely, they may try to pick us off as leaders. I'm closing on our leader now.'

Lancasters began weaving as the wolf pack of Messerschmitt Bf-109s tore among them, picking out victims. To port and below a fighter attacked a Lancaster which, too late, began corkscrewing. Flames appeared in the bomber's port wing, but the fighter, not satisfied, continued firing. The Lancaster turrets did not respond, the fire spread, and a swirl of smoke turned into a shroud as the bomber began falling in a slow spiral.

Another Lancaster, sinking fast, trailed smoke from an engine. Fighters seemed to be everywhere, consumed by an insatiable bloodlust, snarling and snapping. Parachutes floated among the blood bath.

The gunners, eyeing the carnage, attempting to absorb the turmoil around them, tried to anticipate which fighter might turn on C-Charlie. A fighter broke off its attack on a nearby Lancaster and the sound of heavy breathing was heard over the intercom. Turley recalls the moment.

'"Woosh! Wham!" Our aircraft rose, the noise of an explosion deafened me and the cold hand of panic clutched my heart. I heard the sound of metal clattering along the fuselage and tail and felt a blow on the back of the turret.'

The Lancaster had been hit by flak on the starboard side. A chunk of flak burst through the cockpit and nearly hit Tom Waring in the head.

'It's okay,' said the pilot. 'I've got her, we're under control.'

A Bf-109 lined up on their port quarter and began its charge. Ivor Turley, in his tiny turret, turned to face the attack.

'My foot felt a hole in the bottom of the turret. My sights lined up, I had him. The air felt thin. "Crump! Whoosh! Wham!" Another explosion. The aeroplane jumped and shuddered. I heard metal tearing and dimly realised we were trailing smoke from our port wing.'

The flak shells had exploded on the starboard side, damaging the fuel tanks.

'The Bf-109 was still in my sights, its spinner looked enormous. "Fire! Fire the bloody guns!" I screamed at myself. Cracks appeared across my vision, a flash of perspex pieces and cold air hit me and I seemed to have no strength in my arms. I saw the yellow belly of the fighter and gasped into my microphone: "My oxygen's gone".'

He came to forward of the tailplane, sitting on the Elsen toilet. His oxygen pipe was plugged in and he could see a pair of knees which belonged to someone holding an oxygen bottle. It was Joe Naisbitt, the wireless operator. He gestured for the gunner to plug his intercom point to the lead hanging in the fuselage, before struggling back to his position.

'Rear gunner here, Skip. I'm okay now.'

'Good show, we'll soon have you home.'

'How are we doing and where are we?' Turley inquired, shakily.

'We've bombed the target and are on our way home. The starboard inner's been hit, we've got holes in the wing and are trailing fuel, but don't worry. We're under control.'

Turley took stock of his surroundings.

'The fuselage was torn and I could see petrol gushing along the trailing edge of our port wing. I looked towards and beyond my turret. We were leaving a trail of vapour. I tried to crawl back to my position, stretching the oxygen pipe as far as it would go. I couldn't quite reach the turret, but saw it was useless. There was no bottom to it, no perspex, and jagged chunks of fuselage curled in from the tail unit. Oil from the broken servo pipes was everywhere. I crawled backwards and sat again on the Elsen. I felt bloody useless.'

'How are we doing, Tom?' the pilot asked.

'We're losing fuel fast,' said the engineer. 'We won't make it if we follow the stream.'

'Okay Tom.' Then, to the navigator. 'Alex, plot us the straightest course to Woodbridge. Give me a heading, we're leaving the main stream.'

'I've already got it for you,' said Stott.

The Lancaster turned and Turley, looking through a flak hole, saw the rest of the stream flying on the port side. C-Charlie would soon be alone, at the mercy of any fighter.

'How's the fuel, Tom?' Warwick asked. 'Have we enough?'

'I've worked out that we can make it to Woodbridge on three at the present rate.'

Turley, looking through a flak hole on the port side, saw that the port outer engine was stopped and the prop feathered.

'Okay boys, don't worry,' said the pilot. 'We've enough petrol and she's flying okay. Stay on intercom.'

Mac Thompson suddenly announced: 'We've company on the starboard beam. A fighter.' As hearts leaped, he added: 'It's one of ours.'

A Mustang moved in close, tucking his wing in behind and slightly below theirs. The pilot, Flight Sergeant Wright, from

Andrew's Field, Essex, gave them a thumbs-up, before moving out slightly.

'He'll look after us now,' said Warwick. As intended, his optimism infiltrated the rest of the crew. But good news was quickly followed by bad as the Lancaster vibrated, an engine coughed and missed a beat. They dipped to port.

'Port inner's going,' reported the pilot, his voice displaying no alarm. 'I'm feathering now.'

The revs were increased in the two starboard engines and the bomber lurched to the right as the pilot lowered the starboard wing.

'I've got her, we're at 14,000ft now. How's the fuel, Tom?'

'I'm not sure, Skipper,' said Waring, cautiously. 'We're getting very low. I'll work it out again.'

'We're losing height and the air speed is dropping, Alex. We're at 12,000ft. I must keep the nose down a little to maintain flying speed. I'm going straight in at Woodbridge, no circuit. Where are we?'

'Somewhere over the Zuider Zee, Skip.'

'Sorry Skip, we won't make it.' The engineer broke in, glumly checking his calculations.

'Ten thousand feet, Alex, 130 knots,' said Warwick, doggedly.

'We can't make it, Harry,' said the navigator. 'We're too low unless you can glide us in most of the way, or stay at this height for a bit.'

A roar and splutter reverberated through the aircraft as it dipped, pulling up as power was restored. They were now flying above several layers of cloud.

'The starboard inner's going,' said the pilot. The engine noise increased and, just as suddenly, was cut by half. 'Starboard inner engine's feathered,' said Warwick. They were reduced to a single engine, flying over water. The emergency airfield at Woodbridge, Suffolk, might have been on Mars.

With both inboard engines feathered the pilot's normal blind-flying instruments were now useless because they had no suction to operate them. The let down through the cloud could only be done on the turn and bank instruments. It was a dangerous situation, one not relished by any pilot, but he and his crew remained calm.

'We've lost too much fuel,' said the engineer. I'm on wing tanks to starboard, we're losing them. I can't balance the tanks.'

'I'll try to hold her on the starboard outer, but we're losing height fast,' said Warwick.

The revs on the solitary engine were stepped up, the engine screamed. The aeroplane shook and staggered. The pilot's voice remained steady, optimistic.

'Okay boys, do we bale out or stay with the Lanc?'

There was no hesitation. They would remain with the skipper. He would get them out of this if anyone could.

'Right, let's see how far we can go. We're at 9,000ft, just entering cloud. Joe, send out emergency signals. Give us our position, Alex.'

Stott gave their position as over the North Sea, close to the Dutch coast.

'Now at 8,000ft,' said Warwick.

The note of the starboard outer engine dipped, coughed and stopped. The nose of C-Charlie dropped and as the roar of the engine faded they heard the shriek of the slipstream and buffeting wind.

Ivor Turley remembers being lifted from the Elsen seat by G-force as they rapidly lost height. Suddenly, the starboard outer engine picked up and a little surge of power rippled through the Lancaster.

'Don't worry, we'll be okay,' said the pilot, calmly. 'I'll call out the altitude as we go down.'

It was time to go to ditching positions. Turley disconnected his oxygen pipe and intercom plug and moved forward to help Thompson, sliding down from his turret. Bill Perry, the bomb aimer, settled on the bunk Thompson jettisoned the overhead escape hatch and the two gunners lay on the floor which formed the top of the bomb bay. Turley plugged into the intercom point hanging next to him and told Thompson, who did not have one, that he would show him the height on his fingers as it came through from the skipper. Turley recalls:

'I clipped my mask to my face, switched on my mike and reported: "Rear and mid-upper gunners in position, Skipper. Good luck." The crew reported in turn and I lay there with Mac listening to the roar of our one engine, seeing the fuselage twitch as we rolled and yawed and the skipper corrected. There were no other thoughts except what if I broke a leg or arm on impact? Would it hurt much?'

'Four thousand feet,' said the pilot. Turley signalled 'four' to

Thompson just before the engine spluttered and died. The nose tilted forward and the engine roared again. The aircraft straightened and the pilot reported they were now at 3,000ft. The engine died again only to bellow defiantly seconds later.

'It seemed to me,' says Turley, 'that somewhere petrol was swilling into the carburettor pipes when we dipped forward sufficiently to cause the engine to pick up as long as the prop turned it over. I lay perfectly calm now, listening and waiting for the inevitable.'

The pilot again: 'Can't see a bloody thing yet. We're still in cloud.'

The starboard outer cut once more, the nose dipped, and everyone waited for the engine to tease them again by coming back to life. It did not. The cutting wind sounded more sinister.

'Two thousand feet,' said Warwick, unruffled. And almost in the same breath: 'One thousand feet.'

There was a roar in their ears, the engine was back in business and the nose pulled up a little jauntily.

'I see it,' said the pilot, clinging to the controls. 'Four hundred feet. Stand by for impact.'

In the stuttering seconds it took to recover from the shock of ditching and the apparent loss of their dinghy, the fevered scrambling about, bumping clumsily against each other inside the marooned bomber, clambering out on top of the fuselage and sniffing the unaccustomed salt air, they went swiftly through a variety of moods. These touched on any words which equated to catastrophe and hopelessness, how long it would take the Lanc to sink and would there be any wreckage to cling to. They had not wanted to be sailors for Christ's sake. They stared in despair at the vast empty sea and imagined themselves as constituting a tiny nonentity bobbing pathetically upon it.

It took the consistently positive Harry Warwick a single inspired moment of leadership to restore hope and faith. The pilot pulled himself through the escape hatch above his seat and sat on the edge of the cockpit canopy with his back to them. He looked round and as he pulled his legs clear, grinned broadly.

'Well boys, we made it,' he shouted. And there was such a look of triumph on his face, they knew they must get through this one miserable little setback.

Ivor Turley, who found that his watch had stopped at 3.20pm, wrote afterwards: 'For a brief moment I felt that all was over.

Then, just as quickly, I now realised we had to survive.'

The skipper slid down to the starboard wing, joining the others. They looked up at the sound of an aircraft. It was the faithful Mustang, circling his charges.

'Where's the bloody dinghy?' someone yelled.

'Still in the hatch,' shouted Naisbitt, pointing at the dinghy panel in the wing. The sea switch release system had not worked.

In the top right-hand corner of the panel was a rectangle of perspex, with water splashing over it. Naisbitt broke the panel after several hefty kicks with the heel of his flying boot. Alex Stott immediately thrust his hand in the hole. There was a hiss and an explosion as the dinghy inflated. A wave swept over the wing carrying the dinghy and navigator away towards the tail section which was separated from the fuselage by a gap of six feet spanned by sagging belts of ammunition. Stott's head bobbed up, striking the bottom of the tailplane. He was clutching the dinghy.

Turley jumped into the icy water, but hampered by his bulky clothing, struggled to reach his crewmate. He got to the dinghy and tried to swim with it to the others on the wing. He was a good swimmer, but his clothes were waterlogged and his strength was waning. Afraid the dinghy would be swept away, he searched unsuccessfully for the green cord which should have secured it to the aircraft.

Turley says: 'In an ideal situation it should have been floating with its tether so we could leave the aeroplane to step into it, keeping reasonably dry.'

He yelled for the others to help and they thrashed through the turbulent water towards him. Turley found the rope ladder hanging from the side but was too exhausted to use it. Many hands reached down to pull him up, then the inflation lever on his Mae West hooked on the ratline around the dinghy. He was pushed back into the water to get untangled before flopping into the drenched dinghy. Ration boxes, first-aid kit, other vital items for survivors, and tins of Very pistol cartridges were recovered from various tethering points around the dinghy.

It now seemed to be a sensible idea to move away from the wreckage. They undid the hand panels from a ration tin and began a flurry of paddling, but the effort used was disproportionate to the distance covered and after crawling some thirty yards they settled in the dinghy and dreamed of how delicious that first beer would taste back in the mess.

Beneath the lowering cloud, the sea swell became heavier, tossing the dinghy about with increasing vigour. They all sat around it, their feet meeting in the middle. Alex Stott was holding a soaked bloody handkerchief round his finger.

The skipper looked concerned. 'What have you done, Alex?'

'It's nothing to worry about, Skipper. I cut my finger getting the dinghy out.'

The skipper leaned across with a bandage to clumsily bind the badly-cut finger then asked his navigator if he knew where they were.

Stott reached inside his Mae West, produced a sodden and crumpled map, and estimated they were some sixty miles east of Woodbridge. Joe Naisbitt said he had been sending their position since shortly before ditching. Their optimism remained high.

'Okay,' said Warwick. 'In any case our faithful escort up there should be able to transmit our position.'

It took fifteen minutes for the tail unit to be swallowed by the sea. Thirty-five minutes later it was followed by the Lancaster's main section.

Water was becoming increasingly deeper in the dingy and Turley began baling with a first-aid tin as the others erected the yellow weather apron which protected them from wind and spray. Bill Perry was violently sick and Turley soon joined him heaving over the side.

The Mustang circled low, then turned straight for them, waggling its wings before disappearing into the thickening mist. They listened to the fading engine, each with a deepening sense of loneliness, hoping their position had been logged somewhere and a boat would soon be sent out to find them.

Warwick, recognising their disappointment, took up a Very pistol and exclaimed cheerfully:

'I'm going to fire the pistol to test it. The Mustang's fuel must have been very low, but they'll know at home we're alive and kicking.' He raised the pistol, pulled the trigger and they watched the flaming red ball curve into the bank of mist.

Time dragged then came the sound of an engine flying low. It was a Supermarine Walrus Air Sea Rescue amphibian, barely 200ft up. Warwick fired another cartridge and they waved as an Aldis lamp flashed from the cabin. They knew the flying-boat could not land in this heaving sea, but Naisbitt had read the signal.

'Position noted and reported.'

'Good show,' said the pilot. 'They're getting organised, but it may take some time for a boat to reach us because we're bound to drift.'

The Walrus turned and flew straight for the dinghy. Something fell from the aircraft and brown smoke drifted up from the sea. From this the Walrus could determine their drift and give rescuers a more definite line to search. The aircraft circled a few times then disappeared. Light faded. Some suffered more than others from the miserable cold, but they all remained alert for the sound of engines.

The skipper fired another Very distress signal and several heads, showing interest, appeared above the canopy. A few minutes passed then Alex Stott said he had seen a light. They all looked and saw nothing, but Stott was certain and Warwick sent another red flare soaring into the blackness. The navigator again saw a light then, as the dinghy lifted on a swell, the pilot exclaimed:

'I see it, Alex. It's a ship all right. I saw the navigation lights.'

They rose again and the outline of a rapidly approaching ship took shape. Another cartridge fired and they saw in the red glow some of the crew lining the side.

It took longer than expected to get them aboard the corvette, which had been standing by further east, as was normal practice. An icy wind, together with the swell, tossed the dinghy up and down the side of the ship and there were fears they might be washed away into the night.

Eventually a ladder was clipped to the side of the corvette and they were hauled aboard. They stripped, towelled themselves down, received mugs of hot cocoa and cigarettes and, hours later, after plying a zig-zag course, were landed at Felixstowe for medical checkups and dry clothing. They would fly again, and Harry Warwick was later awarded a Distinguished Flying Cross.

Back at Chedburgh the dinghy sea switches on 218 Squadron's Lancasters were tested. None of them worked.

CHAPTER THREE

HAPPY LANDINGS

Victor Wood's 12 Squadron Lancaster was first to arrive over Gelsenkirchen having been over-zealous making up lost time. Earlier on that night of 25 June 1943, Wood's navigator, Pilot Officer Sandy Kirkby, told his skipper that unless they stepped on the gas they would be late over the target. Wood recalls:

'Sandy found we'd be five minutes late if we accepted the met winds given us at Wickenby. He told me the speed I needed to get there on time, so I increased it accordingly. Unfortunately, we were there a couple of minutes before everybody else, including the Pathfinders. I suppose the others thought the met winds were wrong and they'd be late while assuming everybody else would be late too so there would be no problem.

'Everything was blackness. There was nothing to be seen. We knew we were over the target but apart from a few stars, there was not a light showing, no sign of activity anywhere. I turned to port and started a lazy circle at around 21,000ft to lose time before the Main Force arrived.'

Circling a target alone before a scheduled raid was not to be recommended for even the bravest crew. They were in a huge patch of otherwise unoccupied sky, but it would shortly be joined by another 472 Lancasters, Halifaxes, Stirlings, Wellingtons and Mosquitoes, which would converge deliberately into the throat of the narrow bombing run. Now Wood and his crew were a suspicious blip on a German radar screen, gunners on the ground were awaiting the order to fire and night fighters assembled somewhere running up their engines.

Inside the blaring Lancaster DV158 H-Harry everyone was tense, nerves quaking, reflexes sharpened, peering into the darkness for any sign of movement.

Below, the quiet anxious city listened to the faint hum of a solitary bomber. Gelsenkirchen had not been specifically targeted since 1941 although its residents had since suffered bomb damage and loss of life from aircraft which were supposed to be attacking other industrial towns in the Ruhr.

The patient grind of the circling Lancaster came to an end with fearful suddenness as it was violently shaken by an alien force. There was a loud 'kerumph!' and its crew were precipitated into temporary consternation and chaos. Wood says:

'We were still doing our lazy circle when suddenly the aircraft was literally upside-down. The stars were shining in the wrong place, we had gone into a very steep dive and I was wrestling to regain control.

'At first, we didn't know what the hell had happened, although we realised we'd been hit by something because of the aircraft's behaviour. We knew later it was flak but there were no warning bursts of tracer.

'Dave Davis, the flight engineer, helped me pull the stick back after we'd lost up to 11,000ft. Once we'd got the aircraft more or less on an even keel I did a crew check, finding out who was where and if they were all right. We had problems with the mid-upper gunner and fuel could be seen pouring out of the wing, feeding a fire in the port outer engine.

'I instructed Bill Cruickshank, the wireless operator, to check what had happened to the mid-upper as Dave tried to put out the fire, but the gravinger extinguishers were having no effect and he couldn't feather the prop to reduce the drag. I was worried about the rapid loss of fuel and the engineer transferred petrol from the leaking tank into the others which helped cut down the extent of the fire. So now we had three engines, but as the port inner was running rough and hot we really only had two-and-a-half and the fourth was on fire. At this point I didn't think we would get back to England.

'After checking around and realising that the aircraft would fly we circled, did a bombing run and bombed the target from 11,000ft on markers dropped by Pathfinders who had arrived as we were going down.'

Turning for home the pilot told bomb aimer Guy Wood to leave his position and help Cruickshank who had reported over the intercom that the mid-upper gunner, Sergeant Ted Wilkins, was unconscious, but he was unable to lift him out of his turret, which had been hit by flak and a good deal of its perspex blown away. The gunner sat in a swivel seat but his weight had to be removed before it could be swung out from under his behind. Wood recalls Cruickshank's appraisal of the situation.

'The gunner was being sprayed by petrol which had caused the problem. His oxygen supply had been cut off because the fuel pouring on to him had frozen. He had not been injured, although narrowly missed being hit by shrapnel. A fire axe was used on his seat and they lifted him down. He was all right after being given oxygen, but the turret was u/s so he went on the rest bed.

'Everyone else was okay although shrapnel had ripped through the bomb aimer's compartment which fortunately missed Guy. Most damage was done at the forward end of the bomb bay. Later that day we saw a two-foot square hole had been knocked through it and shrapnel must have hit the Cookie. This 4,000lb bomb, which was like several forty-gallon drums welded together in line had a thin skin, so we were very lucky.

'We dealt with the fire shortly afterwards by putting the aircraft into a controlled dive to 9,000ft which blew it out now the flames were not being fed with fuel.

'It wasn't all that far to the coast from the Ruhr. I tried to maintain height and was pleased we kept going. I had no worries about losing an engine because it had happened once during training and I satisfied myself I was still in control. Everybody had told me the Lanc could fly on two engines, and it was possible to maintain height on one, but I very much doubted that.

'On three you would normally keep going but if you tried to gain altitude it would be a very slow rate of climb. We had lost so much fuel I didn't want to waste any through climbing. Besides, our third engine was rather dodgy, it kept going but stayed rough. There was flak en route, we always saw flak, but providing it was a long way off you didn't bother.

'The Lancaster had quite a spindly undercart and ours was certainly damaged, but I didn't know how badly because various controls had been shot away including the feathering mechanism for the propellers. When we were over Lincolnshire I decided to come into the airfield at Wickenby with all engines dead. My reasoning was that if I did a good belly landing at least there was a good chance of the engines being saved because the props would not be turning.

'I hadn't called the control tower to tell them we were in trouble. If I'd done that I would have almost certainly been diverted to one of three crash sites. I didn't want that.

'I cut the engines just at the point where I could glide in from probably between fifty and 100 feet. We touched down on the runway and came to a halt. Control called me up immediately to ask why we had stopped on the active runway.'

Wood prefixed his reply with the call sign 'H-Happy' instead of 'H-Harry', risking another bollocking from Control who did not encourage his persistent cheerfulness in what should have been serious exchanges.

'I said we had a problem but could deal with it quickly. I started up two engines, one on either side, and we made our way to dispersal.'

Before being picked up by a van to go to debriefing they had time to notice the crank case of the engine on fire had melted, the undercarriage had not collapsed but was in bad shape, the bomb aimer's compartment was riddled with shrapnel holes and the mid-upper turret was in need of serious renovation, but the three engines Victor Wood had taken so much trouble to save were not damaged in the landing.

At the outbreak of war Wood, born in Dublin of English parents, was a young apprentice at a Leicester garage which serviced Army vehicles from the East Midlands. After the war he put his engineering experience to good use by building up a successful group of garages bearing his name. At that time his consuming passion was flying but it was the middle of 1941 before he had managed to extricate himself from his reserved occupation. He had joined the Royal Air Force Volunteer Reserve before the war to spend his weekends flying Tiger Moths at nearby Desford. In August 1942 the tall, good-humoured twenty-three-year-old was commissioned and by May the following year he was flying Lancasters operationally from Wickenby in 12 Squadron's C Flight.

'My crew and I were very introvert,' says Wood. 'Some crews mixed socially with others, but I more or less told my chaps that I didn't want us to do that. We went out as a crew and did not make a lot of friends. We had enough to worry about without dealing with the grief of losing a close friend.'

He believed his navigator, Pilot Officer Sandy Kirkby, from the Hull area, to be, at forty-two, the oldest navigator in Bomber Command.

'He was a remarkable man who had dropped rank from flight lieutenant in transferring from Balloon Command to join aircrew. He was streets older than the rest of us, had a paternal influence, and was very keen, but on our first operation his navigation was not all that brilliant.

'Often a pilot on his first op would be sent out as second dickey with an experienced pilot, but the officer commanding 12 Squadron, Wing Commander Richard Wood, DSO, DFC, had a different approach. He was also the bravest man I have ever met. He made a habit of going out with every sprog crew on their first op. Talk about sticking your neck out. So many new crews didn't come back from their first trip.'

As they climbed aboard the Lancaster on the night of 29 May 1943, the Wingco sniffed the air and remarked breezily: 'With three Woods aboard nothing can possibly go wrong.' Something did go wrong however, on their flight to the industrial Ruhr town of Wuppertal. Victor Wood recalls:

'When Sandy thought we were at the target we were forty miles away from it. The wing commander kept quiet and let us get on with it, then said, very quietly, to me, although it could be heard by the crew over the intercom:"I suggest we head north." That's as much as he said. We turned on to a northerly heading and the target started to appear. Sandy was very annoyed with himself for making that mistake, but he didn't make any more.'

The rest of Victor Wood's crew were all sergeants. They included the wireless operator Bill Cruickshank, a dark-haired Scot. Bomb aimer Guy Wood came from Pudsey, near Leeds. Well built he had dark curly hair. Charlie 'Dave' Davis, the eighteen-year-old flight engineer, had been an engineering apprentice at Halton.

His original mid-upper gunner suffered badly from air sickness, only lasting four trips.

'We had to get rid of him,' says Wood, 'but senior officers wanted to make him LMF. I was an awkward sod, only a flying officer at the time, arguing forcefully that he was not LMF. It wasn't that he didn't want to be an air gunner, it was that he was air sick on ops and a danger to the crew because he couldn't do his job. So he was taken off aircrew and put in the caravan at the end of the runway on signalling duty instead of being posted to another station and put on permanent latrine duty.' His replacement, Ted Wilkins, joined the crew for the first time on their trip to Gelsenkirchen.

The rear gunner, Ray Coll, was born into a farming family near the town of Moose Jaw, in Saskatchewan,Canada.

One morning, early in Victor Wood's tour, he and two other young pilots, Flying Officers Weekes and McLaughlin, were called into the Wingco's office.

Wing Commander Wood, looking less cheerful than usual, said,in a low voice:'You seem to have some difficulty in keeping your flight commanders so I'm going to make you three up to acting flight lieutenants.' He hesitated, then added, bleakly: 'Perhaps one of you at least will see the tour through.'

Victor Wood says:

'In 1943 we were getting through our flight commanders quite rapidly because so many were lost on ops.Thereafter, when a flight commander went missing, if they didn't ship a replacement in straightaway, the first of us into the flight office took over and the other two supported him.'

Victor Wood's longest trip was to Turin on 12/13 July 1943. They left in LM321, the new H-Harry, at a time when most people in England were climbing into bed, dropping into Wickenby 10hr 55min later, when the country had been at work for a couple of hours. He says:

'5 Group used to have the privilege of going on these raids in the south, afterwards being routed over to North Africa and returning with crates full of bananas, oranges and booze. We complained bitterly to 1 Group about this because we thought if they can have bananas,why can't we. We were told our aircraft were not fitted with 5 Group's sand filters, which we thought was a bit of a lame excuse.

'We believed this raid was set up to encourage Mussolini to surrender. What was unusual about it was that we were routed down to Turin at only 16,000ft which included the stretch across the Alps. It was a softer target than any we'd been on in Germany, but it was a hell of a long way.'

Raids on Italy normally caused less grief among Allied bombers but bullets and shells can still kill a man and bring down an aircraft. Thirteen of Bomber Command's 295 participating Lancasters were lost on this raid while 792 people were killed and 914 injured by bombs which fell in clear weather north of the city, Turin's worst air-raid fatalities of the war.

'We bombed much lower than usual and flew low on the way back. The rear gunner had a lovely time firing at anything that appeared to be interesting, like trains and military vehicles. Then as we were flying south of the Brest peninsular at 500ft he came on the intercom and said: "Bandit astern! Starboard quarter high".

'The fighter started diving on us with Ray Coll providing a useful commentary. I decided to dive so if he missed me the German would go into the sea. I did as steep a turn as I could, losing height at the same time, making us a difficult target, while the Brownings were chattering away in the rear turret. Then it went quiet and I heard Ray exclaim loudly: "Shit!"

'I replied: "What is it Tail?"

'"I've lost my fucking sight, it's dropped off."

'It was the only time I heard Ray swear. We didn't see the fighter again and had no idea whether it had just cleared off, which some did if we were too watchful, or if it had dropped into the sea.'

We left enemy territory over La Rochelle. We were on a westerly heading, dropping to fifty feet over the Atlantic because it was daylight and we needed to get below German radar. Our landfall was supposed to be Land's End on a north-easterly heading and we'd been told to refuel in Cornwall. It got misty which presented a few difficulties. When we should have been making a landfall we couldn't see any land.

'We were well overdue on our landfall then, at 500ft, realised we were over land and came across a town which we identified as Plymouth. We had seen a lighthouse sticking out which must have been Eddystone. It transpired that we had somehow been flying one-and-a-half-miles east of the English coast which had been covered in mist. We had a discussion about the fuel because we'd been told we wouldn't have enough for the whole trip. We decided that if we landed to refuel we'd probably be in a bloody long queue to get it and I was always reluctant to land anywhere else. I liked to get home, I slept better in my own bed. So we flew straight to Wickenby.

'I was economical with fuel. You could save it by flying with as weak a mixture as possible and I was careful before leaving for a raid. A lot of pilots taxied out early but then had to climb over the base for about forty-five minutes before it was time to leave. I used to be the opposite, making sure I was towards the end of the takeoffs, which gave me more fuel to use on the way back.

'We landed back at base with virtually no fuel left, possibly twenty-five gallons, but we'd made it and I slept well.

'Instead of marking the operation by having another bomb added to the collection on Harry's nose, I had an ice cream painted on; the op wasn't worth a bomb.'

On the night of 2 August they paid their fourth and final visit to Hamburg.

'Our aircraft, JA922, was a stranger to me and the operation was a shambles. Hamburg itself was blotted out by a severe storm, thunder, lightning and heavy cloud. The weather man back at base had not warned us about this.

'Occasionally, if there was any doubt about the weather, a Mosquito was sent over the target before we were due to go to see what the weather was like, then he reported back and the forecasting was based on what he had seen. Someone had made a cockup.

'I tried in vain to get over the storm. We struggled to about 23,000ft, all the time I was looking for an opening in the cloud. Then I spotted a fissure and began flying into it, hoping it would become clearer, but lightning was flashing from both sides of the cloud and the fissure and right in front of us.

'The trailing aerial was jettisoned after being struck by lightning and blowing up the wireless operator's set. I decided we were asking for trouble because other bombers would have been milling about and the aircraft could have been knocked about quite heavily in this turbulence. We turned out of that cloud system the way we had gone into it, then I asked the navigator if there was an alternative target.

'We were not always given an alternative or last resort target in case something went wrong with the main one and we didn't get one at briefing that night. After some discussion we decided to have a go at Heligoland because it was obvious if you were going to see anything you would see that because it really stood out.

'We found the island which looked the shape of a large warship, possibly an aircraft carrier. Then all hell broke loose. We were the only aircraft there and flak poured up at us, everything they'd got. We decided the fight was off, left in a hurry and looked for something easier.

'The bomb aimer and navigator eventually saw a town on the way home they identified as Bremerhaven, which we bombed from 18,000ft. We weren't as lucky as some who hit an ammunition dump when they jettisoned their bombs, but there was no point taking them home. I can't remember what the aiming point photographs showed but I never got a rocket about it so it couldn't have been too bad.'

Thirty of the 740 aircraft sent to attack Hamburg were lost. Only scattered bombing was possible on the river port and many crews turned back early or found other targets to hit.

On 7 November 626 Squadron was created at Wickenby from 12 Squadron's C Flight.

'Nothing was changed on my aircraft which still had PH,the marking for 12 Squadron, on it, and although I was technically on 626, I remained in the same billet.The change of squadron made not the slightest difference to us.'

Their first operation on 626 Squadron was on 10 November, when Wood's aircraft was among 313 Lancasters despatched on a long run into the south of France to smash the entrance to Modane tunnel on the main railway route to Italy. An attempt to bomb the tunnel with a slightly heavier force had failed on 16/17 September.

Wood recalls negotiating the Alps with St Elmo's fire flickering over the aircraft and his blind flying instruments failing.This called for swift improvisation.

'I climbed over the Alps using the navigator's divider box attached to a boot lace which was tied to the light on the top of the canopy for a plumb line. If the box hit me on the right side of my face that meant I'd got the port wing too low. If it hit the engineer in the face I had the starboard wing too low. If it went where we couldn't see it,it meant we were climbing too bloody steeply and we'd be in danger of stalling.

'You could see the railway line pointing towards the tunnel which was lit by moonlight and not heavily defended, so it was an easy set-up for the bomb aimer.

'Some of our bombs appeared to skid into the tunnel mouth, which was blocked as requested, and the railway line was damaged.All Wickenby crews had an aiming point photograph, except one because their camera was faulty.'

Victor Wood's seventh trip to Berlin on 26 November was also the thirtieth and last op of his tour. Earlier that month he had been awarded a Distinguished Flying Cross for invariably displaying 'the utmost determination to achieve the maximum effect on every sortie' and having 'proved himself to possess the greatest skill and resource'.

But he was now without his regular gunners. Wilkins, who had been screened and was now instructing, was replaced by Sergeant Mallin. Ray Coll was suffering from pleurisy. His place in the freezing rear turret had been given to Sergeant Syd Hare. They also had Flying Officer Wilkinson flying second dickey. The officer who had taken over command of the new 626 Squadron, Wing Commander Don Craven, did not share 12 Squadron's Wing Commander Wood's zest in accompanying all his new crews on their first bombing operation.

Victor Wood's memory of this operation is less of the savagery of Berlin's defences, more of their spectacular return to Wickenby.

There was also a long tense interlude during which the bomb aimer and wireless operator struggled to release the photoflash which had jammed over the German capital.

'It was an American photoflash, which I didn't trust, and if it had gone off in the aircraft it would have had the same effect as a 250lb bomb. After they'd jettisoned it the bomb aimer asked if he should return to his position. We were only eleven minutes from Wickenby and it wasn't worth him crawling over the main spar and forward to his compartment so I told him to go to the rest bed.'

'Lincolnshire was covered in thick fog. I thought we would be diverted, but it didn't happen. Other people seemed to land all right and I came in using SBA, the standard beam approach, but I wasn't satisfied with the Morse signals we were receiving and left the airfield for a minute or two, doing another circuit to think ourselves out.

'I told the flight engineer I was going to let down but as soon as I got to 500ft he should give me full power because if I still couldn't see anything I would abort. Dave began counting out the altimeter readings to me. At 500ft we could see nothing below and he pushed the throttles wide open. At that precise second I felt the slightest tremor in the aircraft, something I had never felt before. You must remember we were in landing configuration with flaps and undercart down.

'The aircraft hit something, made a lurch, went over at an angle, then struck something else and lurched the other way. What we didn't know at the time, because of the fog, was that with 500ft showing on our altimeter and all engines going full pelt we had hit the deck. The two obstructions were ditches which had torn off our undercarriage legs.'

The Lancaster roared across several fields before coming to a sudden jolting halt.

'When we stopped the four engines literally fell out of the wings and the propellers screwed themselves into the ground. We got out quickly because we were bothered about fire. Somebody cleared off in the opposite direction, I gave chase and swung him round by the shoulder. I didn't recognise him and said: "Who are you?"

'It was Guy Wood whose face was covered in blood from a bad cut on his forehead. My question didn't please him, although he must have realised if he'd gone to his position he would have been a bit mangled. Other aircraft were circling overhead as we got into a ditch.

'There was no fire and I had to go back into the aircraft to raise help. The radio was still working, I called up control and said: "This is H-Hap – H-Harry requesting assistance." I heard the station commander, Group Captain Basil Crummy, talking in the background.'

Crummy, in a voice mixed with surprise and anxiety, said: 'That's Wood! It can't be Wood.' The young pilot was not known for getting into scrapes like this.

'I took a Very pistol and shells back to the ditch and we sent up the odd one every two or three minutes to let the ambulance crew see where we were.'

Before the blood wagon arrived a WAAF flight officer confronted Wood after a tiresome walk across the fields. She said:

'What's happened?'

Wood replied, a little abruptly at the daftness of the question: 'We've fucking well crashed.' Shuffling her feet the woman said stiffly:

'Well, I can see that, but mind your language.' The two officers had no further exchange but Wood learned later that his aircraft had first touched the ground between a WAAF hut and a haystack, with no more than eighteen inches clearance on either side.

'When the ambulance drew up as luck would have it an aircraft was coming in about to land. We'd just shot up a red Very light. We heard the throttles go on the engines and he went round again. The pilot wasn't very pleased with me about that.'

CHAPTER FOUR

HAS ANYBODY GOT A FAG?

The Lancaster swept in low from the east: dark and purposeful, heading straight towards the Lincolnshire river port of Boston. No one bustling through the ancient market place bothered to look up at first; the county was generously carpeted with military airfields and bombers were a common sight.

But as the aircraft drew nearer and larger, continuing to lose altitude, the bellow of its engines became even louder, edged with menace, and the queues snaking out from several shops wavered, looking up nervously before scattering, believing that the bomber was in trouble and about to crash.

Thundering in over the shuddering fenland town at 250ft there was only time on the ground to confirm that all four propellers were spinning satisfactorily and to wonder why a Lancaster was hell-bent on tearing apart this little community. Then it sank even lower and banked with heart-stopping elegance around St Botolph's parish church, known world-wide as the Boston Stump, before heading off in the direction from which it had come, leaving a glimpse of the pilot's grinning face for those who had been brave enough to watch the entire extraordinary performance.

It was the morning of 10 March 1945, a time when the dwindling German resistance was no longer providing enough excitement for some pilots which meant they needed to go in search of it elsewhere, and a tight turn around the 272ft-high Stump and panic in the streets below was good enough for twenty-four-year-old Flight Lieutenant Peter 'Andy' Anderson.

Anderson's mid-upper gunner was Sergeant John Pearl, nineteen, who recalls the exhilaration of the Stump stunt.

'It was a fine piece of flying, a bit of devilment too. We'd been on a high-level bombing exercise over Wainfleet Sand, followed by local flights. We saw the Stump from twenty miles away and just flew towards it. Our wing tip was a few yards off the church tower and we went round below the top of it like the hands of a clock, then flew off, picking up speed. Andy was not normally a rash pilot. He was a safety first sort of guy, who occasionally broke loose.'

Had anyone reported the Lancaster Anderson would have been in trouble with his commanding officer, but there were no repercussions. Pearl remembers another time when his skipper pretended he was a fighter pilot.

'Leaving one day for an exercise, Andy went straight up from the runway, as if he was flying a Spitfire. It was a spectacular takeoff, the talk of the squadron. He could make a Lancaster do things other pilots would have been afraid of attempting.'

They were based with 207 Squadron at Spilsby at the southern end of the Lincolnshire Wolds where winter winds rushed in from the North Sea with malicious endeavour.

Anderson was not the crew's first pilot. They lost Flying Officer Vernon Ashbolt at 1660 HCU, Swinderby. From Christchurch, New Zealand, Ashbolt, a small man, had handled a Wellington all right at 16 OTU, Upper Heyford, Oxfordshire, but had problems piloting the Stirling. Pearl recalls the pilot's difficulties.

'He could take off and land the Stirling well and fly it straight and level, but had to get out of his seat and stand on the pedals when it came to manoeuvres and corkscrews. He was taken up by the chief flying instructor who said if that happened on an op, Vernon would risk the lives of his crew and he took him off the course. He was sent somewhere to fly lighter aircraft.

'There was some talk that we'd be split up, each of us going into someone else's crew, just after we'd got organised. Then we were given Andy, a Canadian, who had already done his first tour, with 97 Squadron, during which he picked up a DFC and was mentioned in despatches. He had been instructing at Metheringham on 106 Squadron, but was harassing people to get him back on ops. Andy was told he could take over our crew providing he completed the course with us at Swinderby. He was not very keen, having hoped to get a crew of first-tour veterans instead of a bunch of greenhorns.'

Pearl had not, at first, taken to his new skipper, believing him to be aloof, looking down on anyone who was not in the officers' mess.

'I could not have been more wrong. He arranged for us to have a very early breakfast next day and we got to the flights when nobody else was about. We got in the Stirling and off we went. He was marvellous. He did things with that aircraft I had thought were impossible:stalls,dives,corkscrews and two-engine flying. I think it was his way of letting us know what he was like in the air.'

Anderson, the well-built son of a farmer, from Union Point, Manitoba,teetotal and a non-smoker, nevertheless enjoyed going out with his crew, content with a glass of lemonade or orange juice in a tiny room off the bar at The Bull, over two miles from the airfield, in the small town of Spilsby. They became good friends of Sam Dowling, the landlord, and his wife, Sadie, who made up beds for them at night if the weather was bad, sending them on their way in the morning after a free breakfast of porridge and toast.

On Sundays, when they were not flying, the entire crew had a standing invitation to tea in Halton Road with another Bull regular, Bert Smith,his wife,Winifred,and their sixteen-year-old daughter, Audrey who, many years later, confessed to having a secret crush on the pilot.The men often went on leave carrying parcels of sausages and bacon which had been made from one of the two pigs raised and slaughtered in the Smiths' back garden. During the long austerity of strict rationing these were generous gifts.

Twenty-two-year-old navigator Flying Officer Cyril Hewett, from Dartford, Kent, had replaced a flight sergeant who was thrown off the OTU course after being caught puffing on a cigarette near an aircraft in a strictly non-smoking area.

The wireless operator, Sergeant Vic Collins, twenty-seven, from Upper Norwood, a burly former detective with Croydon CID, strove in vain to keep the crew on the straight and narrow.

Flying Officer Ken Larcombe, twenty, the bomb aimer, handsome, with a fine voice, often led the crew singing bawdy songs when they were in the mood. His home was in Walthamstow, east London.

Sergeant Ted Nichols, a former builder in West Hartlepool, Durham, thirty-five, was Anderson's flight engineer. He was married with two children, to whom his crewmates donated all the chocolate from their flight rations.

John Pearl, from Forest Fields, Nottingham, was 5ft 6^1/$_2$in fully stretched, a thin weed of seven stone. In his spare time he enjoyed cycling, going to the cinema and reading books, especially those by Ernest Hemingway and Dashiell Hammett, which stirred his imagination.

His father, Ben, had joined the Great War at seventeen to escape his job as a coal miner, but was seriously wounded on the first day of the Battle of the Somme. Pearl was a sales assistant in a men's wear shop before he escaped into Bomber Command.

Sergeant Eric Matthews, from Smethwick, was renamed by the two Australian crews who shared their billet at Swinderby. One of the Aussies stared hard at the rear gunner's lugubrious face and said:'For a bloke who looks so much like Humphrey Bogart, Eric is a cissy name. We'll call you Eddie.' The name stuck.

Pearl's first bombing operation involved attacking the Mittelland Canal near Gravenhorst on 20 February 1945, but as a spare bod in a crew which had already completed eighteen trips. Flying Officer Peter Passmore's regular mid-upper was indisposed and Pearl, plagued by severe misgivings, climbed into the aircraft surrounded by hard-nosed veterans.

'I was very nervous anyway because it was my first op, but I was even more nervous flying with people I didn't know, aware that they might resent being given an inexperienced bloke.

'The rear gunner was Al Foreman, a prominent English boxer for some years before the war, who was now forty-one, more than twice my age. He took me to one side to discuss tactics and said:"If you see an enemy plane do nothing, but tell me and I'll see to it." His words did not fill me with confidence and I thought:"Are they going to think I'm bloody useless?"

'I was searching the sky on the way to the target, as I had been taught, and saw a Lancaster approaching on the starboard side. I watched it overtake us and disappear. The headphones crackled; it was Passmore, very angry, wanting to know if I'd seen that Lancaster. He gave me a rollicking for not telling him. I thought he was a bit tetchy but later found out why he didn't leave anything to chance. A few weeks before, while bombing Royan, France, they lost a wing tip after colliding with another aircraft.'

The raid against the canal was called off by the master bomber because the target was covered by thick cloud. On the way back the bomb aimer spotted a break in the clouds. Passmore dropped through it and found, spread out juicily below, a built-up area, believed to be Ahaus.

The bomb aimer released the bombs from 9,000ft with the gleeful observation: 'Let the buggers know there's a war on.' Passmore was the only skipper on the squadron to leave his bombs in Germany that night.

Matthews had also been a spare bod to Gravenhorst, rear gunner for Flying Officer Michael Cooke, who did not return from a later sortie. A few days later Cyril Hewett filled in for another navigator to Ladbergen.

Peter Anderson's crew went on their first op as a team on 3 March to attack the Ladbergen aqueduct on the Dortmund-Ems canal. Pearl was nervous, but so were the others. He was more relaxed with his regular crewmates, but well on the way to the target he went to pieces.

'I suddenly became petrified and really fell apart. I couldn't keep still, my arms and legs were shivering and the rest of me trembled uncontrollably. I said nothing, and got rid of it eventually. I gritted my teeth, clenched my fists, clung to my guns and forced myself to get back to normal and for the rest of the trip I was all right. But I couldn't go on like this. What if we were attacked with me in such a state?

'We bombed from 8,000ft through the clouds at target markers. We saw the glow under the clouds and smoke swirled up. Shells were bursting all round us and other Lancs swarmed in like flies to get on the target.

'It was a strange feeling, realising that somebody at a desk twenty-four hours ago had planned this operation, working out bomb loads and the amount of fuel and so on, which had built up during the day and here it was all coming together. I thought it was bloody marvellous.

'When we got back to Spilsby there was a terrific thump as we taxied along the perry track to our dispersal. The aircraft shook, I thought we'd collided with something. We carried on, then heard someone who was landing coming through loudly over the r/t: "There's somebody else in the fucking funnel, what's going on?"

'There was a loud "Crump!" And we knew intruders were over the airfield. Two bombs had been dropped and Lancasters which had not landed were diverted.'

Nine aircraft were lost over Germany and the sea that night with another twenty-two written off, probably twenty of these having been attacked by 200 intruding Luftwaffe fighters over England.

'Next morning all the air gunners in 5 Group were bussed off to an airfield where we were torn off a strip by a high-ranking officer who said:"Not one air gunner fired a shot." He made us feel really small.'

John Pearl lay in bed after the return from Ladbergen trying to figure out what had caused his frightening breakdown in the turret.

'I had experienced a sort of melt down and finally attributed it to my imagination which had been shaped for many years by adventure stories I'd read and films I had seen. While I was in the turret I imagined we were going to be attacked by a fighter and somebody out there had his eye on us. I knew I was putting the other lads' lives in danger.

'I got over it by deliberately scaring myself for five minutes every time after getting into the aircraft, then gradually shutting down the fear by sheer will power. Once I got it out of my head I was all right and when we reached the target I was on a high.'

Two nights later they were sent to Böhlen to attend to a synthetic oil refinery. It was a long trip, almost ten hours.

'We could see the target through breaks in the cloud and bombed from 9,500ft. Black smoke billowed up as the bombs struck. There was not much flak but combats were taking place and I saw several kites going down. I didn't see the actual combat, just a flash in the sky, and there was the impression of the nub end of a cigarette being flicked away as the aircraft went down.'

Their third sortie in four nights was on 6 March to the naval base at Sassnitz, on the island of Rügen in the Baltic. They were tired from the many brain-numbing hours in the air and John Pearl, staring ceaselessly into the never-ending darkness, fell asleep during the 9hr 30min flight.

'The pilot now and again contacted each man to see if he was all right. He got no response from me on this occasion. We had been very close to some flak that night and although it hadn't hit us we were shaken and the others thought I might have been caught by shrapnel. Andy sent Ken Larcombe, the bomb aimer, to see what was wrong. Ken shook my leg and woke me up. It was a crime to nod off in a bomber, but I was totally knackered.

'We flew across the North Sea and Denmark and down over neutral Sweden. The Swedes fired token barrages at us to placate the Germans, but their shells were miles away. We saw mountains and snow, and towns lit up like fairyland, with traffic running along the roads.

'The ships were like models in Sassnitz harbour and though they were firing at us I don't think they could elevate their guns high enough. We bombed at 9,750ft. Three ships were sunk and a lot of damage was done to the town.'

They were back on duty the following night, attacking an oil refinery at Harburg. Their aircraft was caught by searchlights in the Kiel area.

'We were coned for about twenty minutes. It was a weird and frightening experience. We weren't being fired at and assumed fighters were looking for us but none turned up. We couldn't see out of the lights which were all around although for a time it seemed a dozen or so Lancasters were beneath us, but each one was a shadow of our aircraft. The lights went out after we slipped into a cloud and everything went smoothly after that.'

They had a spell of leave, but were busy again on 21 March, attacking the Deutsche Erdölwerke oil refinery in Hamburg from 17,000ft.

Two nights later they hammered Wesel, helping to open the door for Field Marshal Bernard Montgomery's troops to cross the Rhine.

'As we orbited to go home searchlights appeared on our side of the river, directed in a straight line across the water. Tanks and vehicles were lined up on the bank ready to go. This was a raid I was proud to be on.'

Peter Anderson was at the controls of Lancaster III ME472 EM O-Oboe when they took off on 10 April in daylight for the first time. The target was Leipzig.

'Another crew had been up in our plane, O-Oboe, and made a rather heavy landing, severely damaging the undercarriage. There were other problems, and the rivets in the leading edges had all sprung out. We spent the day in suspense, not knowing whether or not we would be going. There was no available spare aircraft, but the mechanics said Oboe would be ready in time. We had the briefing and pre-ops meal, but it wasn't until it was time to get our flying gear on and collect our rations that we were told it was ready. There was no time for an air test, it had been fuelled and bombed up.

'We had been picked to be supporters on that raid. These are the crews who go in with the Pathfinders to make up the number to confuse the enemy radar. We were like decoys, flying eight minutes ahead of the Main Force. We had to go over the target with the Pathfinders, then go round again to join the Main Force and do our own bombing. We were quite excited about this op.'

As soon as they took off at 6.05pm Anderson knew that George, the automatic pilot, was not working. There was no question of aborting, the skipper simply accepted he would be tied to the controls for many hours.

'Pathfinder marker flares were going down as we began moving across the railway yards at Leipzig,' says Pearl. 'Some light flak appeared ahead of us but it was spread thinly around the sky and did not look too formidable. However, black puffs of smoke from the bursting shells of predicted heavy flak seemed dangerously close and as we continued our run across the target it was one of these shells which exploded alongside, between the two starboard motors.

'It shook the plane, throwing us around the sky, causing me to slip off the strip of canvas, hanging like a hammock, which served as a seat in the mid-upper turret. I fell backwards on to the floor of the aircraft. I lay there a few seconds as shrapnel ripped through the fuselage, sounding like hail stones on a tin roof. The skipper steadied the aircraft and I climbed back into my turret to find it badly holed with most of the cupola perspex blown away. A lot of the metal framework which had been supporting the perspex was twisted and mangled and I sat there like a World War One air gunner with my head out in the fresh air.'

He mused on the good fortune of being thrown off his seat, thus preventing the top of his head being sliced off like a breakfast boiled egg. It was freezing in the shattered turret which could now only be moved by winding a handle. His guns did not work so his role had been reduced to lookout.

The pilot checked on his crew and found them all unharmed. Both starboard engines were damaged, losing oil, and were feathered. Ted Nichols, the flight engineer, reported several large holes in the fuselage and at this point the master bomber called the Main Force in to bomb.

'There was a quick discussion among the crew about what we should do before Cyril Hewett, the navigator, said:"We're here, we might as well bomb." So we orbited, came in and Ken released the bombs at 11pm from 14,000ft.

'Leaving the target area we were hit again by flak on the port side, but Ted couldn't find any damage and we kept going, coming down to 4,000ft. With only the port engines keeping us aloft the skipper managed to maintain control. After ninety limping minutes oil pressure began dropping fast on the port inner engine and the pilot told us to prepare for baling out.

'I left my turret, retrieved my parachute pack from its stowage rack and, followed by Vic Collins, the wireless operator, made my way to the rear door. Eddie Matthews had already come forward out of his turret rather than turn it to bale out backwards. He was at the exit point on intercom, talking to the skipper. I opened the door, and we awaited the skipper's command. There was no panic or confusion. We'd practised the drill many times although we had never actually parachuted before.

'We were flying straight and level when Eddie took off his helmet and signalled that we were to go and he jumped out. I followed, tumbling into the pitch-black sky, with no sensation of falling other than a rush of air against my face. I was floating and slowly somersaulting. One moment I saw stars, then blackness, then stars again. Pulling the ripcord I didn't know that it came away and thought:"Christ! It's broken." Then the 'chute opened with a bone-crushing jerk and I began a slow silent descent to earth, although at first it seemed I was going up instead of down.

'I looked up, pulled on the cords and heard the parachute flapping. I believe that increased my speed slightly while sending me off in another direction. I think that's why I landed a long way from the others.

'Descending, I heard the explosion of our aircraft crashing a long way off. A brilliant flash of light lit up the whole area and in the few seconds before it disappeared all I could see below was a vast area of heavily-wooded countryside and I thought I'd be impaled on one of the trees. Nearing the ground I heard the roar of rushing water which gave me something else to worry about. Maybe I would drop into a raging river and be drowned.'

He landed on his feet in a forest clearing, touching the ground so gently he did not even have to do the forward roll. His parachute came down over him like a soft enveloping umbrella. He gathered up his Irvine jacket, Mae West, gloves and parachute and stuffed them out of sight in the undergrowth.

He felt miserable and lonely in the dark, listening to the rumble of the bombers going home to a decent breakfast and a comfortable bed, the unknown stretching before him like a grim obstacle course. He found a narrow stream nearby and decided to track its course.

'I was brought to a halt at the edge of the wood where the stream cascaded over a high bank into a large lake. Peering through the gloom I saw across the water a big factory, and near it river water pouring over a weir, which is what I heard coming down. I decided to wait for daylight to sort myself out and settled down beneath a tree. I didn't sleep, I kept wondering what had happened to the other lads.'

Eddie Matthews landed in an orchard at the side of a road. He walked along it, heading for a glimmer of light, coming from a house in the small village of Brohl, beside the Rhine, near Koblenz. He put his eye to the gap in the curtained window. Inside men wearing singlets and shorts sat round a table playing cards. Hearing their voices he realised they were Americans and walked boldly through the door inquiring mildly: 'Has anybody got a fag?' Table, cards and money went flying as the soldiers dived for the rifles stacked together in a corner. 'Hang on!' he cried, anxiously. 'I'm British.'

The rear gunner told his story and within minutes he was in a Jeep with three GIs searching for his crewmates They found Cyril Hewett, who had been dangling helplessly for hours from his parachute fifty feet up a tree. He was later carried down by an ex-lumberjack.

Later that day the wreckage of their crashed bomber was found together with the remains of a body, near the village of Burgbrohl. The two Britons were taken to the scene.

Each member of the crew had numbers, depicting their positions, from 1, the pilot, to 7, the rear gunner, painted in white on the side of their flying boots.

'I don't know if any other squadrons or groups did that,' says Pearl, 'but the number on the side of the boot found identified Andy, our pilot. The plane had burned out so there was not much left of him, just one boot with his leg in it, and a glove containing a hand. He was found in the bomb aimer's compartment, and might have been close to getting out, but the aircraft crashed into the side of a hill. I think he could have got out safely if the automatic pilot had been working.'

Ken Larcombe, who jumped out of the forward escape hatch, had landed in the Rhine, struggled to a tiny island, the Hammersteiner Werth,and was rescued by three Americans from a tank-landing craft who, believing him to be German,gave him a beating.

Vic Collins and Ted Nichols were picked up separately after walking all night through woods.

John Pearl knew he was in Germany, but did not know if he had landed behind the Allied lines.

'I had no food, relying on Horlicks tablets in my escape pack which also contained a map, compass, fishing line, water carrier, soap, a mini-razor and a tiny mirror of polished tin.Water was no problem, I found many springs with clear sweet water. I was heading west, but couldn't always go in a straight line. I walked through woods and across fields the other side and into more woods.It was not cold but there were heavy showers and once I stripped off my saturated clothes, hung them on branches and bushes and sat naked watching them steam. I put them back on when they were nearly dry but more rain soaked me again and I gave up.'

He was adrift in the countryside for over two days, hiding from woodmen cutting up and transporting trees, creeping fearfully on his stomach out of a farmyard where he had disturbed a dog and roused the farmer, and climbing inquisitively up a long ladder to the top of a fire watcher's tower. His strangest experience was dodging a group of picnicking German civilian men wearing lederhosen, with rifles and hunting dogs.

Despairing of finding a friendly face, he came to the village of Brohl where he met the Americans and was given breakfast, his first meal since leaving Spilsby.

Several days later he left in a truck on the morning mail run to Brussels.

'It was a long haul, taking in Bonn, Cologne and Aachen. I saw at first hand how those cities had been devastated by Bomber Command. We drove through streets banked high with rubble, where footpaths wound over the debris like mountain paths. Groups of people, like tramps, drawn and haggard, gathered round bonfires between tents and tarpaulin-covered cellars and bomb craters that served as homes.But,I couldn't feel sorry for them.

'I left Brussels in a Transport Command Dakota, landing at RAF Down Ampney and next morning a Lancaster was despatched from Spilsby to take me back to base.'

CHAPTER FIVE

FLAMER

The men who were not being violently sick overboard and wanting to die stared in appalled fascination at the small crowded lifeboats, heavy in the water, being roughed up by the swell. Minutes passed before they realised that the bundles of rags dotted about in the cold North Atlantic were human beings: some still alive, struggling; others passed caring.

They watched in embarrassed silence knowing their ship, SS *Otranto*, could not stop to rescue anyone in case a lurking U-boat should send torpedoes plunging into its bows and claim several hundred more victims. Pity fought an uneasy battle with their overwhelming desire for self-preservation.

Peter Payne, a tall slim nineteen-year-old airman, who had been working at the family jewellery and silversmith business in Oxford a few months before, says:

'We hoped the survivors would be picked up by the Royal Navy. There were about fifty boats in our convoy with destroyers circling, trying to make sure no submarines got within striking distance.'

It was January 1942. They had left Liverpool marching proudly aboard to a brass band, cheered on their way by a patriotic crowd on the dockside braving the wintry chill. All pomp and excitement vanished when 300 trainee aircrew were shown their miserable quarters and realised their trip to South Africa would be a long way from the comfortable six-week cruise they had anticipated. Also aboard were over 2,000 soldiers heading for confrontation with the Japanese in Singapore. The *Otranto* was known by its more humble passengers as 'the hell ship'. Formerly a liner of the Orient Line it had been converted into a troop ship and painted grey.

'Our accommodation was in the hold where we were packed like sardines, sleeping with somebody's feet in your face in a hammock, if you could find one, otherwise you curled up on tables or the filthy floor. The food was terrible. You might have mince and potatoes and, for dessert, tapioca and custard; everything dropped into the same mess tin.'

As the airmen's morale foundered they were offered the encouraging little diversion of tinned tripe.

'After we got underway most of us were vomiting all over the place for about three days. Much worse than that, my friend, Terry Walters, another trainee pilot, died of meningitis during the voyage and was buried at sea.

'Officers, nurses and WAAFs, segregated from us common men, occupied the two top decks in some style and we watched them dancing to a string orchestra.'

The airmen disembarked at Durban on 13 February, but weeks were spent kicking their heels at Lyttelton, near Pretoria, before places on suitable courses were available, because of a shortage of instructors and aircraft. LAC Payne was posted in June to 2 Air School, Randfontein, Transvaal, where he encountered South African pilot instructor Lieutenant Tony Lawrenson.

'Tony was a bit fiery, having strongly resented being posted from an operational squadron in the Middle East to teaching raw recruits how to fly. He was pretty rough and firm with us all, and certainly shook me up, but eventually made me efficient. After I forgot to reach outside the Tiger Moth fuselage to check both magneto switches before taking off, he made me run round the perimeter of the airfield wearing my flying suit and parachute while he watched from the control tower. It was a seat-type parachute, hanging from my backside and not very comfortable, but I never forgot those damned switches again.

'I had flown twelve hours before I went solo, which was longer than a lot of people, but I used to panic when I had a flight commander's test. It took three tests before I passed.

'I had a lovely time in South Africa, spending every other weekend in Johannesburg, about twenty miles from the station, with Ness and Donald Currie's kind family whom I had met through the YMCA. Food was important to someone of my age and there was no rationing in South Africa, where I ate rather well.'

Payne, a modest sensitive man, who lacked self-confidence in the early days, moved on to twin-engine Oxfords at 24 Air School, Nigel, Transvaal, where he received his wings with an 'above average' flying assessment on 19 February 1943. He had also been commissioned. Such momentous events were dulled by more time being wasted hanging about until it became administratively convenient for the RAF to present Pilot Officer Peter Payne with a boarding pass for the former Cunard liner *Aquitania*, which sailed from Cape Town.

Accommodation was better than on the *Otranto*, although WAAFs were unhappily in short supply. He also had a job to do with other newly qualified pilots: guard over 2,000 Italian prisoners who were incarcerated in the hold.

'We were each armed with a sten gun and five rounds of ammunition and had to make sure they didn't get hold of razors or knives in case they killed themselves or attacked us. They were sex-starved and newly commissioned young pilots might have been attractive to them. We had daily roll calls, supervised the distribution of rations and stood by when they were let out each day for a breath of air. If the ship had been attacked we were expected to let them all out in an orderly manner through one little hatch.

'The ship did about twenty-two knots, fast enough not to go in convoy, calling in at Rio de Janeiro where we were not allowed to get off, and New York, where we were. Someone there looked at my nice new uniform and asked if I was a postman. The Italians were disembarked here and sent by train to prisoner-of-war camps in Canada.'

American troops replaced the Italians in the hold on the voyage to Scotland and while the Yanks were sniffy about their accommodation the young RAF pilots were not asked to guard them.

'We were sent on 8 June to 19 (P)AFU, Dalcross, near Inverness. The posting was to get us used to flying in Britain after being in South Africa where there was no blackout. It was not entirely satisfactory because at that time of the year up there it hardly got dark at all. No one seemed to have thought of that.'

Payne crewed up at 15 OTU Harwell, Berkshire, in August, before being whipped hastily into Radcliffe Hospital, Oxford for an appendectomy. This proved to be handy for regular visits from his family, but he was upset that his enforced absence led to his crew being given to another pilot.

Fighting fit, he received a ready-made crew who initially displayed some anxiety and Payne discovered that they had experienced several shaky landings, especially at night, with their previous pilot.

'He had managed Oxfords at night, but not Wellingtons. I think he held off too high. It was very difficult and I was always amazed when we got down. You couldn't see the ground, you judged height by the look of the flare-path and hoped for the best. My new crew seemed to get on with me all right, when they knew I could fly and land reasonably well.'

Payne's navigator, Flying Officer Vernon Long, from Shorwell, Isle of Wight, was twenty-three, and, according to his pilot meticulous and extremely accurate. Although he had not flown on a sortie, Long had already been instructing at a navigation school.

From Bradford, the wireless operator was twenty-year-old Sergeant George Leach, stocky, with dark crinkly hair.

Bomb aimer Flying Officer Josh Emery, twenty-two, tall, thin, with a slightly abrasive manner, came from Whitley Bay, Northumberland.

Sergeant Geoff James, from near Stafford, the mid-upper gunner, was slim, animated and talkative.

Sergeant Jim Knight had quit his job as a policeman to join the RAF. At thirty-six he was a father figure to his crewmates. Almost six feet tall it was a squeeze for him to get into the rear turret. He was married with a five-year-old son. Payne's most poignant memory of his tail gunner dates from Christmas Eve, 1943.

'We were all ready to go home on leave at lunchtime when we were unexpectedly put on a cross-country training run. Jim came to see me and said:"My nipper wants to see his dad. Can you do anything about getting me off?" So unofficially, I flew without him and Jim went home to his son and wife, Lilian – who he always called Ginger.

'In February 1944 we flew a brand-new Wellington X across the Bay of Biscay to Morocco and then to Italy where we joined 40 Squadron in 205 Group, based with 104 Squadron at Foggia. James joined another crew in England. The 40 Squadron

Wellingtons did not have a mid-upper turret.

'Foggia was grim: muddy, cold and wet with awful accommodation in bombed-out flats without glass in the windows. There was no hot water and the loos didn't work very well. The airfield had been hammered at different times by the British and the Germans. The runway was made from perforated interlocking steel sheets over grass but full of bits of shrapnel which were not very good for the Wellington's tyres and they had to be changed frequently.

'Foggia Main airfield runway was checked twice a day for shrapnel and other pieces of metal, including rusty nails and spent bullets. This was difficult because it was being used all the time. Americans were also here with Fortresses and Lightnings. We were briefed in a building which was no longer fit to be used as a school. This was our squadron headquarters.

'We did mainly strategic bombing against places like Plovdiv, Bulgaria's second major city, Budapest, and small ports being used to supply the Germans at the Anzio beachhead.

'There was little to do in our spare time. We slept, played a lot of bridge or pontoon and drank asti spumante, a sort of fizzy champagne, and V and C, which was vermouth and cognac, getting very drunk on occasions. Nobody got leave to go home. A lot of people, especially ground crew, had been out there or in North Africa since 1940 or 1941.

'We had a rest home about forty miles away beside the Adriatic at Rhodi where we used to drive in a garry when we had a few days off. Two houses had been taken over by the RAF and the woman owner cooked our meals. It was pleasant there. I also spent a very cold day duck shooting in Manfredonia on the estate of an Italian count who, I think, may have wanted to get on good terms with the Allies.'

Payne's first bombing operation was on 18 March 1944 as second dickey with Flying Officer Johnny Huggler in Wellington LN874 D-Dog, taking off at 7.15pm and attacking the railway marshalling yards at Plovdiv. The flight took 7hr 35min.

'I was very impressed because I was treated as one of the crew. Very often new pilots did their first op and were stuffed up in the astrodome, but Johnny let me fly and told me all about it. We dropped five 500lb bombs and four 250-pounders from around 15,000ft. We didn't have Gee or anything so it was all dead reckoning and in nine-tenths cloud.It was a poor attack with no illumination, and no concentration achieved so this trip was a dead loss, really.

'We were over hostile territory all the way after leaving Italy. We went off together as a squadron although it wasn't as concentrated as it was from England, but we had to keep to our times to bomb and it was impressed on us that if we drifted out of the stream we were liable to be shot down. We also had to keep to the courses and times along the flight but it was difficult when you didn't know where you were.'

The following night Payne and Long, his navigator, flew in JA509 K-King with Flight Sergeant Allen and his crew to Monfalcone in northern Italy, negotiating heavy flak over the Pola naval base to bomb dockyards and submarine building plants successfully.

Payne flew again with Huggler on 23 March, in MF132 B-Baker, when they acted as one of the squadron's two pathfinders, dropping flares over the target.A night fighter was spotted but it did not interfere with their task of dropping nine 500lb bombs and two of 250lb, rearranging the marshalling yards at Padua.

'Johnny was a wonderful chap but he was killed when he flew into a mountain on the last operation of his second tour, helping the Maquis in southern France.'

Payne's first sortie as skipper was on 1 April when he was sent in JA509 K-King to hit the Macchi aircraft factory beside Lake Varese in northern Italy.

'North of Verona on our return flight we were suddenly coned by searchlights at 16,000ft. My heart sank and I realised: "God, I must do something about this". I had seen other aeroplanes caught by searchlights and thought: "Poor sods". Now we were the poor sods. I dived and corkscrewed, went to the left, steep turns and diving turns. I threw the aircraft about all over the place trying to get out of the powerful beams. I remember needing very much to survive. But I didn't want the aircraft to break up. The Wellington was extremely strong but being flung about violently like that put extreme stresses on the air frame and wings.It must have been terrible for the rest of the crew, but we managed to get out of it at around 2,000ft.

'We came down to 200ft, hedge-hopped back to the coast, and reached Foggia Main airfield where they put up three searchlights as there were no German fighters about, which was useful.

'I had heard of some chaps who had not got back after being coned so I was quite pleased we made it, but we didn't talk much about these things at Foggia. It wasn't a question of a stiff upper lip, more a question of not shooting a line. Some people did, but you didn't listen to them.'

Two nights later, in the same aircraft, they ran into heavy ack-ack on the way to hit the Manfred Weiss armaments factory in Budapest.

'The flak was inaccurate but we didn't know that as we saw it ahead of us. You don't exactly get afraid but you wish it wasn't there. After bombing I set a red on blue on the compass instead of blue on blue and after ten miles or so discovered we were heading towards Russia. We came back avoiding the city we had just bombed and tried to catch up with the rest of the squadron.'

Payne was given another navigator for a second trip to Varese in LN562 C-Charlie on 11 April after Vernon Long was taken ill. Flight Sergeant Bob Edmonds, from Toronto, was slightly built, cheerful, and knew how to get an aeroplane from A to B without making a fuss about it. It was, however, impossible for anyone to find the Macchi factory that night through ten-tenths cloud.

'We were carrying six 500lb bombs and six 250-pounders and had to jettison them in the Adriatic. It was a terrible waste, but this is what we had been told to do if we couldn't see a definite target because the Italians were now more or less on our side.'

On the night of 14 April, back in K-King, their target was the dockyard installations at Porto San Stefano on the west coast of Italy.

'The squadron used to send out three aircraft about every two hours during the night to bomb Porto San Stefano and Piombino, and other ports where the Germans were unloading boats. With luck a bomb might hit them but we certainly kept them awake, on their toes and a little worried. These raids were kept going all through the nights, but not during daytime when we rarely flew, except to Yugoslavia. The squadron did one or two attacks and supply drops for Tito, landing on Vis, an island off the Yugoslav coast.'

Payne and his crew continued their determined torment-the-German raids on 16 April when they left Foggia at 12.50am and successfully attacked Piombino's dockyards. They landed back at base at 5.40am and after debriefing and a night flight breakfast of bacon and eggs, got to bed when the rest of the station was busily at work.

'At about lunchtime I looked at the notice board in the school and my heart sank. We were on ops again that night. I always felt like that before I flew, wishing I wasn't going, although it was all right once I got into the aircraft. Flying was, for me, a sort of love-hate relationship.'

They were briefed to attack marshalling yards and oil tanks at Plovdiv, again flying JA509 K-King. There was no time to do an air test and six 500lb and six 250lb bombs were loaded into the bomb bay.

They urinated on the back wheel as usual before takeoff and, sitting in the cockpit, Payne touched the tiny flat piece of New Zealand jade he always carried in his pocket. His father had given him it and because he had returned safely from every trip it had become a lucky charm. He still has it.

They were third to take off and advanced slowly to the head of the runway when the second Wellington rose into the sky, becoming a blur as dusk closed in. Payne revved the engines up against the brakes, they screamed and the aircraft trembled, as if it was excited at the prospect of leaving the ground. The green light flashed at the controller's caravan, Payne opened up the throttles and at 8.19pm they began moving down the runway. Bomb aimer Josh Emery was sitting in the second pilot's seat beside the skipper, the others were at their positions as the Wimpey touched 90mph, seconds from becoming airborne. Peter Payne will never forget what happened next:

'As we went down the runway the bomber gathered speed, with a surge of power magnified by the uneven runway, then suddenly there was the most horrible rattling and thumping and the entire aircraft was vibrating. The rhythm changed before I realised the right-hand tyre had burst. I couldn't keep the aircraft straight and it swung violently and uncontrollably to the right, describing a complete circle, known in the RAF as a ground loop. This all seemed to happen in slow motion though it could not have taken more than a second.

'Ordinary measurement of time meant nothing. Movement stopped but the aircraft sank down and as well as the flarepath light there was another which became rapidly brighter until the whole aircraft was lit up as though there was bright sunlight. The starboard wing had dropped to the ground, the undercarriage had collapsed, its struts puncturing the nacelle fuel tanks, and I saw a little flame appear behind the engine in the starboard wing. In no time at all it had spread all over the place. I thought: "Christ! We're done for. We'll go up at any moment." We had to get out and I yelled instructions into the intercom. But everybody already knew what they must do.

'All I could think of was the fire, the full petrol tanks and bombs and the overwhelming thought that I must get out. I undid the lever holding the escape hatch above the cockpit, not waiting for the navigator and wireless operator. Josh Emery followed but before climbing out I imagined my friends in the mess saying: "Poor old Pete went for a shit at the end of the runway. Let's have another V and C." In my mind I saw my parents and Nick, one of my brothers, having supper, which on Sundays in the kitchen at home was always soup, pickled onions and cheese.

'Although I had turned off the engines and fuel the airscrews were still spinning, fanning the flames. I jumped on to the port wing between the fuselage and the engine and as I slid towards the ground I felt the whirling airscrew just caress my leather helmet. Even in my rush for self-preservation I felt sick, knowing that another fraction of an inch and my skull would have been smashed. It makes me cold to think about that even now so many years afterwards.

'All these things passed in a flash. My body acted without any prompting, and I found myself running as far as I could away from the brilliant light that was enveloping the Wellington until someone grabbed me and I was pushed to the ground by an ambulanceman who cried: "Stay down! Stay down!" He lay on top of me and I was in darkness.'

The ground rocked as several ferocious explosions in quick succession ripped the air. They were followed by the sound of exploding ammunition, and bullets hurtling in all directions. Payne, spread-eagled, heard shouts and the clanging of bells as more fire tenders and ambulances arrived before the ambulanceman released him and he felt hands reach down and gently place him on a stretcher. He had been burned, but the only pain came from his left big toe which had been broken as he fell from the aircraft. The pilot's brain scarcely had time to register the extent of what had happened, but he felt relief he had survived and hoped his crew were safe. Remembering nothing of the actual crash he was admitted to hospital, and told all was well and he should sleep.

'I later felt my face with my unbandaged hand and found that it was swathed in dressings. A sick cold fear took hold of me when I felt my eyes but couldn't see. This was different to the fear I had when we crashed. Then action was possible and fear aided my will to escape. This time I was helpless. I sobbed and grey gloom took over. My initial thankfulness at my survival evaporated.'

Rear gunner Jim Knight got out of the burning Wellington without a scratch. Wireless operator George Leach's hands were burned and stand-in navigator Bob Edmond's ear was so badly roasted it eventually shrivelled up and was lost.

Josh Emery, the bomb aimer, was in a bad way, severely burned and unconscious. Although he had followed his skipper out from the same hatch, in his confusion and haste to escape, instead of dropping down from the port wing, which was not yet blazing, he turned to starboard and was caught in a torrent of fire. He managed to stagger several yards before being found by another ambulanceman who beat out the flames. The injured men were all taken to 30 Mobile Field Hospital, Foggia.

'I thought I would be blind forever,' says Payne. 'I didn't believe the doctors when they said I'd be fine, that the only problem was the flesh around my eyes which had swollen up and was covering my eyes. But after three days I could see again. I believe the burns to my face, on the left side, were caused when my oxygen mask, still hanging on when I got out, had become unhitched. My left hand was burned after a leather gauntlet fell off.

'I saw Josh in hospital, obviously doped with morphine. He was all bandaged up. Only his eyes were visible.'

All except Emery were shortly afterwards transferred by ambulance along a long bumpy road to the white-painted No 1 General Hospital which stood on the slopes of Vesuvius near Naples.

Josh Emery died on 21 April. Neither Payne nor his crewmates were told for some time of the young man's death and Payne was annoyed and upset by the oversight. Emery was buried at Foggia, his remains moved after the war to the big military cemetery at Bari which Peter Payne and Vernon Long have since visited.

The two ambulancemen, LAC W. J. Clarke and LAC R. E. Williams, who risked their lives to save the aircrew after the crash, were each awarded a George Medal.

Payne remained in hospital several weeks before being repatriated to Britain. Bob Edmonds was sent back to Canada. George Leach and Jim Knight both flew again. Leach came home with a DFM, having completed two tours in Italy.

'It must have been very difficult for them to carry on flying operations after that terrible crash and with another crew. Sadly, Jim was killed on the night of 13/14 July when his Wellington was shot down by a night fighter.'

The rear gunner had been flying in LN270 O-Orange, piloted by Pilot Officer C. Charalambous, which bombed Lambrate marshalling yards in Milan.It was later thought that their aircraft had wandered a little off track and found themselves over Verona where a patrolling enemy fighter would have feasted greedily on a single British bomber. All five crew were killed and are buried in Padua war cemetery.

Another three aircraft crashed after tyres burst on the Foggia runway in April 1944. The growing problem motivated the group engineering officer to develop a gadget to remove dangerous debris from the runway.

The *Manchester Guardian* reported on 1 November 1944 that a magnetic sweep, or a 'snifter', had been designed at Foggia using a big magnet hooked to the back of a truck.The power was provided by two generator sets: one picked up among derelict German equipment in the Western Desert, the other found in a dump on the airfield.

Although the four-foot wide snifter, pulled slowly along the ground eventually picked up thousands of pieces of metal, the problem was not solved until March 1945 when the Wellingtons were replaced by Liberators, which had more robust tyres.

After Payne returned to England, a medical officer sent him to East Grinstead hospital where Professor Archie McIndoe had established a pioneering burns unit.

'They took one look at me, laughed, and told me to go back to my unit,which was understandable.I only had second-degree burns. Some chaps I saw there had practically nothing left of their faces.My burns got better on their own.'

The pilot attended a medical board where he was told he was no longer any good for flying because of his eyes.

'I did not fancy being a stores or MT officer and didn't know what to do. Then I contacted my uncle, Ransom Pickard, an eye surgeon in Exeter. He gave me a few eye exercises to do and I was perfectly all right.'

Peter Payne did fly again, but not operationally. He was posted to several units as the war drew to a close, including some in Scotland where they flew Hurricanes and Miles Masters while towing drogues, giving anti-aircraft gunners target practise. In order to do this he had converted on to single-engine aircraft flying a Harvard, Vengeance and Spitfire X.

'But it was more fun flying Oxfords at night dodging in and out of searchlights so the operators could line them up on us as we tried to get away. That was much better than being coned when night fighters were around.'

CHAPTER SIX

THE RESISTANCE FIGHTER

To anyone standing on the small grass airfield at Desford, the Tiger Moth, a dark speck dawdling across the blue sky, sounded like a frustrated blowfly trapped in an empty wine bottle. To Ken Trueman, a twenty-year-old trainee pilot, off the ground for the first time, it was a sensational feeling.

Sitting behind his instructor in the little biplane he marvelled at the view of Leicestershire spread out below and congratulated himself on joining the RAF. Life aloft was spectacularly different to being confined to the ground.

It was the summer of 1942, the sun was shining and he was drifting through the first flight of his twelve-hour selection course.

They spent a few minutes going through exercises, then the pilot said: 'Would you like to do some aerobatics?' Trueman, rather too eagerly said that he would and the instructor asked: 'Are your straps tight?' Trueman recalls:

'I pushed up against my straps, said they were fine and he immediately turned the plane upside-down. I thought: "Oh my God" and felt myself go a little bit as the straps took up the strain. We did two or three loops. Then he did a loop with a flick off the top to turn the plane the other way.

'We plunged towards the ground for a bit of low flying that included going underneath some electric wires which, I believe, was against the rules as was frightening the life out of several people who were working in the fields. It was great fun.'

Their landing at Desford was more spectacular than had been intended, even by the standards of a young pilot whose zest for excitement and speed was matched only by his determination to fully test his pupils' nerve.

'We came into the airfield to land and were almost touching down when the starboard wing struck the ground. The plane did a half turn then went back on to its wheels. Neither of us was hurt. I had a laugh about it with the pilot, a flying officer, not much older than me, and the lads on my course, then put it out of my mind. The plane's air frame was twisted, but it was repaired and flew again in a month.'

'I soloed after 7hr 50min and later took the plane up with the instructor, did all the exercises and landed without him touching the controls. At the end of the twelve hours he said: "You'll be a pilot all right".

'Next thing I knew I was told I could never be a pilot because of bad night vision. Terribly disappointed I had a word with the CO. I wanted to go off flying altogether if I couldn't be a pilot. Then Groupie said: "You know, the navigator is just as important as the pilot". And I decided to give it a go.'

Two years later Sergeant Ken Trueman was navigator for Sergeant Denis Barr, a Yorkshireman, from Cottingham. The same age and slim build as his navigator, the pair became great friends.

Trueman, born in a beer house, Navigation Inn, in Hockley, Birmingham, was brought up in a succession of pubs managed by his father, Bill. Ken Trueman, a slim six-footer, became a carpenter, helping build airfields before becoming an airman. The crew's only married man, his wife, Sylvia, lived at their flat in Acock's Green.

Wireless operator Bill Ezra, from Reading, the crew's only non-smoker, slightly tubby, was twenty-eight.

The bomb aimer, Bernie Harkin, an Australian farmer, was a flight sergeant, outranking, and at thirty-two, older than all his crewmates.

Nineteen-year-old Arthur Goddard, from Cleethorpes, Lincolnshire, was flight engineer. Tall and slim, he was most remembered for a persistent hacking cough.

Barr's first air gunners were both Canadians. Small men with ferrety faces, they were not with him long. Trueman recalls:

'We were at 20 OTU, Lossiemouth, where, after a couple of training trips, they asked Denis if he would mind them leaving to join a Canadian crew. Off they went and not long afterwards we were coming back over the Grampians to Lossiemouth after a training exercise and saw smoke close to base. Denis said he thought a Wimpey had gone down.'

It was the Canadians' Wellington, reputed to be the oldest aircraft in the RAF. The ground crew had been running a lottery on when it would crash.

'They had gone into a corkscrew and one engine cut. The corkscrew turned into a spiral and they were all killed, burned to cinders.'

The two replacement gunners had only been in the RAF for six months when they joined Barr. The mid-upper, Alf Broddle, from Croxton, near Kirmington, had been a farm labourer.

The tail gunner, 'Lefty' Orrick, from Middlesbrough had pursued a successful pre-service career as a poacher. He did not speak much about his furtive employment in the fields near the Yorkshire town, but often demonstrated his considerable skills to the crew.

'We occasionally went for walks in the country and suddenly heard "Plop!" Feathers began flying everywhere and another sparrow dropped out of the hedge. Lefty was deadly with a catapult. Bill Ezra, who didn't agree with killing small creatures for fun got mad with Lefty, who took no notice, snaring rabbits at night.'

This was a happy but mild-mannered crew, easy in each other's company. None used bad language. Ezra was always irritated by Lefty's poaching, but never swore at him. Aware that foul language often coarsens the character of those who use it, none risked spoiling the special relationship they had by launching into a tirade of abuse with each other in difficult situations.

After converting from Wellingtons to the Halifax III at 1652 HCU, Marston Moor, they were posted to 640 Squadron, Leconfield, Yorkshire.

'When you joined a squadron you had so many cross-countries, day and night, to do before being put on ops,' says Trueman. 'They also did clever things like routeing you near the Orkney Islands and Portsmouth so you got fired on by the Royal Navy. They didn't fire too close to us, but it gave us an idea of what it would be like later.

'We'd got two night and one daylight cross-country to do before being thrown into operational duty when Denis and I, walking to the mess for a meal on 5 June 1944, were unexpectedly summoned by Tannoy to the briefing room. We were met by the navigation officer who said we were going on ops that night.

'When I said we still had three exercises to do he smiled and said:"Don't worry, it's an easy one tonight."

Their apprehension was further diluted at briefing, when an intelligence officer said, encouragingly:'There's only one anti-aircraft gun in the area where you will be bombing.'

'We put our flying gear on, collected our parachutes then got on the RAF bus which took two crews to their aircraft. My stomach always dropped into my boots when I got on that bus.

'You were at dispersal for an hour, although we didn't get straight on the aircraft. Some time was spent playing pitch and toss for pennies with the ground crew. I got in half-an-hour before we took off and did my plot with the latest information. I had to work out a climb on course. A fully-loaded plane could not go straight up, climbing was a slow business. You could not get height over the station and you couldn't go much higher than 16,000ft or 17,000ft with a full bomb load.'

'We arrived at the target, a battery of guns pointing out to sea at Maisy, near Cherbourg. We started the six-minute run over the Cherbourg peninsular when what we had been told was the only anti-aircraft gun in the area suddenly put a shell right underneath us.

'My feet turned into blocks of ice as I became frozen with fear, and thought:"That's it, I'm finished. I'll go LMF before I go on another op." I didn't say anything to the others then suddenly they were all saying:"Look down." I looked and although it was dark we could see the wakes from all the ships, an amazing sight. It was D-Day. I gave the pilot the course for base, poured a cup of tea from my flask and in a minute or two thought:"It wasn't too bad", and when we got back to base we told everyone the invasion was on.

'By 9 June we'd been on three ops and were getting a bit blasé. On 12/13 June we were sent to attack a railway target near Amiens. We were never told the name of the town or city we were bombing, only the latitude and longitude.

'We were out in front of the first wave, just before we were due at the target, when we were coned. Two other bombers were also coned. Our pilot immediately put us into a nosedive and luckily, we got out of the cone, but when we levelled out we saw the other two aircraft going down on fire. We had to go round and come back, quite low, on to the target. We didn't bomb at the right height, but we hit the target indicators.'

When Denis Barr and his crew joined 640 Squadron they used other people's aircraft on their early trips. Then they were given M–Mother as their own. Their dispersal point was almost in the village of Molescroft so they called it M–Mother Molescroft Maggie.

'It was the oldest plane on the squadron but became special to us. Every aircraft suffered from what was known as soft iron. You had a compass on the plane which should point north but didn't because it was surrounded by metal. You had to calibrate your compass every so often on the ground with the engines idling. The pilot puts the compass on a north heading while the navigator stands about 100 yards to the rear with a hand-held compass. The pilot signals he's on north, but might be three or four degrees out so he does the corrections for each heading. Maggie suffered with soft iron even more than other aircraft, but we got used to it.

'After five or six more trips we were offered a new aircraft, but Maggie had certain advantages over other Halifaxes, even the new ones. It could go 200ft higher and fly 30mph faster. This was useful if we were late getting to the target or needed to get higher to escape the flak.

'We flew at around 160mph with a full bomb load. After dropping the bombs, pushing the throttles straight through the gate you'd get up to 200mph. One night when we came off the target with a tail wind of 100mph the pilot said we were flying at a ground speed of 300mph, a wonderful feeling.'

The raids mounted: thirteen in June, ten in July. Then, on 7 August 1944, still in Molescroft Maggie – LK757 C8 M-Mother – they were sent to the Normandy battle area, near Caen. Over 1,000 aircraft were briefed to attack five different aiming points less than a mile in front of Allied ground troops. Only 660 aircraft bombed. Strategic German positions and surrounding roads were hit. Trueman explains:

'Our master bombers were not needed because our own artillery was to fire coloured shells on to where they wanted us to bomb. Unfortunately, these did not last as long as the Pathfinders' TIs. We were told that if we were on the run-up and the artillery's lights went out we were not to bomb, but bring our bombs back to base.

'You can guess what happened. We were on the run up and the artillery lights went out so we returned to England with our bombs. In the meantime a sea mist had rolled in through the Humber estuary, covering our airfield, not for the first time. Night after night we had to land away. This night we were instructed to fly all the way up to Scotland and back to get rid of fuel because we were to put down at Boscombe Down and a Halifax couldn't land with a full bomb load and a lot of fuel.

'Boscombe Down, Wiltshire, was an experimental station, with a grass runway and manual flare path. The pilot was told that on his approach he should undershoot the landing "T", which showed the way you should fly in. Just before landing the wireless operator and I had to lie in the rest position behind the main spar.'

Trueman was late getting aft and made the mistake of peering out. What he saw rapidly bearing down on them were two rows of telegraph poles carrying wires on either side of a railway line. The pilot had undershot too much. Molescroft Maggie smashed with great precision into one pole, then another, making a memorable appearance into Boscombe Down airfield trailing two sets of telephone wires, putting down heavily on the grass, tearing out the four engines and the bottom of the Halifax while the perplexed navigator was bounced helplessly round the crumpling fuselage like a bag of laundry.

As they continued their madcap half-mile passage across the grass, bombs began dropping out of the aircraft and rolling in all directions. The fuselage was ripped into three pieces but they stepped from the wreckage without a bruise between them.

As Trueman lay winded on his back beside the pilot he heard the exchange with control.

A plaintive inquiry: 'M-Mother, where are you?' Followed by the pilot, gritting his teeth, replying: 'We've just crashed.'

'Another 100 yards and we would have been all right,' says Trueman. 'Trouble is we had not been told how far we should undershoot.'

The following two nights they bombed more targets in France then, on 12 August, they were briefed to attack the Opel tank factory at Rüsselsheim. They were told V2 rockets were being built here.

Two new Halifax IIIs had been delivered to 640 Squadron. One, MZ345 C8-G, was given to the squadron commander,

Wing Commander M. T. Maw DFC. The second, MZ855 C8–F
was piloted by Denis Barr.

'These two aircraft had been fitted with H2S which I'd been
trained to use,' says Trueman. 'With H2S you sent out your own
radar impulses, picking up the rebound. If you were over water
you didn't get any rebound, although if there was a river you
could find where you were from the bends. Over fields you got
a slight rebound. Over houses it became tremendous. So you
could see the outline of where you were, almost as if you were
looking at it. I was delighted. Unfortunately, it was to be our
downfall.'

They took off at 9.39pm, four minutes after Maw.

'Near the target the pilot and bomb aimer both said: "Look at
this." I opened my black curtains and looked down on a sea of
fire. Our bombs went away and we did our two minutes off the
target and turned. We'd been told to come down as quickly as
we could from 18,000ft to fool the night fighters. It was a
powered dive before levelling out at 6,000ft where we were hit
by flak.

'We found out afterwards that the only planes shot down that
night on our squadron were the two carrying H2S. They'd lined
the guns up on our radar. That's what intelligence told us when
we got back. We were hit first by a shell from a light anti-aircraft
gun standing on the railway.

'The noise was deafening as the shell blew a hole in the side
of the aircraft. The next shell hit the starboard outer engine and
set it on fire. The flames were almost out when a third shell took
the undercarriage away. We were over Belgium and I worked out
the exact position handing it to the wireless operator who sent
out an SOS.

'A fourth shell went through the starboard wing and the
Halifax was engulfed by flames. It was like daylight though, at
this point, there were no flames inside. The next thing I knew
was Bernie Harkin, the bomb aimer, his parachute on, tapping
me on the shoulder and crying: "Get out of the way!"

'I got out of the way and clipped on my parachute as Bernie
opened the escape hatch under my seat, and jumped out. I
followed him.'

Two men died in the blazing wreckage of the Halifax: the
pilot, Denis Barr, and rear gunner Lefty Orrick. The survivors
later speculated what might have happened.

Trueman continues: 'Bernie had been sitting next to the skipper when he said:"Abandon aircraft!" Because the intercom was u/s we believe Denis switched on the automatic pilot. The giros must have been damaged because the bomber flew in a circle and we all landed in the same area. If it had been going straight and level we'd have been miles apart.

'We think the pilot went through the plane checking that everyone had got out, because that was the sort of man he was. There was no way he would jump out himself if he thought someone else might still be there. He had to be sure. I think he found Lefty slumped injured over his guns, or trying to open jammed turret doors to get at his parachute.

'It only took me two minutes to come down which was a good thing because I had forgotten to take my helmet off and the intercom lead got mixed up with the parachute as it went up and got tight around my neck. I had my fingers in pulling at the lead to stop it tightening.

'I looked down and saw I was landing in a field where bonfires were burning. I couldn't understand what was happening, but knew I had to escape somehow. I was drifting to the side of the fires, going backwards. The breath was knocked out of me when I hit the ground as my parachute caught in a tree. It was 1am. I was in a field 6km south of Ciney in the Ardennes.

'A fellow came up and said:"Kamerad." He was, I discovered, a Belgian, but he spoke in German because he didn't know if I was a German dressed up as an RAF airman to catch him out. I was still on the ground and couldn't have knocked over a baby, let alone a man. I said:"English." He said:"Ah, Angleterre." He picked me up and kissed me on both cheeks.

'The Maquis were expecting a delivery of aid from England that night. Instead, they got me. Nothing else arrived for them and they put the fires out before we started walking.

'They looked a bit rag tag and bobtail, ordinary lads who had come from towns and had gone into the woods so the Germans wouldn't take them. But they were armed.

'I wanted a smoke and reached into my battledress pocket. I always took a full packet of Players with me but on this particular op I'd forgotten. I only had seven cigarettes and took one out of a packet and six hands reached out and took the rest. I was on their rations after that.

'One or two spoke a little English. We went to various houses.

Some already had members of my crew and weren't going to take any more. They were all in safe houses except Alf Broddle, the mid-upper gunner. He'd got in with the Maquis when they suddenly disappeared. He continued walking and went over the top of a hill straight into a gang of Germans.'

Wing Commander Maw, who had been flying with a seven-man crew, was killed. Three of his crew also died; another four became POWs.

'At 5am, when I was just about on my knees, I was put in a little room in the roof of a cottage deep in the country. At 8am they got me up and gave me breakfast: an egg, a thick fatty piece of bacon, and bread. I ate it all, I was so hungry.

'That morning I was visited by local dignitaries: the vicar, the postman, the policeman and many more. They all shook me by the hand and with everyone I had to have a little drink of white liquid which I believe was wood alcohol. I didn't want to upset anyone by refusing but for someone who didn't drink it was a bit fiery and by midday I could hardly stand.

'It was then the door burst open and two men, sinister and threatening, appeared, armed with sten guns. I thought: "Oh God, this is the end." But they were also Maquis. They led me across a field in brilliant sunshine. I wanted to lie down and sleep. An open lorry was parked in a lane full of the Maquis, plus Arthur Goddard, our flight engineer, and wireless operator Bill Ezra. It was then we learned that two of our crew had been killed and buried by nuns from a convent.

'We drove through Ciney where I looked over the side and saw German officers walking with their girlfriends. The Maquis were standing brazenly in the back of the lorry. But the retreat was on and the Germans had accepted the presence of the Maquis, providing the Belgians didn't kill any of them.'

That night the airmen were guests of honour at a party in the woods, at which they met the local railway stationmaster, captured by the Maquis, a friendly German civilian who had the freedom of the camp and did not want to leave. They slept in a tent on a floor of straw.

Woken at 2am, the airmen were taken to another Maquis group and met Baron H. De Woot who lived in some splendour at the turreted Château de Jannée, at Pessoux on the main road to Luxembourg. The baron was second in command of the Maquis group. His brother-in-law, a Belgian count, known as

Chief Tom, was in charge. The Chief's wife was liaison officer between the Maquis and British intelligence.

'Chief Tom was pleased to have some RAF lads because they had discipline which was what the group needed. They were aged from fourteen to fifty.

'After four days our bomb aimer, Bernie Harkin, joined us. He had come down into a dung heap and sprained his ankle. He laid under a hedge for two days until he could approach somebody he felt he could trust. We settled down to a life of terrorism.

'They fitted us out with trousers and rough shirts, and I had a sports jacket with sleeves which ended well above my wrists. They couldn't provide boots so I cut through stitches in my flying boots to turn them into shoes. I was armed with a sten gun, 200 rounds of ammunition and a Mills bomb.

'The idea was to disrupt German communications. A driver and four men went out with crosscut saws. We stole a car and drove to where there were telegraph poles on each side of the road. Two worked with a saw on the left and another pair were on the right. I was on a saw and my crewmates were also involved. We cut down the poles, drove a couple of miles and did it again half-a-dozen times before dumping the car.

'We blew up several goods trains on a local line which ran up a steep incline. At the top our men with bren guns stopped the train and the Belgian driver and his fireman ran off. We used plastic explosive to blow up a rail at the bottom of the hill, the last truck was uncoupled to roll down and turn over on the broken rail and we drove the train into it. It kept the Germans busy then, after it had been repaired, we did it again. It was great fun.

'We always relied on villagers feeding us, providing we didn't kill any Germans because they would be made to suffer. But they were also short of food and we once went three days without a meal.

'One day the Belgians brought in two prisoners, suspected of being quislings. They had to be tried. They were tied to a tree and we took turns guarding them. One was ugly and said nothing. The other was a restaurateur from Brussels. After four days he was acquitted and made camp cook. The ugly man was taken into the wood and shot.'

Once, eating their lunch in a signal box they were fired on by seven Germans who had been walking along the main line. They escaped into the top of the steep-sided cutting, dispersing into the countryside.

Another time a New Zealander was killed in a fierce gun fight with Germans after the Belgians and airmen tried to steal lorries before switching camps. The Maquis then melted away as if they had never existed, except two who stayed with the four airmen. They kept on the move for thirty-six hours to make sure the coast was clear before attempting to return to their camp, but after meeting two other Belgians the plan was changed and the little party headed for one of King Leopold's remote hunting lodges. Here they met another twenty Allied airmen, including the entire crew from a crashed Flying Fortress.

They lay low for a week during which they watched four retreating German tanks attacked by two Spitfires. The tanks crashed headlong into the woods unaware that they were being observed from a deep ditch by Ken Trueman and his companion who were trapped there for two hours until the Germans believed the danger had passed.

From here they marched forty miles in fourteen hours to an orphanage where they slept in cowsheds and, for five days feasted royally on venison and trout until early one morning they discovered that German troops were slowly surrounding them. They fled into the woods, chased by gun fire. Later that morning shells whistled over the group from both sides. Then it became quiet. Trueman recalls:

'A Belgian said he would go into a nearby village to see what was happening. He was away ages and we became despondent. We hadn't eaten and our tobacco was wet. Suddenly, we heard a tank approaching and thought that was the end. The "tank" appeared. It was a Jeep without a silencer. In it were two Americans, both drunk as lords. They gave us cigarettes and cognac.'

Trueman and his crewmates scrounged lifts from American drivers to Paris where, a month after being shot down, they were given American uniforms, their first proper wash for weeks, and seats in a Dakota home from Orly airport. They arrived at Hendon at midnight and were dismayed to be sent through customs. All Ken Trueman had that might have interested the dogged officials were photographs taken with the Maquis which he had always kept hidden in his shoe. He did not declare them.

CHAPTER SEVEN

JUST ANOTHER NIGHT OUT

John Sargeant was fourteen, living in the small Lincolnshire village of Frithville, attending Boston grammar school, at the start of the Second World War.

Low-flying aircraft were almost as common as cars in Bomber County and no one was surprised when he joined the RAF as soon as he could, volunteering for aircrew. He trained as a flight engineer and was a stocky nineteen-year-old when posted to 106 Squadron at Syerston, Nottinghamshire, in 1943.

Early on the morning of 4 September 1943, Sargeant's crippled Lancaster ditched in the North Sea after attacking Berlin. It was his third sortie.

After the war he ran his own tyre-fitting business in Boston. A shy modest man, who hated fuss and show-offs, rarely talking about the war, he died from leukaemia in 1970, aged forty-six.

When Sargeant's grieving widow, Terry, was going through his desk she was astonished to find in a box, his Distinguished Flying Medal and an old notebook with his pencil-written account of that traumatic trip to Berlin. She had been unaware of their existence. This is John Sargeant's secret story which he called *Just Another Night Out*.

★ ★ ★

It was rather a dull day on Friday 3 September 1943 when we went down to the flights as usual at about 9am. After roll call we waited for any gen about flying for the day which mostly came out at about 10.30.

It came as we had all expected. Operations Tonight and we

were down to fly. We immediately got started on our own necessary preparations.

In our crew there were Mac, [Les McKenzie] and Jock [Ron Kelly], our two gunners. Mac, in the rear turret, was from Cambridge, a real old timer with eight years' service compared with us sprogs. He was well above the average age for aircrew, twenty-eight as far as the RAF knew, but about thirty-four I always thought. He looked much older, with such a huge old-fashioned moustache he had cultivated on his top lip. Mac was a good type, quiet and reserved, but he enjoyed coming out with Jock and myself in the evenings.

Jock, our mid-upper gunner, was my pal. We were both new members of the crew. I joined them just before they left Swinderby, their heavy conversion unit – 1660 HCU.

Jock arrived a few days later when we got to 106 Squadron at Syerston. He had been separated from his old crew because of a wound received while returning low over the Baltic from Stettin one night. Hit three times in the leg he was off flying for about six months. We palled up together right from the start and got to be like brothers, as someone once remarked to me. We shared the same room and rarely went out unless together, and I must say we had some grand times which I shall never forget. Jock was from Newton Mearns, a small place just outside Glasgow.

Chap [Doug Chappell], the wireless operator, was also a good type and very interested in his job, keen in all respects. Chap was from Kent a policeman before joining up. He was also above the average age for aircrew. He got on quite well with Sax, [Tom Saxby], our air bomber, a flying officer, another ex-policeman.

Dave, [Pilot Officer Tom Davies] the navigator, another old fellow at thirty-four was a quiet Londoner, a good friend of Mac.

Our skipper [Squadron Leader David Howroyd, their flight commander, from Kelvedon, Essex], was even older. He had been in the service some time and was married with one child. He was a keen and very experienced flyer, strict on discipline.

After hearing we were on ops I went down to dispersal to the kite we were taking, JA893 ZN C-Charlie, better known as Bar Charlie. I had a gossip with the ground crew as usual about the night's loads; the fuel load especially, because from that we could estimate where the target might be.

The ground crew had the gen. It was 1,700 gallons, from which we deduced it must be east of the Ruhr. We had heard on that morning's news bulletins that the Army had landed in Italy which made us think we might be going to give them a hand.

We went to briefing thinking it was not Berlin, which had been attacked two nights previously, a thought which,I must say, was very comforting. At our engineers' briefing we established that the fuel load had been increased to 2,000 gallons, definitely backing up our hopes of Italy and wiping out any chance of The Big City.

One thing we had not thought of was a special long–distance route to Berlin and boy, were we shaken when we got to main briefing. Berlin it was.

'Blimey!' everyone said.'Now we're for it.'

Main briefing went off as usual with all the necessary gen from the met man about altitudes,wing company, and so on.

Our next stop was the mess at 6pm for a tea which was to last us until about 5am the following morning, or so we thought. It was the usual eggs and bacon. We also filled our flasks with tea, which we usually drank after crossing the English coast on the way home because, after wearing oxygen masks for long hours, our mouths became parched and dry.

We had very little time left as takeoff was 7.50pm and the skipper always liked us down at the flights at least an hour before.

Jock and I rushed up to the billet to do our last-minute odd jobs in case we might not return, although we never thought that we wouldn't. Jock left sooner than I, having so much extra clothing to put on when he got to his locker. I just put on my boots and another sweater and ambled down at about 7pm.

Everything was peaceful and quiet around the flight offices and locker room except for sudden outbursts of: 'Where's my bloody so-and-so?'

We stood around outside the flight offices waiting our turn for the transport to take us out to our kite as other crews kept leaving. Now and again, from somewhere around the dispersals, came the sudden outburst of engines as the first wave were running up their machines before takeoff.

With the roaring of engines all around us, it was our turn to get into the transport and go to Bar Charlie. As we climbed aboard the bus the wing commander and others wished us luck and shouted, as usual:'See you in the morning.'

There were no apparent signs of nervousness in any of the

crews. If there was, they did not show it, they were just one big joking crowd.

We got out to the aircraft and lay about chatting to the ground crew. We had plenty of time before takeoff, so while the rest of the crew did the chatting the skipper and I walked around Bar Charlie doing certain checks and having a general look over to see that she was all right.

The time came for us to climb aboard and get the engines started for the ground testing. They started a treat and all tests were satisfactory, so we gave thumbs up to the ground crew and taxied Bar Charlie out to follow the other kites around the perimeter track to the takeoff point.

While we were lined up waiting our turn I looked around and there, as usual, were people watching from a nearby farmhouse and, at the head of the runway, a crowd of WAAFs, ground crew and aircrew waving at each aircraft as it left, roaring down the runway.

Then it was our turn. The skipper and I made sure everything was all right as far as we were concerned to get the huge aircraft airborne.

Takeoff is rather a tense moment because, as you might imagine, any engine trouble at such a time can be serious, especially with bombs aboard. Luckily everything was perfect and as soon as we were airborne everyone relaxed and settled down for the long trip into darkness. From now on we were just a team of seven men who seemed cut off from the rest of the world, with one job to do before we could return to earth. We circled around with many more aircraft for company, gaining height, until it was time to set course for Germany.

An hour after takeoff we were flying at about 12,000ft, our course almost direct to Berlin. By this time the sky had turned dull and the night darker, so we set course, climbing steadily all the way.

There was thick cloud now and it was almost pitch black. Before leaving England we had seen aircraft all round with lights from each wing tip but now, out over the North Sea, it seemed we were on our own. Those comforting lights had gone after leaving the English coast, but we knew aircraft were still around.

We flew on for about three hours, all quiet and undisturbed, except for a few searchlights which tried to pierce the thick cloud below us.

The flak over the coastline was also clearly seen, but nothing to put us off, the sort of welcome we always got on reaching the enemy coast. Not until about half-an-hour's flying time from Berlin did we see much sign of life from below. The dense cloud and darkness which had covered and comforted us suddenly ended. We were now flying in a clear sky lit by searchlights, fighter flares and explosions of all kinds above the suburbs of Berlin. Looking out everything seemed almost as clear as day.

When we were due south of the city we went in on our briefed compass heading of 180 degrees. From the navigator's calculations we were eight to ten minutes behind the correct bombing time. Knowing this was not very comforting. The Main Force would have bombed and be well away by the time we arrived and all the defences of Berlin would be able to concentrate on us few stragglers.

We arrived on our heading after avoiding a few searchlights and near misses from flak bursts that seemed pretty close on the starboard side. When we turned on I saw quite plainly two or three aircraft each coned by twenty to thirty searchlights on our starboard side, having hell knocked out of them by flak. It was the same on the port side where half-a-dozen searchlights were doing their best to pick us up in their beams.

As usual, combats with fighters could be seen going on all round by the lights of tracers from each aircraft.

Now it was our turn for the run up to the target. As we got to our positions the skipper's voice came over the intercom:

'Everyone okay? Turning on.' Then the bomb aimer's voice:

'Bomb doors open, Skip.'

Suddenly the whole aircraft shuddered and Mac, the rear gunner, called out:

'They've got me, Skip. I can't get out, the doors are jammed.'

The aircraft shook, lurched, rolled and dived steeply as the skipper took evasive action to get away from the oncoming fighter. The bomb aimer had already dropped the whole bomb load without a moment's notice. Then Chap's voice was heard:

'Okay Mac, going down.'

We were still doing violent evasive action when the fighter attacked again, this time from below, raking the aircraft from stem to stern. I was on the floor, having seen the fighter attacking the first time from the rear starboard quarter with his tracers entering the rear of the fuselage. I stayed on the floor, after being thrown there by the sudden evasive manoeuvre. Unable to do anything to help I waited for my 'packet'if it was coming,while watching my panel of engine and fuel gauges for any trouble that may suddenly break forth. Luckily, they were okay.

As I lay there during the second attack,an explosive shell burst immediately below my position and shrapnel whirled through the floor and out through the roof. A few pieces of shrapnel ripped into the back of my left knee. The lower part of my leg immediately went numb and I thought I had lost it, but I managed to stand up on my right leg. My other leg was intact but I was unable to stand on it.

I later discovered that Sax,the bomb aimer, had been seriously hurt in the same attack. By now the intercom had become unserviceable. Whether Sax said anything I don't know. I saw him climb out of his compartment and fall in front of me.

I thought he had done it on purpose at first, but as we were again attacked, without any serious damage being inflicted, he did not move from his position on the floor. I went to examine him and found he was unconscious.His body was still warm and his pulse quite strong.

Still in a strongly defended area north of Berlin, we had lost considerable height, down to about 10,000ft. I had to leave Sax and keep a sharp lookout for more trouble.

We seemed to have lost our fighter [shot down in a fierce exchange of fire with Jock Kelly],so I reported everything okay as far as I was concerned.The skipper shouted for power so I opened up and we left the area pretty quick, climbing hard.

While Dave tried to find our correct position and get a course for home the skipper pulled the kite up hard on a course due north and I tried to clear up a little and check for any trouble we might not have noticed.

Chap had, by this time, helped by Dave, got Mac to a more comfortable position against the rear spar. Jock was okay and trying to do two gunner's jobs.

Dave was taking astro shots, doing his best to pinpoint our position as the sky was clear above and below. We crossed the north German Baltic coast to Sweden and followed the west coast up to what we thought was Copenhagen.

Whatever town it was it had quite a few flak batteries firing up in our direction, but the shells did not come very near, making us think we were not alone, even at 27,000ft.From there we turned due west, knowing we would reach Britain somewhere along the east coast. We crossed Denmark without any trouble and set out across the North Sea.

About eighty miles from the west Danish coast Dave managed to get a Gee fix and immediately worked out our course and distance to base. I checked on the fuel situation and found we only had enough for three hours' flying. It was impossible for us to make base. The skipper had to decide whether to turn back, bale out over Sweden, or carry on and ditch.

Because of Mac's serious injuries, making it unable for him to bale out, the skipper decided to carry on and ditch. The actual thought of ditching and the dangerous consequences it might incur did not seem to worry anyone. I had total confidence in the skipper and thought nothing of it, no more than I had in landing.

From then on we all got prepared. Dave got an approximate ditching position and Chap bashed out the position on the W/T right to the end. We closed down the engines and undertook a steady controlled descent.

I looked at Sax carefully, found him completely helpless and stone cold and reported his condition to the skipper. I went to the rear of the fuselage and warned Mac and Jock what to prepare for, after trying to cheer Mac up a little.

I immediately got to work throwing out all unnecessary heavy equipment, such as the pyrotechnics and ammunition, as the rear turret magazines were completely full.

While I was doing this all four engines cut due to lack of fuel. Everyone immediately prepared for the worst and began rushing about. By everyone I mean Dave, Chap, Jock and myself. The aircraft lost height quickly and rather uncomfortably fast in that half minute. I ran from my position in the rear to the fuel cocks on my panel up in the cockpit and luckily, just in time, managed to change the cock and the engines immediately responded. We were only twenty feet off the water when the engines restarted and the skipper pulled up the nose.

After that shaky do I made a rough check on the fuel situation and told the skipper we could go on for about another half-hour.

As time was so short the skipper told me to warn the others to get in ditching positions and prepare for the worst. They went aft and I got organised up front. What with the skipper's harness, and hatches to release and check, I did not have much time to myself.

I told the skipper when I was ready and we waited for the big splash. He gave me three minutes to get settled in the back and I went to my ditching position behind the main spar. It was 4.50am.

I shouted the position and time to the rest of the crew and we waited. I had just got crouched up in the corner when the skipper waggled his wings as a last warning and the engines gave their usual cough when he throttled back for the glide in. The last half-minute seemed a lifetime.

Two violent bumps came as we hit the water. I felt very little but Dave was not quite ready for it and he was thrown around violently. Fortunately he only had his watch knocked from his wrist. Immediately water rushed in everywhere, through the damaged fuselage at the rear and a huge spout rose from the flare chute. In a matter of seconds the fuselage was half full and both Chap and I leaped for the hatch together. I, being the smaller, wriggled out on to the starboard mainplane to the dinghy, only to find it already out and half inflated with Jock waiting to get in.

We were all out on the starboard mainplane within thirty seconds, gathering ourselves together and ready in case Bar Charlie made her last plunge. But she remained afloat so the skipper suggested we went back for the packs, also to inquire about Mac's condition. No one seemed to know exactly so three of us went back to drag him out. He was conscious but in a pretty helpless state.

We got him in the dinghy, also one pack, a pigeon and the radio. As soon as possible we started to paddle away from Charlie in case it sank suddenly and took us under too. We soon drifted away but Charlie remained afloat and we drifted with it, more slowly than if we were on our own.

We arranged ourselves as comfortably as possible, especially Mac who had lost his boots. We had brought a parachute with us and wrapped his feet in it. He looked terribly ill but was quite conscious at the time. At around 5.30 he went into a coma and died soon afterwards. He had lost a lot of blood and the shock must have been too much for him. We covered Mac up with the parachute having decided to bring him back with us, not knowing if we would see old England again.

After rigging up the dinghy mast and aerial Chap attempted to send an SOS with the radio and to launch the kite aerial. His first attempt failed because the rocket was not properly connected to the kite and it shot into the sky on its own. The second rocket was launched okay, taking the kite well up and we managed to keep it airborne for about five minutes when it suddenly dived into the sea for some unknown reason.

At about 6am, when it was really light, a huge sea bird which had been following us flew off and we released the pigeon with a message. It got off pretty well and after circling the dinghy a couple of times set course. But where to? We still do not know because it never arrived at base.

As we had had nothing to eat for about twelve hours we opened our emergency rations, bearing in mind to conserve as much as possible.

By 7.30am we had seen no signs of life except the smoke from a convoy miles away on the horizon. We thought we should get some sleep and the skipper took the first watch.

I was just dozing off when I heard aircraft. I could not believe it at first and thought I was hearing things and took no notice until the skipper mumbled something about aeroplanes coming our way. We looked up and saw three twin-engine Lockheed Hudsons roaring straight towards us at about 150ft. This was the most exciting moment I have ever experienced.

We had been seen and they began to fly over us. Each time we waved and they came back which was very thrilling.

They threw out smoke floats to obtain drifts and wind directions, then dropped five containers in line, known as Lindholmes. Each one contained waterproof sleeping suits, warming bricks, cigarettes, matches, chewing gum, Horlicks tablets, cans of drinking water and condensed milk. What a feast we had.

The Hudsons remained in the vicinity, one flying higher than the others which, we supposed, was to wireless our position to base. The other two circled us more widely than before.

Relieving Hudsons came at intervals during the morning. Then, at 12.30pm, three additional Hudsons [from 279 Squadron], came into view. They made several flights over us into wind at about 1,000ft, each time dropping smoke floats. To our astonishment one suddenly released an airborne lifeboat which was something we had heard so much about but never seen before.

It came straight towards us on three parachutes but, carried by the wind, hit the water about 100yd away. The parachutes were released on impact when three rockets, with 150yd long lifelines attached, were launched automatically, landing fifty yards on either side of us. Rockets and lines floated very conveniently.

We paddled to the nearest line, pulled ourselves to the boat, scrambled into it and made ready to sail. We towed the dinghy, with Mac still aboard.

We soon got everything fixed, including buoyancy bags, and struck up the two small two-stroke engines. They burst into life really well, but after five minutes both cut dead and we were unable to turn them over by hand. This puzzled us for a time as there did not seem to be any mechanical problem.

We thought one of the lifeboat's parachutes – which were designed to automatically release and float free – might have caught in the propeller, but this had not happened and we were unable to discover any fault which could be put right to benefit unfortunate types who might ditch in the future. We had no alternative but to attempt to rig sail and get underway. After a struggle we managed to get moving, but slowly.

It was raining quite a lot by now and most of us were feeling the worse for wear and sat in the corners of the boat looking rather lifeless and saying nothing.

Apart from the constant circling of the aircraft all was quiet and we gave casual glances at the circling Hudsons knowing that we were not completely lost and alone.

Suddenly, as I was looking towards the horizon I imagined I saw a black speck and had to ask the others to make sure I was not seeing things. It was a launch, two in fact, and they were getting closer. It was very exciting for all of us and we suddenly found the strength to sit up and watch them getting larger.

Just to make sure they had seen us we fired a Very cartridge and they answered with an Aldis lamp.

The excitement was growing and it was comforting to see the launches coming to pick us up. They came within fifty yards of us and Jock could not contain his excitement any longer and gave one loud cheer. One launch moved towards us while the other headed for our Lancaster which was still afloat. They were both Air-Sea-Rescue launches.

While we were helped aboard one of them and were settling down in the sick bay, the other launch spent some considerable time attempting to sink Bar Charlie with machine-gun [and cannon] fire. The last we saw, as we pulled away, Bar Charlie was still floating proudly in the water, resisting the bullets and shells to the bitter end.

Our launch took the airborne lifeboat in tow and lifted our dinghy aboard. We were all shaking from head to toe with the cold, having been in wet clothes all day. I had not realised how cold we were until we were stripped off in the warm sick bay, having a brisk rub down before getting into bed. A bowl of hot soup was followed by bacon and eggs. Strangely, no Naval rum, which was a relief to me, I hate the stuff. [None of his crew knew John Sargeant had been injured until they were taken aboard the launch].

It was not long before I fell asleep, but I soon awoke with a start, reared up in my bunk, banged my head on the roof and almost fell out. For some unknown reason the launch's engines had spluttered and stopped. I subconsciously thought the engines of the Lancaster had cut again, and rushed forward to my fuel cocks.

They calmed me down to sleep again and I was woken at 7am at Immingham Docks. I was carried ashore on a stretcher and taken to the local hospital where I was treated like a hero when they knew my story. After a few days I was transferred to RAF Hospital Rauceby, Lincolnshire.

While there I learned that the remainder of my old crew had received fourteen days' survivors' leave, before getting three new crew members and going straight back on operations.

My crewmates: Squadron Leader Howroyd, the skipper; Flight Sergeant Kelly, Pilot Officer Davies and Flight Sergeant Chappell, were reported missing on the night of 8/9 October 1943 on an operation to Hanover. Much later I learned there were no survivors in their aircraft. [In fact, one new crew member did survive and became a prisoner of war].

* * *

Tom Saxby, the dead bomb aimer, is thought to have been thrown into the sea by the impact of the Lancaster striking the water.

An unsuccessful attempt was made to bomb the floating Lancaster, which was a danger to shipping. Not until the Royal Navy brought in its big guns was the defiant aircraft sunk. Bar

Charlie was one of twenty-two Lancasters lost on the raid to Berlin.

Sergeant John Sargeant received the DFM, having been praised for his efforts in recovering Sergeant McKenzie from the floating Lancaster, but he did not fly operationally again.

CHAPTER EIGHT

THAT'S MY BOY!

Three weeks after Doug Fry was reported missing over Germany, in the summer of 1943, the nineteen-year-old air gunner was spotted on the screen of an Islington cinema.

Winnie Fry, a widow and mother of eight children, was astounded to hear that a neighbour had seen her son in a short film, *The Biter Bit*, which dealt with the thorny issue of war propaganda.

Winnie was a regular weekly visitor to the Carlton cinema in Essex Road, whatever film was showing. She went there that night, nervously clutching her handbag and a handkerchief.

For a woman, who had not received a scrap of good news after the loss of her son's Stirling bomber on 31 July, desperately clinging to the hope that he was still alive, it was a surreal, but unforgettable experience. She endured several chilling minutes of strutting German arrogance, before the black and white film suddenly switched to an unnamed airfield where cheerful and relaxed young RAF aircrews were seen emerging into the sun from the briefing for that night's bombing raid.

Suddenly she saw him, gazing steadfastly at the camera and her eyes filled with tears. 'That's my boy!' she whispered, and slumped fainting to the floor.

Helped to the manager's office she told her poignant story and learned it might be possible to arrange a private viewing of the film. A few days later Winnie sat nervously in a small Wardour Street cinema, a guest of the Ministry of Information, which had made the film. She had been warned that the young fresh-faced airman she had seen fleetingly might not be Doug, but Winnie returned home elated, even though the film offered no proof he was alive.

Little more than three hours after they had been filmed four of Doug Fry's crew would be dead and it was to be October before Winnie Fry knew the truth, when a card arrived from her son in Germany.

Doug Fry, tall and skinny, became an office boy with a marine insurance company after leaving school at fifteen, often walking through the debris and fires still burning in London from the previous night's raid during the Blitz to get to his office in Fenchurch Street. One morning he saw, amidst the rubble, five feet of the wing tip from a Dornier. A member of the ATC, with a keen interest in aircraft recognition, he yearned to be in the RAF.

Now he was flying Stirlings as George Judd's mid-upper gunner stationed at 15 Squadron, Mildenhall, with a pair of gleaming Browning machine guns he cosseted more lovingly than any woman, doing the job he had dreamed about.

Pilot Officer Judd, twenty-two, an only child, came from a well-off family in Reading. Engaged to be married to a girl called Joyce, he was garrulous and good-humoured, joining his crew on their nights out at the Bird in Hand pub, near the airfield's main gate, or in Cambridge where the Dorothy Café had a dance hall upstairs. Here, their minds could be briefly prised away from the war by the company of pretty women and nights of simple fun, which included contests for the knobbliest knees and the most sensational moustache.

There are few situations which could bring seven men closer than sharing regular brushes with death. Fry says:

'We were always together, spending all day at dispersal with the ground crew when we weren't flying. They included Curly, Jock and others, all good blokes, but the flight sergeant in charge was a nasty piece of work. He was a regular and regulars didn't like young aircrew because we got our stripes so quickly. It had probably taken him ten years. We had a tent there and a tethered goat, Billy, we had inherited from Flying Officer Hawkins and his crew who did not come back from Mülheim. I nearly went on that raid.

'There were only two of us in the crewroom on 22 June when the gunnery leader said Hawkins' mid-upper was missing for some reason and a replacement was needed. I hadn't even been on an op but immediately said I would go. I wanted to get cracking. I reported later with my kit to Hawkins who told me his mid-upper had turned up so I wasn't needed. They were all lost. It was their sixth operation. We took over their replacement aircraft, A-Apple, and Billy. Another Stirling from the squadron was lost the same night. The pilot and his rear gunner were killed.'

Judd's navigator, Dennis Brown, twenty-one, a trainee journalist from Chester, had fixed a date to be married on his next leave. All the crew were invited. He had hidden half-a-bottle of whisky in a cupboard in the billet to be opened on his stag night.

Wireless operator Sergeant Bill Wells, from Willesden, was twenty-three. The bomb aimer, twenty-six-year-old quietly-spoken Sergeant Syd Long, came from Chatham. Sergeant Dick Richards, the flight engineer, married, with a building business in Bridgend, South Wales, was the crew's old man at thirty-eight. He and his skipper each owned a small car into which their crewmates crammed for nights out.

Pilot Officer Ken Banks, thirty-three, was British born, but had settled with his family in Winnipeg, Canada. Tall, slim with a small moustache, he had been an insurance rep before joining the fight against Germany. He always wore a peaked cap inside which he carefully recorded each operation. He did not fly with the crew on their first five operations, languishing in RAF Ely Hospital after an operation to exterminate haemorrhoids.

'We carried spare bods in Ken's rear turret,' says Fry. 'One was a Canadian who had a reputation for falling asleep on operations. He said nothing to us when he got into the aircraft and just grunted as the skipper called through to all the positions. We never heard any more from him on the flight.

'Another chap we had in the tail fired on a Beaufighter which was coming up on the starboard side to escort us home after we'd attacked Cologne on 28/29 June. The bloody fool didn't say anything, he just opened fire and, luckily, didn't hit it. He'd already caused us some grief on our bombing run over the target, mistaking a burst of flak for an attacking fighter.'

Their first op had been 'gardening' off the Frisian Islands.

'It was exciting because it was the first and we were very tense because we didn't know what to expect. We felt terrific when we got back to base.'

Another eight trips followed, including three to Hamburg, on the last of which they had an extraordinary run-in with a Ju-88 over the North Sea.

'We were breezing home and Bill was listening to the German frequencies on his radio when he heard loud voices coming from their ground control to a fighter pilot. Bill told us to keep a special watch and blow me if a fighter flare didn't come down almost on top of us. Then a Ju-88, at roughly the same height as us, slightly to starboard, came in from the rear and flew past the flare, illuminating himself, which was a bit strange. I was unsighted by our fin and rudder but Ken in the tail had a clear view and let rip, but at 800 yards, he was too far away. The German sheered off into the mist below without firing a shot, I think we'd put the wind up him.

'The general impression is that all German fighters came in gung-ho and shot everybody down. But reading some of the combat reports you realise that very often, if you got in the first burst they cleared off because they were just as scared as we were.'

Wartime aircrews were not widely known for wasting precious spare time in the gymnasium honing their bodies to the peak of fighting fitness. They had their own well tried and tested methods of maintaining their condition in which figured nothing more physically invigorating than enjoying huge fried breakfasts, lifting pint glasses of beer, smoking plenty of fags, and enjoying the regular company of amiable popsies. They saw no compelling reason for change.

So it was a formidable shock during one of 15 Squadron's weekly meetings in the crewroom to learn from their CO, Wing Commander D. J. Stephens, that an urgent message from 3 Group called for greater fitness among aircrews. It had to be acted upon with the utmost diligence for the outcome of the war depended on it. Stephens' remarks, delivered with fervour, were received with prolonged groans but the men were told to report to two PTIs on the airfield at 6am next day. No one could be excused although the CO, for reasons never adequately explained, was unable to accompany them. Fry, a non-smoker, rare among aircrews, who believed he was extremely fit, says:

'We arrived, cussing and blinding long before breakfast in shorts, flying socks and sweaters, swinging our arms about. Early mornings could be chilly in East Anglia even in summer. We were of all ages and a corporal PTI said cheerfully that we would warm up by running round the airfield perimeter. A squadron leader pilot who was there didn't look pleased. He told the corporal:"Sod you, I'm not running anywhere." And he set off walking back to the mess. The squadron's fitness programme collapsed before it had begun. We all buggered off leaving the PTIs standing there. We never heard any more about it.'

They went up for an air test on the warm afternoon of 30 July. They knew there was an op on that night but had not yet been told the target.

'We were a bit miffed about being on the Battle Order. On the previous six nights we'd been once to Essen, and three times to Hamburg. We'd only got back from there at 4.10 that morning. We were hoping for a night off, but we couldn't pick and choose, there was a job to do.

'After tea, when everything was dead quiet, I went out to our aircraft, EF427 LS A-Apple, which was still at dispersal. I got my pans, one over each shoulder, humped them over to the armoury, which was like a big shed — it wasn't far — and topped up the ammo that I'd used while test firing earlier over The Wash. I liked to mix my own rounds myself and put in a couple of tracers, then one each of the others: ball, incendiary and armour piercing. The mid-upper pans each held 250 rounds.

'I don't know any other air gunner on the squadron who did this job, normally done by the armourers, but it was routine for me. I wanted everything to be just right and it wasn't a difficult thing to do, a piece of duff, really. I carried them back to fit on either side in my turret and cleaned my guns again. I occasionally checked the harmonisation of my Brownings because vibration could easily make them slightly out of alignment. The aircraft was later towed to the marshalling point and lined up with the others at the head of the runway near the control caravan and bombed up.'

Twelve crews from 15 Squadron were among a force of 273 aircraft sent to attack the industrial Ruhr town of Remscheid, south-east of Düsseldorf.

'Not long before this raid Butch Harris had given us a pep talk, we thought he was a smashing guy. He said Churchill wanted us to make a film of Bomber Command's work. When we went into briefing that day arc lights had been set up for the film unit. Later, when we were waiting to be taken out to the aircraft, I turned round and saw a cameraman filming us.'

The crew bus was driven to A-Apple from the back of A Flight hangar by an airman in shirt sleeve order wearing a peaked cap. Fry remembers how smart he looked.

They took off at 10.42pm, carrying a load of 30lb and 4lb incendiaries.

In the second wave, flying at 14,000ft, much lower than the Lancasters and Halifaxes, they encountered few problems crossing the enemy coast, apart from desultory flak and a few searchlights. The Germans set up a few dummy markers south of Brussels.

'We altered course near Cologne to bring us on to the final leg. It was not long before I saw the glow of the target ahead and the usual hell of bursting shells, weaving searchlights and photoflashes going off. Syd Long was in position, preparing for the bombing run and Ken Banks and I were trying to look into every corner of the sky at once. It was an edgy time. The bombs were due to be released at 1.06am. Not long.

'Then we heard Syd's quiet voice: "Bomb doors open" and the skipper's response: "Okay". By this time we were into the outer defences of Remscheid. Searchlights were probing, although the flak barrage was not all that heavy, and I turned my turret forward to see the target already well alight.

'Suddenly, as I was searching to starboard, the radar-controlled master searchlight, with its brilliant beam, flicked across our starboard wing tip. Even as I reported it, the searchlight swung back, locked on to us and was immediately followed by a dozen others. They had us cold. I kept up a running commentary about the number of searchlights and their positions as we pressed on with our bombing run. The flak began to get our range but George did not attempt any evasive action.

'We heard Syd again. "Bombs gone, let's get out of here, boys." Then, the skipper, remembering the drill, said: "Let's get our picture." This meant another ten seconds or so flying straight and level and the flak was still coming up. I could hear stuff bursting all around, a lot of it hitting the aircraft. As George spoke I heard a different louder noise in my earphones, above the normal roar of the engines and exploding shells. I looked down and saw flames streaming past inside, pressed against the port side of the fuselage.

'I was not doing much good in the turret at that time, fighters would not be attacking us through the flak, so I decided to do something about the fire, which I think had started in the priming boxes behind the wireless operator. The flames had already burned fiercely through the wooden bulkhead and were consuming my K-type dinghy which had been hanging there.

'I had one foot on the floor and the other on the bottom rung of the short ladder leading into my turret when there was a shell burst astern and I felt as if I'd been kicked in the stomach. It didn't hurt at first although I doubled up and fell to the floor, close to the flames.'

At this point the world of seven men was being brutally rearranged, and some were already dead or badly wounded. But Doug Fry was still alive. He had to act immediately. Just then another terrible explosion ripped through the front of the aircraft, the nose tipped over and they went straight down at terrifying speed. Fry believed his time had come.

'I thought that was it, the end. The nose was near vertical and I was pinned by G-force to the ceiling and couldn't see us pulling out then, amazingly, the nose started coming up. The skipper slowly pulled Apple out of the dive with what must have been a superhuman effort, for George had probably been hurt in the explosion. He had given us a chance.

'I fell to the floor, saw the flames were now roaring like a blow torch and began passing out only inches from them. Then Dick Richards, the flight engineer, walked straight past me, without pausing, to the rear escape hatch. He opened it and was gone. Dick had been throwing out Window from the other side of the bulkhead when we were hit. I gathered my wits about me and got up, although I was feeling pretty ropey. I was injured but didn't know how badly.

'I had stowed my parachute on the starboard side, in a rack just forward of the turret. It wasn't there – I supposed thrown out during the violent dive – and I resigned myself again to death, before thinking lucidly: "It has to be somewhere." And it was. It had slid along the fuselage and lodged against a tiny step, part of the bulkhead. I crawled past the flames, retrieved it and sat on the step created by the bomb bay fiddling about trying to clip it on as Ken came out of his turret.

'He looked tiny, as if he was a long way away and something strange was happening to me. He told me years later that I was groggy and he'd helped me on with my parachute. I saw him roll out and I followed. We were at around 5,000ft. My parachute opened immediately and I saw the aeroplane flying away, nose down, flames streaming from her, and wondered how many of my chums were inside.'

Ever since that grim night Doug Fry has regretted not struggling to the front of the aircraft to see if he could help but, realistically, knows he would not have had the strength to get there.

Floating down, he seemed to be drifting towards a huge lake and pressed the gas button on his Mae West which inflated immediately and held him in a stifling grip. The water was a field of wheat, moving in a breeze, reflecting starlight, and nearby was a brick wall. He kicked up his feet as he fell towards it.

Fry made a perfect landing in the back garden of a small cottage owned by Frau Margarete Framzen in the village of Mannheim, thirty-five miles from Remscheid. He released the Mae West and parachute because he wanted to be on his way. But he became faint and disorientated and remembers leaving the parachute draped over the wall while scratching, with curious determination, a hole under a bush in which to bury his escape kit.

He failed to find a way out of the walled garden and collapsed, roused later by the wail of an all-clear siren and the sound of people, presumably leaving an air raid shelter. A man was calling out.

'It was a soldier on leave. He helped me into the house where several people, including three or four children, crowded into the kitchen looking apprehensive and white faced. A little woman, probably Frau Framzen, shook her fist at me before sitting me in a chair at the table. She gave me a glass of water and made signs for me not to drink, only rinse out my mouth, because by now they were loosening my clothing and had found a hole in the right side of my stomach, dripping blood.

'A man who looked about ten feet tall, wearing a black uniform, holding a Luger pistol, burst in, yelling and shouting and said:"Wo ist der Englishch Schweinhund?" I'd thought they only said that in films. I believe he wanted to take me out and bump me off. They argued with him and he left, muttering. He was probably a Gauleiter, a Nazi official. I tried to find the chocolate I'd kept in my flying boots to give to the children, but it had gone, lost when I baled out.

'Two lads of about sixteen, wearing tin helmets, brought in a stretcher. They gently laid me on it and took me to a house where a doctor put a pad on my wounds. I'd also been hit in the wrist. He gave me an injection, put me in the back of his car, and drove off into the night, but I kept falling off the seat. I hung on to a tasselled hand grip, fell off again and it came away in my hand. Funny the little things you remember.'

He was eventually transferred to the bottom shelf of an ambulance and before slipping again into unconsciousness, heard from above the unmistakable voice of Ken Banks.

After an operation, at M-Stammlager VIJ, Gerresheim, a reserve hospital near Düsseldorf, Fry endured many days of terrible pain, delirium, drainage tubes, drip feeds into his back passage, and innumerable changes of dressings, while lying on a bed with a mattress stuffed with sawdust and wood chippings, attempting to shut out the constant chatter of other patients around him.

'When the pain subsided Ken, who had been wounded in his leg, said he saw me being undressed, looking as if I was made of marble, well on the way to being a corpse. The Polish Army doctor, another POW, Captain Polakowski, who operated on me, said I'd been saved by my youth and fitness.'

In September Fry, Ken Banks and a Canadian whose foot had been amputated, were moved from the hospital. Fry was admitted to Hohmark sanatorium in Oberursel near Frankfurt while the others went to the nearby interrogation centre.

Still in bed, Fry experienced hours of questioning, learning from a Luftwaffe officer that George Judd, Dennis Brown, Bill Wells and Syd Long had all died on the night of 31 July, incinerated in the wreckage of the Stirling. The pilot's mother had died shortly afterwards, convinced her son would come home safe and well. Fry was given a card on which he could send a brief message to his mother in Islington.

Weeks earlier, Winnie Fry's hopes had received a crushing blow in a letter from the Red Cross, which told her that information supplied by the Germans claimed five men had died in her son's aeroplane.

'When they had enough people to make up a transport we were off from Oberursel to a permanent camp. We were five days and nights in cattle trucks travelling to East Prussia and Stalag

Luft VI, Heidekrug, where we were put into K Lager, a brand-new compound.'

Life as a POW settled into a dreary routine although Red Cross parcels arrived regularly and each prisoner was given a card every week and a letter form each month to send home. By now Fry had got fit walking round the compound, playing football and volleyball. It was here he met Dick Richards who apologised for not helping him in the burning Stirling. He said: 'I thought you were dead.'

'In July 1944 we were moved from Heidekrug to Memel on the Baltic. We spent three shocking days and nights battened down, crammed into the filthy hold of an old collier, the *Insterburg*. We had a single light bulb. Buckets came down with water and for use as a toilet. We were not given food.

'We disembarked at Swinemünde and sirens went off as we were shovelled into cattle trucks on the quayside before Yank bombers went over on their way to Peenemünde.

'We ended up at Stalag Luft IV, Grosse Tychow, Pomerania, which was overcrowded, providing less food and comfort, fewer Red Cross parcels and mail deliveries.

'Early on the morning of 6 February 1945 we started the forced march that would take us 600 miles across Europe. It was bitterly cold, snow was thick on the ground and a blizzard was blowing. Rumours had previously abounded so we had prepared ourselves as best we could. I still had the uniform I was shot down in, plus the RAF-issue boots, underwear, greatcoat and cap I'd got at Heidekrug. I'd sewn my two thin German blankets together to make a sleeping bag.

'I also had gloves, a change of socks, and my grubby white flying sweater which I swapped on the march for a freshly-baked loaf of bread from a young pregnant woman who said she would unpick it to make baby clothes.

'As we moved out we were each given a piece of bread and two Red Cross parcels. I remember being issued with three more parcels on the march, but the only liquid we could get was melted snow.

'Many prisoners died. Others dropped out with terrible feet, bad legs and dysentery. Anyone who collapsed was given a lift on horse-drawn carts which carried the armed guards' equipment.

'In one village three old women put buckets of water by their front gates so we could grab a drink as we passed. The guards kicked over the buckets, but we warmed to the women's courage and kindness.'

The marchers, their clothes perpetually damp, growing weaker through lack of regular food, often stayed overnight at farms,occasionally in frozen fields.Fry was lucky to escape being shot after stealing a turnip.

The weather improved in April.The German guards,knowing their war was almost at an end, began showing photographs of their families to the prisoners, and Fry joined his pals bathing naked in the freezing water of a stream.

In Cammin, locked for the night in a big thatched and timber-framed barn, the prisoners were wakened at 1am by aircraft cannon shells smashing into the building. Fry was cut in the back by a sliver of shrapnel, the men on either side of him were killed, others were wounded, but the burning barn was evacuated without panic. Fry was among the wounded taken by a horse-drawn cart for treatment at a small POW camp outside the town of Schwerin. RAF aircraft regularly strafed a German airfield a few kilometres away and several 20mm cannon shells fell and exploded in the compound.

Their ordeal ended on 2 May, the day before Doug Fry's twenty-first birthday.

'The Germans had fled the camp at Schwerin. We saw our first American soldiers as thousands of Germans — civilians, and columns of deserting servicemen, some with their families — flooded through nearby woods into a huge field behind us. Former Russian POWs, having armed themselves, roamed the countryside, seeking retribution. We were eventually fed and waited patiently to be sent home.'

Fry flew to England from Lübeck in the mid-upper turret of a Lancaster. Looking out from the special train from Cosford to Paddington he was moved by 'Welcome Home'signs painted on houses, and banners in gardens alongside the track. In Islington, his mother was waiting anxiously on the top step outside their house in Northchurch Road.

Incidentally, Billy the goat was taken over by another 15 Squadron pilot, Len Miller, who sometimes took him up for a flight.

Years later Fry heard of two German eyewitnesses who had seen A-Apple, trailing flames, sinking low over the countryside but clearly veering away from the village of Mannheim. It crashed in a field 4km from the village near the main road to Bergan at 1.29am. Doug Fry likes to think that the deliverance of Mannheim was the last act of his courageous skipper.

CHAPTER NINE

BACKWARDS INTO BATTLE

Sergeant Chum Rees thought he had been posted to the wrong unit when he arrived at 21 OTU, Moreton-in-Marsh. He recognised the clapped-out Wellington IC twin-engine bombers stumbling with trainee crews above the Gloucestershire countryside, but could not see an RAF uniform anywhere.

Rees, who stood half-an-inch above 5ft 4in, when straining every sinew, says:

'I thought: "There's something wrong here. What the hell is this place?" There were massive Australians, big chaps from South Africa, New Zealand and Canada, but mainly Aussies, all bigger than me, yet no Brits.

'I was feeling a bit lost when an Australian came up to me, grinned, and said: "Where are you from, Sport."

'I said: "If I told you you wouldn't know it." "Try me," he said.

'"Well, you've got somewhere called New South Wales, I'm from old South Wales."

'"Oh, you're a bloody Druid." And so I became The Druid or Dru to the Australian crew I joined. My new pal was their wireless operator, Warrant Officer Frankie Weston, known as "Snakehips": good looking, dapper, immaculately turned out, a great character and renowned charmer of women.'

Rees, christened Charles, had been known as 'Chum' from the day he was born in 1923, the eldest of five children, brought up in a cottage without electricity or water in the small Pembrokeshire market town of Haverfordwest. As he grew older it became his job to take buckets to collect water from a well four fields away.

'My father, Sidney, a great man with boxing gloves, taught me to look after myself, and after regularly playing rugby, a game which teaches a boy to take and give knocks,I was ready to take on the world. Dad had served on the ground with the Royal Flying Corps in the Great War and I joined the RAF to find I was the right size for the rear turret of a bomber.Years later my son,Michael, would become a squadron leader pilot in the RAF.'

There were even more Australians at Driffield, Yorkshire, when they were posted to 462 (Australian) Squadron in the autumn of 1944, having been converted to Halifaxes at Dishforth.

Their skipper was Pilot Officer Maxie 'Thrasher'Taylor, from Perth, Western Australia.

'You had to do your job with him. He did not condone slackers or moaners.A big man, he kept a tight well-disciplined crew whose lives depended on each other being on the ball.He was a good pilot, very careful, not afraid of anything and talked about little else but flying.

'Our navigator, another Max,Warrant Officer Maxie Smith, a huge bloke, with dry wit, not yet twenty-four, was the oldest man in the crew.We called him "Dad" to annoy him.He'd been a school teacher.

'Warrant Officer Arthur Lobb was even more handsome than Frankie, a six-footer, with an appealing baby face. Whenever we went to our favourite pub,The Buck,in Driffield, girls would be all around pawing at him.He thrived on it.He'd been a baker in the family confectionery business just outside Melbourne. Now he was dropping our bombs.

'There was nothing Mick Manning, a Londoner, didn't know about engines. He had worked for an aircraft production company before the war and if he sensed something was going wrong with an engine it went wrong,there was no guessing.He was also a warrant officer.

'When I met our mid-upper gunner, Dennis Somerville, I thought he was a Canadian,he certainly had the accent.Then he told me that although he had spent a long time in Canada he was originally from Newport, Monmouthshire. He'd joined Bomber Command to kill as many Germans as he could as a pay back for his brother who had been killed flying bombers.Den was a flight sergeant.'

A short stocky man Chum Rees possesses a keen intelligence, with the Welshman's innate ability to sum up people quickly.

Blessed with a spiky sense of humour, he remembers more of the funny side of war than many of his comrades, and in particular the torment of his skipper as they approached the Ruhr Valley one night.

Being taken short in civilian life can be regarded as an uproarious joke by those who are not squirming in distress. But it could be a matter of life or death for men with a bursting bladder or erupting bowels while heading through the sky in a bomber over hostile territory. Men have died while sitting aft on the chemical Elsen toilet when their aircraft has been hit,or after their pilot, taken ill, has handed over the controls to another member of his crew before staggering through the fuselage. Rees recalls the moment when pilot Maxie Taylor was desperate to urinate.

'I heard Maxie say, in a not very polite way, that he wanted to spring a leak. There was uproar as the others visualised him struggling to get to the Elsen. Someone shouted: "Don't you bloody leave your seat we're nearly in the target area".'

The engineer acted swiftly to construct a modest portable toilet by hacking a length off the broad flexible piping that drew in warm air from an engine. He flattened the ends together, bunged it up and sealed it with Window.

After expressing extreme relief Taylor stood the makeshift pot at his feet and ran the Halifax smoothly into the target.

'We had forgotten that on the Halifax the wireless operator sat with his head virtually underneath the skipper's feet. The inevitable happened, Frankie complained of rain splashing on to his head and his log then, as the truth dawned, yelled angrily at the skipper, accusing him of doing it on purpose. He dropped the soggy paper down the flare chute.That incident became a big joke with us teasing Frankie on future trips by asking him if it was raining.'

Being a tail-end Charlie was no joke for Rees, sharing the responsibility with the mid-upper of defending the aircraft against the Germans.

'People have asked me since the war how I could go into danger backwards. I got used to it although I couldn't see any part of the aircraft, stuck out as I was beyond the tail unit.It was like sitting in a glass box, continually staring into space or down at the ground. I couldn't see any of my crew, but I heard them talking.The skipper worried about me because he was a caring bloke. He would call up and say:"Dru, are you still there?"We'd heard a story that the Halifax's rear turret was only held on by four bolts and that they occasionally snapped off.

'Some reckoned rear gunners had the loneliest job in the war, but what they didn't realise was the fantastic view I had. But to say I wasn't frightened would be a damned lie. I was scared stiff and on our first trip I nearly died of fright and thought: "My God, what the hell have I got myself in to?"'

That first sortie was a daylight raid in a Halifax III against Le Havre on 10 September 1944 and he recorded in his logbook, after the 4hr 40min-flight: 'No flak or fighters. Very quiet. Bombed from 10,000ft.'

'I was very excited, but a bit scared. We were just supporting the Army but when we got back to England I felt a real bloody hero. What impressed me were the battleships below. I'd only seen them at the cinema before. When they were firing they heeled over to one side.

'One thing never changed in the rear turret, it was always cold,sometimes fifty degrees below freezing.It took me an hour to put on my flying clothes before an op, not because I was slow, but if I was quick I would sweat and in the turret that froze on you. I wore five pairs of gloves but if you inadvertently took them off and got frost-bitten hands you were put on a charge for self-inflicted wounds.

'When we got near the target area I often flew with one eye closed so I didn't lose the night vision in that eye. If fighter flares drifted down or searchlights caught you your night vision was gone straightaway.

'I had a Boulton Paul turret with a joystick control. I invariably flew with my doors open even when turning the turret.This was because of the danger from icing.You could fly through heavy rain taking off, or the aircraft might have been standing in rain at dispersal.The sliding doors, which led to the fuselage behind me, ran on little gutters. When you got to heights where it was minus forty or fifty degrees they froze and you wouldn't be able to open them.My parachute was just inside the fuselage as there was no room for it in the turret. Being trapped in that tur ret was my greatest fear.'

They flew into heavy flak for the first time on 12 September near Gelsenkirchen.

'The flak was a bit scary, but I didn't really understand it.I saw puffs of black smoke when shells were bursting some distance away. I occasionally heard some rattling but didn't realise at the start that was flak hitting the aircraft.Afterwards I did.'

As the sorties mounted, so did their experience and Rees soon learned to recognise the two kinds of flak.

'There was either barrage flak, which is a mass of bursting shells hoping to hit an aircraft,or it was predicted and you would see it following you, usually from behind. There would be a pattern with it.That was the one you had to watch.

'We were near the bombing run one night when I could see the flak following us and warned the skipper: "We are being predicted, be prepared to take evasive action."

'Arthur, lying on his bomb sight, said: "Take it easy, Dru, there's nothing there. I'm just starting the bombing run, it'll be all right." As he spoke there was a tremendous "Crump!" just above or below one of the wings and the aircraft was thrown on to its side. All I heard from the bomb aimer was:"Shit! Bombs gone!"'

Most men who survived the war can speak nonchalantly of near misses and Chum Rees is no exception. Once, when the pilot was unable to get a coherent reply from his rear gunner he sent a man hurrying aft with a spare oxygen bottle.

'A piece of shrapnel had shot into the turret, smashing the oxygen regulator and cutting my supply of air. If it hadn't hit the regulator the shrapnel would have gone through my head. I didn't realise what had happened until I started to talk a bit queer, as if I was very drunk. Being connected to the oxygen bottle cured me, but without it I would soon have been in trouble.'

The routine of a daylight raid turned into a fleeting nightmare when Rees saw a Lancaster loom into view no more than 100ft above his Halifax.

'We were approaching the target area and I was watching this Lancaster crossing over the top of us from port to starboard with his bomb doors open. He suddenly let the bombs go and an 8,000lb Blockbuster came tumbling towards me. A bomb which exploded on contact,it went so near my turret I could count the rivets and read the letters on it. If I'd wanted to I could have reached out to touch it.Other bombs from the same aircraft fell clear, but it was the big one that interested me.

'Dennis, the mid-upper, said:"I thought you'd had it, Dru." I said:"Not just me, boy. The whole lot of us." If the bomb had hit us it would have taken us out of the sky and the Lancaster, too. There must have been a lot of aircraft lost through bombs coming down in that way. I'd have shot the devils if we'd found out who they were. They just let them go. They got too excited, you see. And we were in the way. Too bad.'

Rees remembered this incident when a badly shot-up Halifax returned to Driffield, its rear turret crumpled and the gunner trapped inside.

'Some of us went over to the rescue lads and offered to go inside because we knew how to move around in there, but they had to cut the turret in half with oxyacetylene to get him out. It was Snowy Whitehead, but he was dead, butchered really. It sickened me. It was at such a time when your spirit of adventure was replaced by the awful reality of war. It also happened when you were being hit, or saw other aircraft being hit, and seeing blokes being lifted out at our airfield dead or cut in half.'

They saw a German jet fighter for the first time on 30 October as they moved in on Cologne. Arthur Lobb called Rees up from the nose. 'There's a huge streak of light coming up and round in a massive curve like a rocket. Keep your eyes open, Dru.'

'We didn't know what it was,' says Rees, 'and, of course, the Germans had jet fighters in the war long before we did at a time we were messing about with Gloster Meteors at Manston. When this one swept past I thought I'd never seen anything move so fast in all my life. We seemed to be standing still.'

The tail gunner spotted a single jet fighter two nights later when they attacked Düsseldorf.

'It came rapidly straight at us so I opened fire with my four machine guns. The fighter swung away and we didn't see it again. I'd used up over 200 rounds in a very short time.

'We had to be vigilant the whole time on an op because the Germans were absolutely ruthless. Fear kept you alert, sharpening your mind. My job, and the mid-upper's, was to try and defend the aircraft, quite often against pairs of fighters. I was always reckoned to have exceptional natural eyesight and one night I spotted a German coming above us about a mile-and-a-quarter away. He hung fire, but was flashing lights, drawing our attention. I reported him to the skipper and said I thought he was keeping our attention because he had a mate somewhere who was probably planning to sneak in underneath us.I got the skipper to dip the wings so the mid-upper gunner could have a good look below.

'I told Den: "Don't hesitate. If there's something there you don't understand open fire at once." Luckily nothing was there but there could have been and that was one of the ways the German fighters operated.'

Their first major test came on 28 November 1944, during their third trip to the Prussian city of Essen,probably the foulest of German targets. Chum Rees frowns at the memory. Few former aircrew who visited Essen in a bomber have forgotten the experience.

'I think Essen was a worse prospect than Berlin. In Krupps, Essen had the biggest armament works in the world and the city was very heavily defended.Nobody liked going there because of the warm reception they knew would always be waiting for them. On this occasion we got through the flak, bombed and turned to come home.There were no searchlights. Perhaps they didn't need them because it was a full moon.

'Suddenly I saw a pair of FW-190s coming quickly towards us from the rear, more or less one behind the other.To have one was enough trouble but to find two coming at you meant it was difficult to decide what evasive action to take. There was only time to report: "We've got two visitors, prepare to corkscrew, Skip."

'I gave him their approximate position and he said: "Okay, Dru, tell me what to do".

'Corkscrew starboard!'And he was already into it.

'I was firing as they came in so low down, the mid-upper couldn't see them.They shot past and went away. They didn't come back.The whole combat took less than a minute. At the time I did wonder if they had been trainees,sprog pilots,because they didn't press home the attack. On the other hand, I had driven them off and maybe they didn't much care for the attention.

'Next day I went up to the flights and met the flight sergeant armourer who had been re-arming our aircraft. He said: "You had a busy night last night,Taff."

'I replied:"How the hell do you know that?" "Because you only had forty-two rounds left in the entire turret." We carried around 5,000 rounds for each machine gun.'

Rees was later awarded the Distinguished Flying Medal for his outstanding ability as an air gunner, the only member of the crew to be decorated.

'I told the boys it was as much theirs as mine because we were a team. We had a good time with the forty-quid bounty that came with it, and none of us was drinking milk, believe me.'

Maxie Taylor's Halifax was among a force of 523 aircraft sent to drop several hundred early Christmas presents on Duisburg on the night of 17/18 December.

They were caught by a serious blast of predicted flak on the way and the flight engineer, having been sent back to check on the damage, told the pilot: 'We might have trouble with the undercarriage when we're landing.'

It was a subdued crew who flew out of the Ruhr without further mishap, apart from being prodded unsuccessfully by a few searchlights, but reflecting sombrely on the words of Mick Manning,who was never known to be pessimistic without good reason. Well out over the North Sea they were advised by Driffield control to head for the emergency landing ground at Manston. Few nights went by without at least one aeroplane, having dragged itself miserably across the North Sea, flopping down at the Kent airfield where there was a 9,000ft-long concrete runway, with extended over-runs of cleared grass at both ends.

The engineer had difficulty getting the undercarriage down and they were within sight of the airfield when he was still struggling with the wheels. A few feet from the runway they creaked down and Manning gasped:'You might have a problem with one of the wheels, Skip.'

They touched the concrete and seconds later the pilot observed calmly:'I think we've lost a wheel.'

'Yes,' said Rees laconically. 'It's just rolled past my turret. I'm watching it now.'

Nearly sixty years later Chum Rees recalls the moment:

'The skipper had hold of her and for a few seconds she was riding nicely on the starboard wheel.Then the law of gravity took over and she started to tip. The skipper shouted:"Hang on boys, we've had it." There was a hell of a crash and crumping as we landed and a horrible screeching noise as she dragged herself along,and suddenly we were in a heap on the runway. It was one of the biggest frights I ever had in bombers.'

There was a lot of swearing among the crew as they scrambled to get out. Rees, bulky and clumsy in his flying kit, had not imagined he could move so quickly to escape a broken aircraft and avoid being singed by fire. They scattered in all directions, but when fire crews moved in with professional detachment and it was clear that all the fight had gone out of the Halifax, they returned sheepishly to gaze at the wreck which had carried them to Duisburg and back in 5hr 20min and was now lying on its side with a hammered-in nose and ripped-off port wing. No attempts would ever be made to patch it up and get it back into the air. Its crew climbed sadly, but relieved, into a truck which took them away for breakfast and a few hours' sleep before returning to Driffield.

Towards the end of December 462 Squadron was moved to Foulsham, Norfolk, and absorbed into 100 Group, which had the motto 'Confound and Destroy'. The squadron immediately began training on special equipment for its new role, radio-countermeasures duties.

From the early days of January 1945 the Australian squadron, and other units based in Norfolk, became specialist carriers of Window, bundles of metallic foil strips which were so effective in creating false radar signals, making the Germans believe a large force of Allied bombers was approaching. Spoof raids by a handful of aircraft could be launched deep into Germany confusing radar operators, controllers, and fighter pilots who had been hastily despatched to intercept what was thought to be hundreds of incoming bombers. Sometimes, but not always, the spoofers were attempting to create a diversion away from the Main Force. If they were lucky the 100 Group bombers could slip away unnoticed by the German pilots. Not all were successful.

Aircraft in 100 Group also carried lighter bomb loads than they were used to, often being briefed to drop them in the first wave of a raid.

'The Germans had beacons along the French, Belgian and Dutch coasts. They plotted which way our bombers were approaching over the Channel or the North Sea and got their fighters to orbit the beacon to which we were heading.

'Our people used German-speaking Britons to pretend they were the controllers and broke into radio transmissions, ordering enemy fighters towards another beacon miles away from where our bombers would be. The German controllers got angry and lost their tempers. The Luftwaffe brought in women operators, but we followed this up with girls from the WAAF who spoke impeccable German.

'The fighter crews were puzzled. The controller was just a voice to them, but they were having to deal with so many voices they often didn't obey the Germans because our girls sounded so full of authority. These girls were known simply as Y-Force, it was all very hush-hush.

'Sometimes we carried a special bod. None of us was allowed to ask what he was doing on the aircraft or what he was listening in to. They were briefed and debriefed separately from the rest of us.'

Maxie Taylor's first sortie in 100 Group was dropping Window over Heligoland on the night of 5 January and bombing from 16,000ft. Two nights later they were sent on a prowl into the Ruhr Valley but returned early with the starboard inner engine feathered.

Both gunners' roles continued as before. The wireless operator and flight engineer dropped Window out of the aircraft on the approach to the target. Chum Rees continued to be searching the skies constantly and he was oblivious to what was going on nearer the cockpit.

His circumstances changed on 8 February when he flew as a spare bod with another pilot, Flying Officer A. M. Lodder.

'Maxie Taylor had done one more trip than the rest of us as a second dickey and I wanted to make that up so I could finish on the same number of ops. My job that night was pushing out Window, which was at least 100ft long and floated down on little parachutes. It was very cold and boring.

'I'd been doing this a while when Lodder called up the tail and as there was no answer I said I'd see what was wrong. The rear gunner, Sergeant Casterton, was ill and he went to thaw out at the warm-air inlet while I took over. Some thirty minutes later I heard one of the crew saying something was wrong with Cas who had taken off all his clothes and I realised he had a stomach upset.

'I got word that he was on his way back to his turret and when I caught a whiff of him realised he'd messed himself. It happened sometimes. Cas had his flying gear back on. He gave me his dirty clothes in a big bundle and I dropped them out on

Germany from 18,000ft through the clear vision panel.

'With the help of Maxie Smith, I wrote in Latin in my logbook: "*Casterton Excretare Ab Altidudino Magna*", meaning "Casterton excretes at a great height", which puzzled my squadron commander when he came to sign it.'

Lodder, who sustained burns, and Casterton, were among three of their crew who became POWs on the night of 16/17 April when their Halifax crashed in Germany. Five men, including the specialist equipment operator, were killed.

On 23 February ten Halifaxes from 462 Squadron were sent on a diversionary raid to Neuss.

'Five aircraft, including ours, were leading, the others were higher, some distance behind. They were all weaving, dropping the special Window and giving the appearance of a large bomber force. There was no reaction by the Germans on the first night, but the following night when the same aircraft and crews went out to the same target, they hammered us. I saw four aircraft in the second group explode in balls of flame, one after the other. That tactic was never tried again.'

Twenty-six men died, another five became prisoners.

On 7 March, following a spoof raid on Berlin, returning over the Baltic, they dropped to around 200ft to shoot up an airfield in Denmark.

'I had a whale of a time, shooting at buildings and aircraft,' says Rees, 'but we didn't hang around to admire the damage.'

They once took an air vice-marshal on a night operation.

'He wanted to say he'd been over Germany. After debriefing he stood up to address everyone. He said he was a very disappointed man, appalled at the way the crews spoke to each other, using nicknames instead of Sir or rank, a terrible lack of discipline, he really laid it on. There was a chilly silence as he walked to the door and turned, I can see the bugger now.

'He said:"I hope I've made myself clear to you people. I want you to increase the discipline. I'm sure you don't misunderstand me".'

As the AVM puffed himself up one voice, loud, clear and lacerating rang out from among the wrathful Australians:'Wind yer bloody head in,Sport!'

The great man, red-faced and aghast, hesitated then, as the room erupted with gusts of uncontrollable laughter, dignity and common sense marched his feet away from the terrible scene.

Rees learned later that Maxie Taylor had told the AVM: 'That's the way we do it, we're still here and I've got the best crew in Bomber Command.'

Chum Rees's only regret was that no one knew they were on their final trip, to Lübeck, on 23 April 1945, until the skipper told them after landing back at Foulsham. They went on leave, Rees, after thirty-one ops, to Wales, the others to London. He returned and drifted, a small forlorn figure, around the airfield for three days, until he learned they had all been posted straight back to Australia.

'I didn't even get chance to say goodbye.'

CHAPTER TEN

THE HEAVY GLIDER

Everyone stopped what they were doing one day in Ponsanooth in 1934 when a small aeroplane appeared in the sky and whined lazily over the Cornish village.

One of the upturned faces belonged to Don Moore, a miller's son, who was nine years old, an age when his already fertile imagination was ready to be boldly stirred. Transfixed, he watched the aircraft disappear and an ambition was born.

'Aircraft were rare down there in those days,' he says, 'and I remember turning to a friend and saying:"One day I'm going to be up there".'

During the grinding austerity of the Thirties there were few opportunities in the extreme South-West for youngsters who craved excitement. Cornwall was quiet, largely undiscovered by tourists who would, years later, flock here in their shuffling millions to clog roads, fill beaches, and become known by exasperated locals as emmets.

'Money was tight, we didn't exactly have a hand-to-mouth existence at home, but there wasn't much to spare, and when the war came along it offered a way out.'

The aeroplane represented glorious freedom, an opportunity to explore the world, and after joining the ATC he went with them on a camping weekend at RAF Portreath and was taken up in a Tiger Moth.

'We took off across the cliffs and went over the sea at about 1,500ft. It was only a circuit but it was really exciting; that *was* flying.'

A month before his fourteenth birthday war was declared and shortly afterwards Moore became an apprenticed mechanic in

Falmouth. He followed the war with increasing interest and impatience until 17 January 1944 when he joined the RAF to be trained as a flight engineer.

He met Flight Sergeant Ivor 'Johnny' Johnson in November 1944 at 1668 HCU, Bottesford, where the pilot, and several other skippers, only needed an engineer to complete their Lancaster crews. Johnson and the five men he had been flying with on Wellingtons at OTU studied the form as the unattached aircrews filed in. Moore recalls:

'It was what we used to call The Marriage Bureau. Crews stood in huddles to see what was on offer while the engineers milled around like wallflowers at a village dance. Johnny and the boys eventually picked me and after completing the Lancaster course we were posted on 10 January 1945 to 218 (Gold Coast) Squadron at Chedburgh, Suffolk.'

Johnson, shortly afterwards to be commissioned, was a Londoner who lived in Ludgate Circus with his parents in the top flat of a building of which they were caretakers for the Methodist Church.

'He was three years older than me, about my size, slim and 5ft 6in. He was a good bloke and a pretty good pilot. We were all quiet chaps, keen on the job we were doing and we knitted together well.'

Sergeant Moore was the youngest of the crew and Flight Sergeant Roger 'Mac'Makin,from Chesterfield,at twenty-three, the oldest, and recently married. Liverpudlian Flight Sergeant Harry Christian, who had been an apprentice draughtsman at a structural engineering works, was Johnson's navigator.

The wireless operator was newly commissioned George Robinson, who had gone to even greater lengths than usual among earnest young pilot officers after removing the wire strengthener from the peak of his cap then crushing it into the required bedraggled state, to suggest he had been flying in bombers an impressively long time. He took it with him on every bombing operation.Robinson,from Coventry, never went out on the booze with his crewmates, preferring to chat up young women or get involved with church functions where food was being served. Robinson had a way with words and an insatiable appetite.

Nor did Flight Sergeant 'Jimmy' James, from Uxbridge, the bomb aimer, join his crewmates on their nights out.

'He was a bit of a loner, a mystery man, disappearing before we went out. It was only five years back when I was unsuccessfully trying to trace Jimmy that another former bomb aimer told me he used to go to an Army camp near Bury St Edmunds and teach soldiers to read and write.'

Twenty-year-old Flight Sergeant Alf Spence, whose home was near Paisley, was the rear gunner.

'When Alf got excited in the air it was impossible to understand a word he was saying and the aircraft was put into a corkscrew, just in case there was a fighter on our tail.'

They began their tour with an attack on marshalling yards at Krefeld on 29 January in Lancaster PD439 XH J-Jig, leaving Chedburgh at 10.26am with a load of thirteen 500lb bombs and a 4,000lb Cookie. The 148 Lancasters had an escort of fighters, a luxury not enjoyed by bomber aircrews earlier in the war, who had suffered grievously at the hands of German fighter pilots.

'We were subdued and apprehensive on our first op, but pleasantly surprised that there was less flak over the target than we had anticipated. Although the German fighters were still around at this stage of the war you didn't see them when you had escorts. It was Gee-H bombing which meant we were bombing through cloud. We bombed from 20,000ft and were back at base at 3.51pm. It was a piece of cake, although we never stopped being apprehensive before a raid.'

Other trips followed, including those to Mönchengladbach, Wiesbaden, Chemnitz, Dortmund and Cologne, during which their status shifted considerably from sprog to near veteran.

'The weather was a big problem. Very often when you got over the target it was nothing like what you had expected. On 7 February, heading for Wanne-Eickel, we went into cloud at our normal height of 20,000ft which had not been forecast by the met man during briefing at Chedburgh. Normally the cloud was below us at that height. Even on Gee-H bombing we bombed through the cloud not in cloud.

'That day we went towards the target with absolute full power on to clamber out of the clouds. At the end we were barely climbing and when we broke out at 24,000ft we could only see two other aircraft. We had been on 3,000 revs – which were the takeoff revs – for over twenty minutes. We dropped our bombs from 24,000ft on Gee-H.'

On 5 March they paid their first visit to the industrial Ruhr town of Gelsenkirchen, where they bombed successfully, but their wings and fuselage were spattered by flak. They were not unduly disturbed by the experience and after their return to base that afternoon the holes were soon patched up by the ground crew. One of 170 Lancasters from 3 Group on the raid against the Consolidation benzol plant was lost.

Flak was unpredictable, often striking when aircrew thought they were safely out of a target, but in early 1945, as the Germans were being ground down, their big ack-ack guns were the least of Don Moore's fears.

'Worst of all was another aircraft coming over the top of you with its bomb doors open. They got very close at times, sometimes no more than thirty feet above us. It happened often, and to an awful lot of chaps. There might have been a slightly different wind above that had blown them marginally off course and they tended to drift across the front of you. We also drifted over other people, you couldn't help it; you all had your times to bomb, but a lot of aircraft were pouring into the target, which could make it difficult. You hardly saw these near misses at night, but you saw them during daytime all right: always Lancasters. Halifaxes and Stirlings couldn't get above you.'

Warnings were not generally given to the pilot. 'It depended on the situation. If the other aircraft are coming in on a steady run they're going to drift across the top of you to the other side, so what's the point in your moving on to the rest of the gang? You kept an eye on them, but there wasn't a lot you could do about it because aeroplanes were all around you. Even so, it was always a worrying situation.

Johnny Johnson and his crew returned to Gelsenkirchen on 19 March, joining another 78 Lancasters from 3 Group having another crack at the benzol plant. It was their fourteenth bombing operation.

They lifted off the runway in Lancaster RA532 XH L at 1pm after an early lunch. Their run over Holland and Germany was without hassle, and although vigilance was maintained all the signs pointed towards this being another routine trip. Some remembered their last visit and wondered if they might avoid the flak this time.

'As we approached the target area at 20,000ft, predicted radar-controlled box flak containing sixteen to eighteen shells opened up in front of the formation. We started a gentle weave in an attempt to avoid these bursts but eventually, as we got nearer, we collected a few stray bits of shrapnel, rattling against the wings and fuselage, which sounded like stones being thrown against a length of corrugated iron. There was no serious damage to the aircraft and none of us was hurt, but you never got used to flak and it was, we hoped, our lot for this trip.'

There was nothing scientific about weaving. It all came down to the experience and judgement of the pilot who had to make a sequence of instant decisions, aiming for what he thought might be the safest patch of sky and where the next heavy burst might come from. They could have been safer going straight in, but felt more secure weaving. The box flak had become a nasty form of Russian roulette as practised by the Germans. Turn this way you might be safe; that way you could catch a terminal blast of shells. But rather than do nothing they felt safer doing something.

They got to the target where Jimmy James released one Cookie and fourteen general-purpose bombs into the fires below.

'The bomb doors were closed and we turned sharply away from the flak ahead only to be caught in the middle of the next salvo and all hell broke loose. Shrapnel came up from the throttle box, clipped the skipper's helmet earpiece and went out through the canopy.'

The aircraft's perspex nose blew in bringing with it the stench of hydraulic oil and cordite fumes, and a rush of cold air. The pilot quickly learned that no one had been injured except Jimmy James who had a cut hand from jagged pieces of flying perspex. He left his windy position in a hurry to apply a dressing. But both inboard engines were on fire.

They were immediately feathered by engineer Don Moore and fire extinguishers operated as they stopped. Increased power was applied to both outboard engines, but the fires continued. Moore says:

'We stuck the nose of the aircraft into a steep dive and after losing around 4,000ft succeeded in blowing out the fires, although by then the fuel might have stopped feeding them anyway. We got back on an even keel and under reasonable control.'

They briefly talked about their options. The intercom was not working and information between positions had to be confirmed on paper. Former navigator Harry Christian says:

'We could bale out, go for the North Sea and ditch, or try to get behind the Allied front line and hope for the best. I believed we would make Allied territory and gave Johnny a course to steer. We sent out a Mayday and were eventually contacted and directed to Brussels Evere airfield. We had strict instructions to pancake on the grass alongside the runway to avoid the possibility of closing down the airfield. I made only a slight course alteration and gave Johnny an ETA.'

Moore admitted that they were all frightened, but as the pilot and the engineer worked together at the controls, nursing the Lancaster over Germany, there was no time to think of failure. They had trained exhaustively for this and needed to work calmly and methodically to put things right.

Jimmy James, with a great wad of bandage applied to his injured hand, joined Christian on his long bench seat, where he normally assisted the navigator by operating the H2S equipment when he was not employed in the nose.

'The situation was now reasonably stable,' says Moore, 'and I started to relax when I realised something was trickling down my legs. I remember panicking and being overwhelmed by embarrassment. Bloody hell! I've wet myself. Instinctively I reached down and felt wet and sticky. I pulled my hand away and it was dripping red. Hell! I'd been hit. I felt shock but couldn't feel any pain. What on earth was it? Realisation dawned. It was the red hydraulic oil which fed the front turret. What a relief.

'All this time we were going slowly downhill but getting nearer the British battlefield lines which were marked by fires. Johnny was complaining that the aileron controls were getting heavy and he already had full trim on to pick up the port wing. Of course, eventually you get to the end of the available adjustment. From then on you have manually to pull the control to try and keep that wing up and attempt to keep the aircraft level.'

The perilous situation seemed to emphasise their trudging progress, but smoke from the British lines was now more than a dark smear on the horizon. They could see the occasional flash of flames and were dragging themselves towards it.

'A check on the fuel system showed we had lost most of the petrol from the starboard side. It was necessary to open the cross-feed to run the starboard engine off the port tanks in an attempt to get the aircraft back into balance.

'George Robinson, the wireless operator, opened the cross-feed cock, the starboard outer continued running smoothly and everything appeared to be under reasonable control. We had abandoned any idea of walking home as the front line was only a few miles ahead, then the cockpit began smelling heavily of fuel. We immediately shut down all electrics as petrol was flowing into the cabin from the cross-feed line by the main spar.

'The two gunners continued to search for fighters and because everything electrical was shut down the wireless operator had nothing to do except keep watch through the astrodome.'

The crew's crisis suddenly deepened.

'The starboard outer engine started coughing as it was running out of fuel on that side where the tanks had been holed and we couldn't open the cross-feed again because of a danger of explosion. The starboard outer died and full power was applied to the remaining port engine as we started losing height even more rapidly.

'This required me to assist the pilot to hold up the port wing which was getting heavier all the time. It was a question of heaving the ailerons hard over and kicking a bit of rudder on to keep things straight.

'The pilot had full rudder on, full trim on. The port outer was pulling us to starboard and I was hanging on to the control column trying to keep that wing up because all the weight was on that side. The aircraft was a bit lopsided, but not too bad. The starboard wing was higher than the port. Johnny said: "If anybody wants to get out, get out". But nobody wanted to go. We'd got some sort of control. We were in a bit of a desperate situation going downhill but we were not totally out of control and kept going down slowly until such time as the engine was developing enough power to hold us at a speed and altitude at which we were no longer descending. The engine was going flat out and we were not done for yet.'

No one cheered when, at around 7,000ft, they passed over the British line of fires, although now Germany had fallen behind, each man behind the main spar felt the welcome lessening of fear that an enemy fighter might hasten their demise. However, being above friendly territory was one thing, getting down safely on one engine was something else and if they landed in one piece, saturated with fuel, there would still be the danger of fire and explosion. All the pilot could do was follow the drill, remember advice given by old sweats who had been in similar hairy situations, and hope for a little wedge or two of luck.

In retrospect the odds were stacked heavily against a satisfactory end to their op, or of them recording one of Bomber Command's many little unheralded triumphs in an air war in which grim resolution, courage and heroism were not part of an aircrew's vocabulary. But Johnson and Moore remained positive. Moore says:

'When we got over the smoke we thought at least we were not going to get caught and started looking round for an alternative landing ground because by now it was clear none of us was going to bale out and we were going to ride it down.'

'There appeared to be no hills in the area but we kept going as far as we could. We were still flying that aeroplane. But it was far from a smooth ride in the aircraft which was rocking a bit. It was also hideously cold with the gale blowing through the shattered nose and up our trousers, but that was the least of our worries.

'Johnny was a strong man on that day. He had the rudder full on to counteract the swing of the engine. That was a terrible strain on his legs, but I couldn't help him with that and there wasn't room for anyone else to come in and give a hand, but he was coping, although the last engine was getting warmer all the time. The others were waiting for the bang, there was nothing else they could do. The men not involved with flying the aeroplane jettisoned the escape hatches and went to their crash positions.

'The port outer began overheating badly, with puffs of coolant coming away from the relief valve. As we watched anxiously it spouted out all its coolant and, with a final shudder, ground to a halt. We now had a lovely four-engine glider to play with.'

The noise of the screams from the Lancaster's last tortured engine died and was lost in the constant whoosh of air rushing into the fuselage, which carried its rattling and whimpering echoes blundering past the five men crouched behind the main spar who glanced at each other furtively.

People working below in the flat fields of Belgium looked up inquisitively as the bomber's roaring engine cut out and imagined the panic inside the great dark ghost drifting across the sky, crossing themselves for the young crew who had fought bravely for the freedom of their country.

There was not even the whiff of pandemonium aboard the silent Lancaster for at 4,000ft, even with no engines, they were still moving forward. The two men in the cockpit had spotted Brussels Evere airfield directly ahead in the distance, which promised better facilities than a farmer's field which they had, at one time, thought they might be forced to drop into. No one had received training for flying a worn-out Lancaster several miles without engines and landing on a patch of ground which might normally be used for cultivating turnips. Johnson and his engineer had reacted well to each new emergency, but now they were within reach of a proper airfield.

'We did have a problem which we had to do something about otherwise we would have had our own hole in the ground to go into,' says Moore. 'You've got to work yourself into such a position that you don't go into that bloody hole. Our experience and the RAF discipline gave us that. We had to dive occasionally to maintain speed, that was essential. We had no flaps so we had to keep the flying speed up.'

The world's biggest glider slipped down towards the airfield and, rather splendidly, they were on line for the main runway. Without a radio they were unable to contact the airfield and ask for seven more places to be set for dinner. Moore recalls the growing tension as they fought with the controls and the runway came up to meet them.

'We had no hydraulics and no undercarriage. Johnny and I had talked about putting the undercarriage down but we didn't know what damage had been done and whether the tyres had been punctured. There was an emergency air bottle to blow the wheels down but would they unlock and come down? We didn't know and were not prepared to take a chance because one leg might come down and not the other and that would have been a worse predicament. We decided it would be safer to belly flop the Lanc in.

'An aircraft was at the head of the runway but we were going for the grass. We didn't know at the time but the Americans were based here and they had a controller's caravan at the top of the runway with the fire engine and blood cart alongside which sat there when flying was on. We decided that if we put down near the caravan on the port side of the duty runway it would be useful for the rescue services.

'We came in low over the airfield boundary, at around 110 to 120mph with a reasonable amount of control. We were keyed up, coming in on instinct. Your reactions are quick, there's no time to think, you know what you've got to do. Johnny pulled back on the stick just before hitting the ground and this had the effect of lifting the nose. The tail met the grass in the best attitude followed by the bomb doors which pulled us down on the nose and she sank on her own. She just greased on to the grass near the start of the runway, the best landing he ever did, real text book stuff.

'The nose escape hatch blew inwards and the lip of the hatchway scooped off the top surface. Earth, grass and stones flew up between Johnny and I and went out through the roof escape hatch. Luckily, we weren't hit by any of it. As we were decelerating, throwing bits and pieces into the sky, we overtook a twin-engine Douglas Invader light bomber which was just starting its takeoff along the runway.

'Presumably its pilot had no idea that we were coming in. He swung off wildly to starboard and disappeared down a line of parked aircraft, much to the consternation of the ground staff servicing them.'

They arrived at Brussels Evere airfield at 5.30pm, at least twenty miles from the point at which the Lancaster had been abruptly converted into a heavy glider. It was a triumph for the pilot and his engineer but there was no time for hearty slaps on backs. Johnson and Moore quickly climbed out of the top hatch, slid down the starboard wing and joined the others who had left by the rear door at the speed of light from an aircraft which might at any moment turn into an inhospitable fireball. After a short gallop across the grass they turned and watched the American fire crew, very much on the ball, who were spraying foam all over the starboard wing, the one which contained the empty fuel tanks.

The crew assembled well clear of the aircraft and discovered they were a man short. Roger Makin, their mid-upper gunner was missing. Don Moore and the navigator, Harry Christian, hurried back to the dead aircraft, pursued by an agonised bellow from George Robinson, the wireless operator, who had forgotten his precious cheese-cutter: 'Don't forget my hat!'

'We went back through the rear door,' says Moore, 'but Mac wasn't there and we weren't going beyond the main spar to George's position to look for his bloody cap. There was a stench of fuel, the aeroplane was creaking and groaning and we got out damned quick.'

It was then they saw Makin trudging towards them alongside the deep 300yd furrow ploughed by the sliding Lancaster. Afraid of being trapped in a burning aircraft he had rolled out soon after the aircraft had hit the deck while it was blasting along at about 60mph and was lucky to sustain only a sprained wrist.

'Our aircraft was damaged beyond repair. It stayed on the grass a long time before it was pushed into the dump for scrap. We were carted off to tell our story to the intelligence officer before being packed into a couple of Jeeps and taken to the nearest bar in Brussels. We had no money, but drinks flowed like water and cost us nothing. The Belgians were in celebratory mood.

'The Red Caps collected us around midnight and tossed us into the local police cells. We were very drunk and happy, without a care in the world.

'Next morning we were taken to Brussels Neuville airfield and climbed aboard a Dakota, KG615, piloted by Flight Lieutenant Clark. When we were taxiing round the perimeter we met a bloke thumbing a lift. That happened all the time when fellows were going home on leave. He came with us to Down Ampney, near Swindon. We were collected there by one of the squadron Lancasters which took us back to Chedburgh in time for tea.

'I don't suppose there are many crews who can claim to have been shot down in the afternoon, spent several free boozy hours at a pub in Brussels, and the night in police cells, before returning to their squadron next day.

'The aircraft we lost had been on its thirteenth trip that night. It belonged to Flight Lieutenant Harry Warwick, C Flight commander, who was not best pleased with us for wrecking it. He made us go across to Wratting Common in our own aircraft, ME438 XH H. We were flown there by Pilot Officer Hamm to collect Harry's new Lancaster, which he promptly changed to XH L. The same aircraft forms the background to the official photograph of 218 taken at Chedburgh in July 1945, just before the squadron was disbanded. Next day we went on survivors' leave.'

No one received an award for the part they had played during the remarkable flight from Gelsenkirchen. 'Our squadron was a bit tight with decorations,' says Moore, laconically.

Johnson and his crew flew another five sorties, the last to Bremen on 22 April. They also flew three Operation Manna trips, dropping food to near-starving Dutch in western Holland, and four on Operation Exodus to Juvincourt, France, carrying former POWs back to Britain.

Johnny Johnson, seconded to the Indian Air Force to train its pilots to fly Dakotas, was killed in a crash in 1946.

CHAPTER ELEVEN

THE HERO FROM MARYLAND

Unseasonable rain was falling heavily in June 1999 when Al Boothby stood, head bowed, beneath the dripping trees of a German forest,gazing at the simple wooden cross which marked the spot where the wreck of his Halifax burned out after crashing fifty-six years before.

His mind slipped back to that freezing December night: jumping out of the blazing aircraft,the traumatic unreality of the situation, and the staggering courage of his pilot.

As a group of German historians were rooting patiently through the damp undergrowth, looking for more relics of the wrecked aircraft,Boothby recalled how he and his brother Frank volunteered to join the RAF on the same day in March 1941 to train as wireless operators/air gunners.

The Boothby boys – Frank was the elder by eighteen months – were brought up in Boston, Lincolnshire, Bomber County, home to nearly fifty military airfields during the Second World War.

'Frank and I were like twins,' says Al Boothby. 'We did everything together including joining the Scouts, and the Local Defence Volunteers, which became the Home Guard, and training as musicians with a British Legion military band. We persuaded our parents it would be a good idea to let us join the RAF and we did all our training together until we went to gunnery school: Frank to Pembrey, South Wales, on Blenheims, and me to Walney Island, Barrow-in-Furness, on Boulton Paul Defiants. Later Frank was posted to 76 Squadron on Halifaxes at Holme-on-Spalding-Moor,Yorkshire. He completed two tours, the second with a Pathfinders squadron, and was decorated with a DFM.

'I eventually went to 78 Squadron at Breighton, near Selby, about ten miles from my brother. My skipper was Flight Lieutenant Jim Lucas, a pre-war accountant from the Midlands. He was a good steady pilot and had the respect of the crew.

'But first, we were among crews to be detached to St Eval, Cornwall, to assist Coastal Command in the anti-submarine patrols, flying twin-engine Whitleys. We did six patrols to the Bay of Biscay, some of which lasted ten hours.

'The subs were coming out from Brest into that area and heading straight for the Atlantic. Unfortunately, we only sighted one sub and he went down before we got to him. One of the most dangerous spots was off the coast at Brest because the German Arado sea planes, faster than the Whitleys, were on the wing waiting for us. It was known as Arado alley.

'The trouble with the Whitley, an outdated aircraft, was that if we had lost an engine and were a long way from home we would never have made it back to England. Luckily, we never had that problem. But I always say the most frightening experience I had before moving to Breighton was going on one of these patrols, when I needed to use the toilet.

'We carried enormous overload fuel tanks on either side of the fuselage to give us the range and these left a narrow central metal catwalk about eighteen inches wide. The Whitley, known as The Flying Coffin, had a long thin fuselage and I was off intercom for four minutes as I crawled down it. I was sitting happily on the Elsen, inches away from the rear turret, when the aircraft was put into a tight bank, the stick pulled back, the tail gunner firing his four Brownings and the smell of cordite swirling around me.

'I thought: "My God, I'm the only man who can contact base and tell them what's happening." I began struggling back along the fuselage, still pulling up my trousers. When I got through to the cockpit they were laughing their heads off. It was a joke planned when I was off intercom. I wasn't very pleased, but joined in the laughter when I saw the humour of it.'

While Sergeant Boothby was based at St Eval he first experienced the Americans' casual approach to war.

'A Catalina dropped in one day after losing an engine and a wheel. It crashed at the end of the runway and we dashed out to

RESCUE

DITCHING

1. LAC Larry Lewis, rigger. *(Lewis)*

2. Rear gunner Sergeant Larry Lewis (right), and front gunner Sergeant George Groves. Both flew with Cab Kellaway on 12 Squadron. *(Lewis)*

3. Paddy Thallon crash-landed on the beach at Terschellen Island. George Groves had baled out. Two men died. German soldiers inspect the Wellington. *(Lewis)*

4. Flight Lieutenant Larry Lewis receives his pilot's wings from Group Captain Kennedy in Canada. *(Lewis)*

5. Rescued from ditching. From left to right: Mac Thompson, Bill Perry, Alex Stott, Joe Naisbitt, Harry Warwick, Ivor Turley. *(Margery Griffiths)*

HAPPY LANDINGS

1. LM321 H-Harry, occasionally referred to as H-Happy, poses obligingly with aircrew and ground crew. Standing, far left, is Guy Wood. *(Wood)*

2. Victor Wood and his father, Albert, taken while Victor was on leave before departing for pilot training in Canada. *(Wood)*

3. Victor Wood with his wife, Kathleen, his mother Agnes and father Albert outside Buckingham Palace, after Victor had received his DFC. *(Wood)*

HAS ANYBODY GOT A FAG?

1. The original crew. From left: John Pearl, Vic Collins, Ted Nicholls, Vernon Ashbolt, Ken Larcombe, Cyril Hewett, Eddie Matthews. *(Pearl)*

2. John Pearl: 'We were thrown about the sky.' *(Pearl)*

3. Pilot Peter Anderson buzzed Boston Stump in a Lancaster. *(Pearl)*

FLAMER

DECEMBER 14TH, 1944

George Medal

L.A/C. W. J. CLARKE, R.A.F.V.R., No. 40 Sqn.—This airman has been employed as an ambulance driver for 12 months. These duties have led him into dangerous experiences during which he has acted with great coolness and disregard of his own safety In November, 1943, L.A/C. Clarke took his ambulance right up to an aircraft which had crashed and caught fire. Disregarding the probability of bombs and ammunition exploding, he rescued a member of the crew who was lying beside the aircraft seriously injured. One night in April, 1944, he again drove his ambulance up to a blazing aircraft which was loaded with bombs and, with the assistance of a nursing orderly, extinguished flames on the clothes of three members of the crew by rolling the airmen in blankets. He then got them away from the scene just before the bombs exploded.

L.A/C. R. E. WILLIAMS, R.A.F.V.R., No. 40 Sqn.—This nursing orderly has been employed on ambulance duties for 18 months and has displayed considerable gallantry and devotion to duty In June, 1943, an aircraft, on taking off, crashed before the ambulance reached the scene, some of the bombs in the first aircraft exploded. Despite the danger of further bombs detonating, this airman went direct into the wreckage and rescued one member of the crew and undoubtedly saved his life. In February, 1944, an aircraft, fully loaded with bombs, crashed in flames. When the ambulance arrived at the accident many bombs had not exploded. With great gallantry, L.A/C. Williams searched all round the blazing wreckage for members of the crew, knowing full well that the bombs might explode at any moment.

Again, in April, 1944, this airman and an ambulance driver were soon on the scene when a bomber aircraft, which was carrying a full load of bombs, crashed and caught fire. Three of the crew of the bomber had been splashed with petrol as they left the aircraft and their clothing was alight. L.A/C. Williams and his companion extinguished the flames by rolling the three airmen in blankets, and succeeded in getting them away in the ambulance just before the bomb load exploded. L.A/C. Williams has set an example of courage which has been an inspiration to all members of the squadron.

1. Peter Payne was twenty when he qualified as a pilot. *(Payne)*

2. Peter Payne (extreme right) enjoys a drink at Jack Dempsey's Bar on Broadway, New York, in April 1943. *(Payne)*

3. They bombed the dockyards at Piombino on the night of 16/17 April 1943. *(Payne)*

4. Ambulance driver LAC Clarke and LAC Williams, a nursing orderly, are congratulated by Wing Commander Kirway, CO of 40 Squadron, after being awarded George Medals. *(Payne)*

5. *Flight* magazine reports the award of George Medals to two airmen who acted bravely after Peter Payne's Wellington X crashed at Foggia. *(Payne)*

THE RESISTANCE FIGHTER

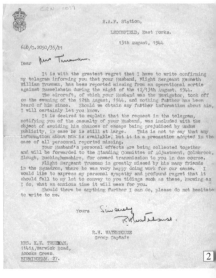

1. Brothers Stan and Ken Trueman. Stan was an officers' cook aboard a Royal Navy frigate. *(Trueman)*

2. Sylvia Trueman received this letter after her husband Ken went missing. *(Trueman)*

3. This Maquis fighter was first on the scene when Ken Trueman parachuted into a field. *(Trueman)*

4. This battered photograph of a Maquis hideout was among those kept hidden in Ken Trueman's shoe. *(Trueman)*

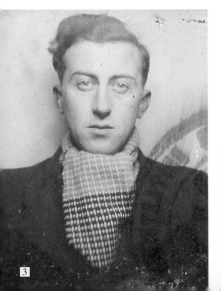

JUST ANOTHER NIGHT OUT

1. John Sargeant, aged seventeen, became a flight engineer. *(Sally Farman)*

2. Pictured before joining 106 Squadron. From left: Douglas Chappell, mid upper gunner Sergeant Woodcock, Tom Saxby, Tom Davies, Leslie McKenzie, David Howroyd. *(Des Richards)*

3. Bar Charlie: damaged but defiant. Photographed from a Lockheed Hudson. *(Des Richards)*

4. It is a little more comfortable in the lifeboat than in the attached dinghy. *(Des Richards)*

THAT'S MY BOY!

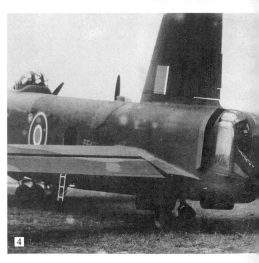

1. They went to 1651 HCU, Waterbeach on 13 May 1943. Back: second and third from left, within the 'B', are Dennis Brown and Sid Long. Middle, second from left: Dick Richards. Fourth and fifth from left: Bill Wells and Doug Fry. Front, sixth and seventh from right: Ken Banks and, with peaked cap, George Judd. *(Fry)*

2. A film still from *The Biter Bit*. From left: George Judd; unidentified, half hidden; Doug Fry (hatless); Ken Banks, in peaked cap, half-hidden; Dick Richards in a white sweater. *(Fry)*

3. The letter which confirmed to Winnie Fry that her son Doug was alive. *(Fry)*

4. The gunners' positions can be seen clearly on Stirling EF427, which took them to Remscheid. *(Fry)*

5. Kriegies (POWs), at Stalag Luft I, Barth. Front, extreme right: Sergeant Vic Clarke, wireless operator, the camp leader. *(Fry)*

BACKWARDS INTO BATTLE

1. Between operations. From left. Chum Rees, Frank Weston, Dennis Somerville, with cat, Arthur Lobb. *(Rees)*

2. Girls flocked to the charismatic Arthur Lobb. *(Rees)*

3. Gunner boys Chum Rees (left) and Dennis Somerville watched out for fighters. *(Rees)*

THE HEAVY GLIDER

1. Time to laugh after a remarkable escape. From left: Jimmy James, George Robinson, Johnny Johnson, Harry Christian. *(Margery Griffiths)*

2. Navigator Harry Christian. *(Christian)*

3. Crew bus driver Margery Bullock drove hundreds of 218 Squadron men to their waiting aeroplanes and, hours later, hoped to count them all back. *(Margery Griffiths)*

THE HERO FROM MARYLAND

1. Al Boothby: witness to an unforgettable scene. *(Boothby)*

2. Breighton: the long wait for the crew bus. *(Boothby)*

3. The best meal of the day: bacon and egg breakfast after debriefing. Centre table, third and fourth from left facing camera, are Al Boothby and Tom Reilly. *(Boothby)*

4. Lachlan Kelly's crew and ground crew. Kelly is at back, second from right, with peaked cap. Rigby is at back, third from left. *(Boothby)*

THE AGONY OF O-OBOE

1. Cyril Baldwin (front, sixth from right) believes he was one of only four men from this gunnery course at Morpeth to survive the war. *(Baldwin)*

2. The survivors. Front, from left: Jim Norris, Bill Reid, Cyril Baldwin. Back: Les Rolton, Frank Emmerson. *(Baldwin)*

3. Touring A. V. Roe's Woodford factory. From left, front row: Les Rolton, Frank Emmerson, Cyril Baldwin, Jim Norris, Bill Reid. *(Baldwin)*

HELL OVER WARSAW

1. Ted Ruman: he and his crew faced impossible odds. *(Ruman)*

2. The crew got out unhurt from this wrecked Liberator. *(Ruman)*

3. Feted in Poland. From left: Former bomb aimer Alan Bates, Ted Ruman, Lech Walesa, president of Poland. *(Ruman)*

THE OLD LADY OF SKELLINGTHORPE

1. The bomb doors of Lancaster X-Ray gape open behind a tired crew, from left: Bob Pettigrew, John Murray, Bob Gillanders, Laurie Pearse, Dave Baker, Alan Barker, Bill Perry. *(Perry)*

2. They had a scare after attacking the Urft dam in December 1944. *(Perry)*

THE WRONG CODE

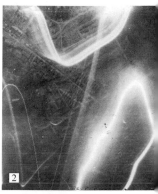

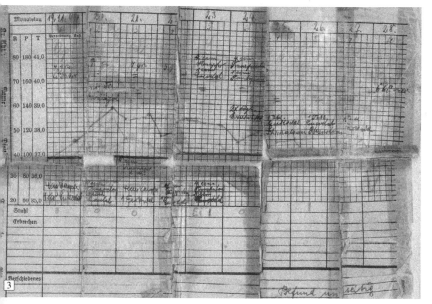

1. David Ward's first tour was on Wellingtons. From left: Calder, rear gunner; Ward; Slash Grover, wireless operator; Tucker, and the Canadian navigator. *(Ward)*

2. David Ward's aiming point for the attack on Naples on 6/7 August 1943 was said to be the best in the group. *(Ward)*

3. This medical chart was used by David Ward as an alternative to his lost dog tags. *(Ward)*

4. The two evaders take it easy at their last safe house. From left: David Ward, Mrs Van de Berg, Major Gordon Sherriff, Mrs Van de Berg's sister, Hendrikus Van de Berg. *(Ward)*

A GROCERS'S BOY GOES TO WAR

1. July, 1944. This photograph was taken
by Alec Stadnyk. To the right is the
Morris 7 Stadnyk won from the
armament officer in a game of dice.
Back, from left: Norman Mason, Ray
Colquhoun, Bill Cooper, Jack Shrapnel-
Ward. Front: Tom Callaghan, Adam
Cragg. *(Mason)*

2. Admission card for York Military
Hospital. *(Mason)*

3. Norman Mason, pictured in flight by
Alec Stadnyk in August 1944. *(Mason)*

THE KILLING SKIES

Navigator Bob Guthrie spent much of his training at seaside resorts. *(Guthrie)*

East Kirkby. Back, from left: Alan Drake, Geoff Jeffery, Hermann Goring, Bud Coffey. Front: Bob Guthrie, Jock Langlands, Benny Bryans. *(Guthrie)*

3. Another course. Navigators at Sidmouth. Bob Guthrie is front, second from left. *(Guthrie)*

THE FATEFUL SWAP

1. Ted Mercer (middle row, fourth from left), did his initial training at Newquay, Cornwall. Bill Reid (back row, second from right), also became a pilot and won the Victoria Cross. *(Mercer)*

2. Clewiston, Florida. Harvards and young trainee pilots. A happy combination. Ted Mercer is just left of the landing light beside the leading edge of the nearest aircraft. *(Mercer)*

3. Ted Mercer overcame one setback to make a long successful career in flying. *(Mercer)*

4. It was never like this in Civvy Street. Bert Baker (left) helps extricate a crewmate from his sweater. *(Mercer)*

COLLISION

1. Letting off steam. From left: Les Duggan (trousers only); Taffy, McMurday's wireless operator; Squadron Leader McMurday; Sammy Sambrook; McMurday's rear gunner; Bert Boos; Bill Cameron. The cameraman's hands wobbled, as they all did, after the night before's binge. *(Duggan)*

2. Les Duggan. The smile of freedom. *(Duggan)*

3. Les Duggan. The despair of imprisonment. *(Duggan)*

4. Fellow-prisoner at Mühlberg Trev Trevett drew this picture of Les Duggan's Halifax in flames. *(Duggan)*

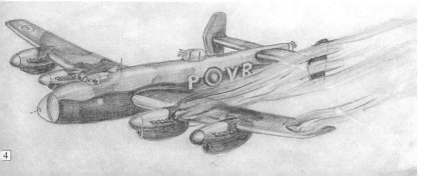

A FUTURE BEYOND TOMORROW

1. June 1942. Wireless operator John Banfield at his position in the Lancaster. *(Banfield)*

2. John Banfield enjoyed exploring the countryside around Bottesford on his bike. *(Banfield)*

3. Bomb aimer John Banfield shows off his gear in the family garden at Hayes, Kent. *(Banfield)*

4. Photo call, 9 October 1943. Location: Stalag VIIIb, Lansdorf. Smiles, please. John Banfield is front row, extreme right. *(Banfield)*

do what we could and found the American crew, all unhurt, calmly frying breakfast in their little on-board kitchen.

'On another occasion the aircraft ahead of us started to move down the runway when its depth charges suddenly dropped out. They didn't explode on impact because they had a sea-water fuse, and were soon cleared away by armourers, but it shows the sort of thing that could happen. The old Whitley did not have bomb-bay doors which opened mechanically. The depth charges dropped on the doors, opening them with their weight. The controls for the depth charges' release were on the pilot's control stick. Instead of pressing the r/t button he had pushed one the other side by mistake.'

Lucas's crew were converted to Halifaxes at 1658 HCU, Riccall, near Selby, then went on to 78 Squadron.

One of a wireless operator's duties before a bombing operation was to take charge of two pigeons which were taken on the aircraft, before the practice was discontinued later in the war. Al Boothby still has the remains of an egg laid by a homing pigeon in its yellow box during a trip to Berlin. He blew the egg, pasted RAF roundels on either end of the shell and wrote the names of the crew on it in ink.

'My last trip with Jim Lucas was to Kassel on 3 October 1943. We flew about twenty ops from Breighton as a crew but because we were hammered so many times by flak and chased by a number of fighters they decided to screen us and we all went our separate ways.

'I stayed on the squadron because I had just been commissioned and there weren't that many commissioned wireless operator/air gunners those days. They needed a commissioned man as signals leader. I was deputy leader and probably being groomed to be leader.'

Boothby began going up with new crews on training flights and on 25 November 1943, on his first operational trip since Kassel, he flew to Frankfurt with Flight Sergeant Rolfe and found that trips with sprog crews could be unexpectedly scary.

'On the Rolfe op someone said:"Oh look, there's an aircraft going down on the starboard side." And the Halifax was suddenly banked to starboard so everybody could have a look.'

Al Boothby was in the wireless operator's seat on 3 December for the tiring 8hr 50min trip to Leipzig with an experienced skipper, Warrant Officer B. Bolsworth DFM.

On 20 December, two days after his twenty-first birthday, Boothby climbed into Halifax II LW320 EY Z–Zebra, piloted by American Lieutenant Lauchlin Kelly, whose wireless operator was indisposed. The target that night was Frankfurt.

Apart from Kelly's mid-upper gunner, Pilot Officer Denis Booth, from Selukwe, Southern Rhodesia, who had been commissioned at the same time as Boothby, the relief wireless operator did not know the pilot or the rest of his crew.

Kelly, a skinny young university student from a comfortable home in Maryland, a small town just north of Baltimore, Texas, had been inspired by the action in Europe and tried to join the US Army Air Corps. Three times he was rejected because of not meeting minimum weight standards and his dismay deepened when, for the same reason, he was turned down by the Royal Canadian Air Force. To his delight he was accepted by the British and joined the RAF in December 1941.

Two years later he had completed fifteen sorties, having several times dragged his faithful LW320 back to Breighton, holed by flak, without its wing tips and bits of the tail. Al Boothby recalls the trauma of that night.

'It was an uneventful takeoff at 4.24pm and we were soon winging our way towards enemy territory. The enemy coastline appeared looking cold and uninviting with many searchlights probing the sky like silver fingers, trying to cone our bombers to bring in night fighters and anti-aircraft fire. Flak became more intense as we approached the target and there were a number of night fighter flares being laid. Our gunners reported several bombers going down and exploding on the ground.

'Suddenly there was a blinding flash and a huge explosion lifted and rocked the aircraft. We had been hit by a heavy anti-aircraft shell at about 18,000ft. To add to our problems we were still carrying a full bomb load. The shell knocked out the port outer engine, while the port inner engine and the wing were ablaze. We were carrying phosphorous bombs in the wing bomb bays and some had been ignited. I tried to speak to the skipper, but realised as I switched on my mike that the intercom was dead. Before I could check it out there was another explosion and the aircraft went into a spin with two engines and one of the bomb bays on fire. The pilot with superhuman effort and skill managed to level out the Halifax at around 14,000ft.

'When I looked over my shoulder towards the rear I saw

flames in the fuselage and both gunners emerging, coming to the main cockpit. The aircraft was flying in circles. The first I knew we were going to bale out was when Denis Booth, the mid-upper gunner, tapped me on the shoulder and passed me the skipper's last command: "Abandon aircraft." The navigator, Jim Rigby, lifted up the escape hatch.'

Rigby was first to fall through the dark hole, followed in quick succession by bomb aimer George Wilson, rear gunner Sergeant R. C. Wellard and Booth.

'Before Denis baled out I recall him getting halfway down the hatch when he remembered something. He pulled himself back and shouted: "Al, have you released the trailing aerial?" I told him I had. The aerial was about fifty yards of wire with lead weights on the end, trailing under the aircraft. If you didn't cut off the aerial you could be decapitated when you baled out. It was one of the first things a wireless operator does in that situation. Denis grinned and was gone. I moved to follow him out.'

As he shuffled forward Boothby turned, looked up, and to his dismay saw the anguished face of flight engineer Paul Westcott. His parachute was open, spilling a torrent of silk, yards of it, into the cockpit. Boothby believed it had opened prematurely. In fact it had been holed and torn by shrapnel, impossible to use. The skipper, clinging desperately to the controls, waiting for his crew to save themselves, read his engineer's fear and gestured for the man to take his own portable parachute from beneath the pilot's seat. As the engineer reached for it gratefully and clipped it on Lauchlin Kelly bellowed defiantly into his ear:

'I'm going to put her down.'

'I was witness to an unforgettable scene,' says Boothby, still staggered by the moment. 'A man giving away his one chance of life to another, an incredible act of bravery. As the fires, growing more intense in the wing, crept towards the fuel tanks, I said a prayer and jumped.'

He was followed by the relieved engineer, a Cornishman, Sergeant Westcott, from the village of Trenance, two or three miles south of St Eval.

'The next thing I knew,' says Boothby, 'I was floating towards Germany. The cold still night air seemed totally peaceful and calm after the thunder of aircraft engines. Then, with a jar that nearly broke my back, I landed in the middle of a track which led through a forest. My parachute was caught up in trees on either side of the track. I was lucky. It was about 7.45pm.

'For a few minutes after hitting the ground my brain seemed to have stopped functioning. I slowly realised where I was and how I'd got there. Overhead I could hear the hum of aircraft,the boys on their homeward leg. I could visualise my friends, on landing, asking:"Who's missing?" How many times had I asked that question and been told that one of my mess pals had failed to return?

'Then I thought of my parents,who would soon be preparing to go to bed. What would their reaction be to a telegram received just before Christmas.

'The wailing of sirens brought my mind back to earth. I was alone as far as I knew in a forest somewhere in Germany. As to my position I could see the target burning in the east and guessed the French border should be sixty miles to the west. I started walking.'

Alone in the burning Halifax Lauchlin Kelly concentrated on his pledge to get the aircraft down,hopefully without sustaining severe injuries. He was a good pilot, but in such a dire situation even the best aviators need luck.He needed a lot of luck:a long flat field without the aggravation of tiresome obstacles. The bomb load had been jettisoned near Löhnberg, setting fire to a barn, but now flames were eating into the aircraft, making it increasingly uncontrollable. The pilot's brave struggles were witnessed by two excited schoolboy brothers, Erwin and Walter Keul,aged thirteen and fourteen,who lived in Odersberg Forest. Walter takes up the story:

'On the evening of 20 December a large enemy force flew over. We were very concerned and kept watching the sky with binoculars and the naked eye. The air was filled with the loud droning of aircraft engines to the extent that the chickens in the coop became upset and began cackling loudly. Now and then we also heard the unease of cattle in the stalls.

'We watched as the air battles started, the red streaks clearly offset against the night sky. As one grew larger we assumed that a plane had been struck. The fire became even bigger and the bomber continued to fall. It flew towards Rasenberg, did a turn and appeared to be heading for our village. In the meantime it was flying so low the flames were illuminating the old school. Time appeared to stand still as the sky was painted red.A huge shining fireball seemed to be falling on us. The plane fell lower and lower, turning again behind the old school and we awaited the crash. When it came the ammunition on board exploded.

'Two men, Helmut Petrowski and a French POW, little Pierre, ran up to the plane but couldn't get near because of intense heat and exploding ammunition. They recorded the exact location of the aircraft: on the edge of the forest between Odersberg and Haiern, but within the Odersberg boundary.

'Two days later we saw the spot with our own eyes. A large wheel had come off the chassis and rolled along the fields. We were amazed by the size of it. Scores of people had come from surrounding villages to see the crashed plane, which bore little resemblance to an aircraft, such was the devastation caused by the fire. The outline was still identifiable. The four engines had been buried deep in an incline within the forest. The fuselage and cockpit, burned beyond all recognition, still sizzled and crackled from the intense heat.

'The wreck was guarded by armed territorial soldiers, older men, incapable of fighting, who had been called up for such duties.

'In the wreckage it was just possible to make out a crew member, still in his seat. He had been decapitated and was without a left hand.'

Lauchlin Kelly, who was posthumously promoted to major, was buried in Odersberg cemetery on Christmas Eve.

It was a terrible night for 78 Squadron and Bomber Command. Among the forty-one aircraft lost, five came from 78 Squadron. The losses included Lancaster LW338 EY Q Queenie, piloted by Warrant Officer Bolsworth, who Al Boothby had accompanied to Leipzig earlier that month. Bolsworth and his entire crew were among the twenty-one men from the squadron killed.

Meanwhile, Boothby was walking cautiously through the forest when his feet smashed through a covering of ice over a narrow stream. Saturated, they became colder and more uncomfortable as he continued trudging westward.

He paused at the edge of a clearing in which he saw several strange animals.

'They were wild boar and frightened the life out of me. I skirted them rapidly and quietly.'

He walked through the night and next morning, as the sky

brightened, became aware of the countryside beyond the forest.

'I was facing a range of hills with small villages on their green and wooded slopes. I heard children laughing and shouting and the sound of church bells. The children, talking German, reminded me where I was. Yet it was peaceful and pleasant, so like England, although the buildings and layout of the villages made them seem as if they had been lifted from the sixteenth century.

'About midday I was climbing a wooded slope when I saw a man dodging through the trees. He was in RAF clothing. I shouted and as he turned I recognised Jim Rigby, our navigator. We sat down and compared notes. To my dismay he said we were eighty miles from the French border.

'All that day we walked towards the west, avoiding the Germans, especially children. We never knew when they might pop out and see us.'

They spent that night in a small barn, lying together for warmth, shivering and shaking from the cold. Boothby said later it was the most miserable night of his life.

About 4pm next day Boothby and Flight Sergeant Rigby, from Southport, Lancashire, spotted the small town of Abhausen, a railway track, and a bridge over a river. They had already talked about sneaking aboard a goods train which offered a swifter alternative to tramping across the frozen landscape. Had he been alone Boothby would have waited until dusk, but the cold was biting and Rigby was eager to keep moving.

'To get to the railway we had to cross the bridge which was in full view of Abhausen,' says Boothby. 'Unknown to us, as we talked we'd been spotted by farm workers who gave chase. We tried to double back but having been on the hoof for three days and two nights, eating no more than Horlicks tablets and a rotten turnip, we were in a pretty bad condition. My wet feet were giving me trouble and I was worried about frostbite. An armed policeman appeared and, suddenly, it was all over.'

They were held an hour at the local police station until a lorry with four armed guards took them to Limberg prison where they were questioned before each received two slices of black bread and potatoes boiled in their skins.

On Christmas Eve Boothby was in the interrogation centre at Dulag Luft, near Frankfurt, where he learned that Kelly had been killed trying to land his aircraft. On the afternoon of Christmas

Day he was moved to a transit camp where he met Denis Booth and enjoyed a festive dinner prepared by other POWs from Red Cross parcels.

Boothby was unable to walk at Stalag Luft III, Sagan, after a two-day railway journey in a cattle truck. Examined by British Army Captain Twee-Mont he was swiftly given a bed in the prison camp hospital where he remained for eight days while his wretched feet were treated for frostbite.

Discharged on 18 January, he and Booth joined a group of fifteen officers in Room 16, Block A, in the Belaria compound, a recent extension to the camp.

All six of Kelly's crew became POWs. Rigby and Wilson were also held in different compounds at Stalag Luft III. Wellard and Westcott were taken to Stalag IVb, Mühlberg. The Germans had driven Westcott to see the wreckage of his Halifax, a chilling moment for the flight engineer.

The next year dawdled by. The prisoners talked a lot about home which seemed more remote as winter drifted idly into spring. Conversation centred mainly on food which was basic and monotonous. Boothby remembers, without nostalgia, semolina and prunes.

German rations given to the prisoners included two ounces of sugar each a week and the same amount of 'synthetic jam'. They each had one-sixth of a loaf of black bread a day and, weekly, 4oz of margarine, two of ersatz cheese, two of sausage, thirty of potatoes and three cups of barley. Each month a man could rely on 4oz of fresh meat livening up his diet. There was an unlimited supply of salt, which raised few hurrahs.

They cooked food from the shared Red Cross parcels in the little kitchen which was at the end of each hut.

'Two people were nominated as cooks and cleaners every week. When the Germans brought us marrows I stuffed them with corned beef and thought that was my best recipe. I was known as "Junior" the youngest chap in the room, for which I was the official tin basher. I made utensils out of the tins. Klim tins were the favourites. They came in the Americans' parcels and contained milk powder. Round tins with biscuits also came from the States. These were useful for making baking dishes and plates.'

A wide range of books was available at the prison library. Boothby read a lot, eventually rigging up a gadget at the end of his bed so when laid prone he could read a book on the wooden rest nailed a few inches below, above Denis Booth's lower bunk. Wooden Red Cross boxes nailed to the wall, held metal mugs, beside pin-ups of girls, and frying pans.

Boothby kept *A Wartime Log* given him by the Red Cross when he arrived at Sagan. In it he recorded life on the camp, illustrating his prose with drawings. On 27 January 1945, he wrote that a continuous stream of refugees fleeing the Russians was passing through.

'Every type of transport is being used from high-powered staff cars to bullock- and horse-drawn vehicles, in their hundreds, and children pulling sledges. They are mostly women, children and old men. The aerodrome nearby is crowded with every type of German operational aircraft and our excitement is at fever pitch.

'Tonight, as I was preparing a brew of coffee in rushed the lager officer shouting:"Everybody pack your kit, you are being moved in half-an-hour."

'Out came the emergency rations we had prepared for the move: one box of sugar, one of biscuits, prunes and cheese, half a loaf of bread, a pat of butter and three squares of chocolate barley cake.

'Then I packed my kitbag. It held three blankets, a change of underwear and socks, about 100 cigarettes and six cakes of soap for trading, two packets of tobacco for smoking and a pair of light slippers.

'We were ordered outside where we stood for an hour. It was snowing and I envied the chaps who had made sledges. The Germans were panicking all over the place before we were ordered back into our blocks. Immediately Stan Stanbridge, an RAF pilot, and I got cracking making a sledge. We emptied the coal box and nailed on two bed boards for runners. For ropes we tied sheets into strips.'

Early next morning each man was issued with one Red Cross parcel before 1,200 POW officers were lined up on the road facing 300 armed guards. The German commandant told them they must march 20km that day. The sick were left behind with hospital orderlies and two padres.

'What a shambles: a long straggling line of men pulling sledges of all kinds, big ones carrying eighteen men's kit, down to one-man efforts made from two hockey sticks. The main camp had been evacuated earlier that morning which meant 10,000 more POWs were somewhere ahead.'

Snow turned into a blizzard and the start of the long march became an agony of endurance. German tanks, guns, lorries, refugees, prisoners, soldiers and guards were mixed into a long confused white stream of fleeing humanity, all tense with anxiety. The POWs tried to make their guards' job more difficult by weaving back and forth across the road.

They spent nights in huge draughty barns. In two days they walked 38km and on the third were allowed to rest at a farm. Many POWs took the opportunity to plunder. Someone stole the commandant's goose and small suckling pig, another ripped the head off a chicken which he liberated from an SS lorry while Boothby squeezed a little milk from a friendly cow. He was wakened in the night by a German couple making passionate love.

Heavy rain had fallen during the night of 31 January after another 20km trek, a thaw had set in, sledges were abandoned and shoulder packs or rucksacks constructed. At Spremberg they joined 500 officers from Sagan's main camp on 3 February and were loaded on to trucks for the slow grinding 24-hour journey to the overcrowded Stalag Luft IIIA, Luckenwalde. Here conditions were deplorable with 180 men packed into a hut, poor and diminishing rations, and no Red Cross parcels.

On 21 April as the sound of gunfire drew nearer many Germans slipped away from Luckenwalde, wire cutters were used by POWs to cut fences separating the lagers, the camp was peppered with shells from fighter aircraft and a white flag was hoisted.

Next day they welcomed the first Russian soldiers to the camp. Their war was over, and although some prisoners broke out and walked to the American lines across the river Elbe, several weeks passed before the bulk of them were released by the obdurate Russians. It was well into May before Al Boothby got home for a family party.

Over the years five German amateur historians have researched several wartime crashes near Herborn, including that of LW320. Sifting through debris on the forest floor they found many relics from the Halifax, including the pilot's burned watch and a pair of aviator's scorched silver wings, eventually identified as those worn by Lauchlin Kelly.

The pilot's remains were transferred to the American war cemetery in Margraten, Holland, at the end of the war, and taken home to America on 3 August 1948.

Kelly's brother, Kenneth, was traced to North Carolina and a meeting arranged between him and one of the researchers, Rainer Klug, who told him of a plan to set up a memorial museum in Herborn. The meeting led to all the memorabilia of Lauchlin Kelly amassed by his family, including photographs, logbook, a diary, letters, medals, career details and newspaper clippings being sent to Klug for display in the museum which has been created in the town.

On that damp summer's day in 1999 the German historians presented their guest, Al Boothby, with Kelly's logbook and a replica of his wings, plus an electrical knob and bits of Window found that day and, from the Keul brothers, souvenirs they had collected in 1943.

Boothby says: 'I was moved and amazed by the friendliness shown me by the people I met in Germany. After all, we were bombing them all those years ago. It shows that it is possible to forgive, and that war is a horrible and destructive waste of human life and energy.'

CHAPTER TWELVE

THE AGONY OF O-OBOE

Everyone interested in Bomber Command has heard of Bill Reid,the tall, slim Glasgow-born pilot with the neat moustache and engaging shy smile who received a Victoria Cross after a traumatic raid to Düsseldorf in 1943. His story has been told many times.

This one focuses more on Cyril Baldwin, an ordinary bloke reluctantly thrust into the limelight because he was Flight Lieutenant Reid's mid-upper gunner on that fateful night.

Baldwin was five when his mother, Mercy, died. Brought up by his father, Robert, in the small market town of Colne, north of Burnley, they moved the short distance to Nelson two months before he left school at fourteen to work in a mill.

Robert Baldwin was a sniper in the First World War, wounded five times, left with a crippled hand and the inflexible opinion that the only good German was a dead one. Not surprisingly his son grew up loathing Germans and, when the war loomed, wanted to be an air gunner to carry on the honourable family tradition of killing them.

Standing five feet four-and-a-half inches, Baldwin's caustic sense of humour, delivered in a harsh accent as broad as the Pennines, was not always understood by some officers who believed his voice only emphasised a lack of intelligence. In fact, it acted as a mask for a sharp mind and a sabre-like wit which raised the good-humour level of the crews with whom he served. Extremely self-conscious about his accent, having developed a hard-man image to compensate for it,he was always on edge ready to explode if anyone laughed at that rather than his jokes.

139

Brought up by his father, without mollycoddling, he was stubborn, blunt, and contemptuous of indiscipline. He rarely experienced fear during a bombing raid, but was cynical about the RAF in circumstances which he perceived as being organised chaos.

He signed up to be a wireless operator/air gunner but at Blackpool the rudiments of the Morse code defeated him and in January 1942 he was among twenty other men who, after failing to handle the perplexing dit–dit–dah–dahs, were posted to Martlesham Heath, perched on the flat heathland east of Ipswich. Spitfires were based here, including those of the American 71 (Eagle) Squadron.

Baldwin remained in a curious state of limbo for five months as the war rampaged on and he waited to be sent to an air gunnery school. His duties at Martlesham were not onerous and included walking round the camp picking up paper, making out Form 295s – leave passes – in the orderly room, and, before important inspections, whitewashing coal which was stacked in bunkers outside accommodation huts. There was nothing quite like the gleam of white coal to gladden the eye of senior pre-war officers.

After the top brass had left the parade ground to imbibe hearty gin and tonics in the officers' mess, Baldwin and his humble companions returned to paint the coal black. This was bullshit at its finest, admired by visiting dignitaries while obliquely focusing the erks' minds upon winning the war.

The airfield was near the coast and, inevitably, became a convenient emergency landing ground for badly shot-up bombers and fighters. This led to less agreeable work for the air-gunners-in-waiting who had to remove the mutilated remains of crews before hosing down the interior of their aircraft.

Baldwin was not surprised that only four of the original twenty remained when postings came through. The others, having changed their minds about flying in bombers, had quietly re-mustered to safer ground jobs.

Nothing dissuaded Baldwin from his ambition to be an air gunner and he was sent to 4 Air Gunnery School, Morpeth, joining the unfortunate men still being trained on the under-powered Blackburn Bothas. There was a steady turnover of air gunners with over 18,000 getting the chop. Baldwin believes he was one of only four men to survive the war from his course of sixty.

'We were posted in alphabetical order. I was sent with two big lads from Wiltshire: Sergeants Banbury and Bradbury, to 1660 HCU, Swinderby where 50 Squadron was flying Manchesters. We arrived on a Friday. The first thing we asked for was a forty-eight-hour pass which would have run from midday until 2359 Sunday. The gunnery leader said he could only give us a thirty-six from midday Saturday. That was no good for the other two but as my married sister, Margaret Bradwell, was living in Lincoln I went there for the weekend.

'When I got back to the billet the bedding and kit of Banbury and Bradbury had vanished. They had both been killed. There'd been a trip on Saturday night and two gunners had gone sick. A sergeant had gone into the mess looking for air gunners. These two silly buggers shot up their hands and went off as spare bods. That was the end of them. They hadn't even been home on leave after training in Morpeth. It was sad but knowing they were dead didn't bother me. To be honest, you couldn't let it worry you because if you did you'd go potty. It was easier to think of the time, however brief, that we'd been together as mates.'

Baldwin was given a week's leave which he spent at home in Nelson. He returned to Swinderby to be crewed up as a mid-upper gunner with an American, Pilot Officer Todd, whose crew was mainly Canadians.

'We went up for a few circuits and bumps and bombing practise, then one day took off for a cross country in an old Manchester. After three hours it lost its brake pressure and we were diverted to Wittering which had an extra-long runway. In this situation you were always ready to get out in a hurry. I was at the rear door and thought the aircraft had stopped, but it was still creeping forward. I jumped out holding my parachute and rolled for a couple of yards, but luckily wasn't hurt apart from a few bruises.'

If this was an unnerving shake up, worse was to follow. Todd and his crew were given a lift by an RAF van that night into Stamford where they relaxed and refuelled at a welcoming pub. On the walk back to Wittering they turned on to the Great North Road, now the A1. It was dark and they did not see the path set back beside the road. Nor did the driver of a lorry see the seven men on the road in front of him. Baldwin says:

'I can remember being thrown across the road by the lorry

and as it hit me, breaking my leg, the driver must have jammed on his brakes and squashed two of my crewmates. All three of us were taken to hospital in Stamford. The others were Davis, the other gunner, a small Welshman, and McPhee, a Canadian wireless operator, a big fellow of about fifteen stones. I'd only been with them a few days. They were in beds beside me and both died in the night from multiple injuries.

'I was transferred to RAF Hospital Rauceby where they had men with broken legs upstairs and those with broken arms downstairs. No lifts. Typical RAF. It was difficult getting down those stairs. I spent some time at a convalescent home at Hoylake, Cheshire, had a month's leave, then returned to Swinderby. That's where I got crewed up with Bill Reid in August 1943. We went from there to 61 Squadron at Syerston on Lancasters.'

Baldwin, then aged twenty-two, says:

'We were just average people, but Bill Reid was a good pilot, quiet and unassuming, but strict. Discipline was important aboard the aircraft and there was no frivolous conversation. He was a typical Scot, a bit on the tight side. We used to have what we called crew nights, when we took our ground crew out, often to pubs in Nottingham. If Bill could get away with it he didn't pay for a single round.'

The navigator was Flight Sergeant Alan Jeffries, a former teacher from Perth, Australia who, rather inconveniently, suffered from air sickness.

Sergeant Jimmy Mann, the wireless operator, came from Orrell, near Liverpool. The cherubic features of bomb aimer Sergeant Les Rolton, from Romford, Essex, led him to being known as 'Baby Face'.

Twenty-two-year-old Sergeant Jim Norris was Reid's second flight engineer. He was three years older than the man he replaced who, too frightened by his first operation to go on a second, was sent in disgrace from Syerston without his stripes.

Jim Norris, from Cardiff, had worked in the city's railway goods yards before submitting himself to the dubious pleasures of Bomber Command.

Baldwin, now a flight sergeant, known as 'Blondie' on the squadron because of his almost white hair, alternated rear and mid-upper turrets with the other air gunner Flight Sergeant Frank Emmerson, from Enfield, Middlesex, known as 'Joe' for his dark moustache which had been compared to Stalin's. The most experienced man in Reid's crew, Emmerson had been awarded the DFM after completing his first tour.

Some aircrew pretended that their first operation need not be much different to training flights, except that when they turned on to the North Sea they continued heading east and real ammunition was in the guns which fired at them. Baldwin says mildly:

'It was obviously strange the first time. As we approached the target in Hanover a German fighter flew about thirty feet over the top of us going in the opposite direction. As I turned my turret he disappeared. Reid said:"What was that?"

'"A Ju-88."

'"Did you hit it?"

'"I hardly saw it." Well, it went that fast.

'We flew at around 23,000ft. They reckoned the higher you flew the safer you were, but that was a fallacy, the fighters could get you just as easily. It was the same when anyone asked:"Did you shoot any down?" My answer was "No." How did they expect you to knock enemy aircraft down with bullets that small?'

'At 200yd our bullets were dropping At 400yd a German fighter could knock you out of the sky with cannon shells. Our Brownings had .303in bullets. They were only rifle bullets. The Germans had point-fives, that made the difference.

'I did get some bursts in at the Germans, but you'll never convince me we were there to shoot them down. Our principle was evasive action. As soon as you saw one you cried out:"Dive port!" Or "Dive starboard!"

'Later, as the war progressed, the Americans were shooting them down and that started our lot trying to do the same. I reckon that was entirely the wrong tactics. A lot of lads could have been saved by relying on evasive action.'

Bill Reid and his crew went on seven more raids: to Mannheim, a return to Hanover, Bochum, Munich, Stuttgart and two trips to Kassel, none of which Cyril Baldwin regarded as remarkable.

While on leave in Nelson on 16 October Baldwin was married to Marion Stead, whom he had met in London. She was in the ATS, working on an ack-ack battery in Primrose Hill. A few days later he and Frank Emmerson were in Liverpool for wireless operator Jimmy Mann's engagement party.

On 3 November 1943 Reid's Lancaster was among 589 crews briefed to attack Düsseldorf. They were in their regular aircraft, LM360 QR O-Oboe which lifted off from Syerston at 4.59pm. It carried one 4,000lb Cookie and scores of incendiaries.

As they climbed towards 21,000ft Baldwin, in the mid-upper turret, fretted about the icy draughts penetrating the ventilators which were intended to prevent the perspex misting up. He knew that later he would be wiping ice off his eyes.

There was a quarter moon, with patches of cloud hovering at around 17,500ft, when, just after crossing the Dutch coast, a pair of orange flares drifted down behind O-Oboe with the innocence of two bright Roman candles. Knowing this indicated the presence of German fighters the gunners' turrets were constantly on the move, intensifying their search for predators. Reid weaved the Lancaster, allowing them a better view of anything slinking along below.

Cool discipline switched into a new dimension when a Messerschmitt Bf-110 hurtled in to attack them from the rear. If Frank Emmerson's electrical suit had not developed problems they might not have been forced to endure a night of such endless horror. The rear gunner had seen the approaching fighter but was unable to warn his skipper immediately because he had lost all feeling in his frozen hands. He could not operate the switch on his intercom, nor fire his four Browning machine guns.

On previous trips they had seen other unsuspecting bombers set upon by night fighters, but it was never possible to imagine the savagery of such an attack until they experienced it for themselves.

Reid gasped as a sudden explosion in the front of the aircraft tore out the windscreen and wicked splinters of perspex ripped into his head, face, shoulders and hands. Emmerson, desperately forcing his stiff icy hands to do his bidding, and Baldwin, both opened fire on the Bf-110, driving it away.

The bomber plunged, out of control, losing 2,000ft. Reid whipped off the oxygen mask which had become a gruesome receptacle for the blood oozing down his face, and dragged on his goggles to protect his eyes from the violent inrush of air. He thought they had been caught by predicted flak but Baldwin said: 'No, it was an Me-110. I couldn't get him because my turret was turning. He's gone, but I'm watching out for him.'

Over sixty years later Baldwin recalls:

'All I heard during the attack was loud rattling underneath the Lanc. The fighter passed underneath and I heard Bill say:"Oh, hell!" over the intercom and we began going down.'

Alan Jeffries, the navigator, asked if Reid was all right as the pilot recovered to drag it back on to an even keel.

Reid said he was fine even though he was not, and the numbness of his head made him feel as if he had been scalped. He added as cheerfully as possible:'Is everybody okay?' One by one his crew reported in and both gunners said they thought they had hit the fighter.

The Lancaster had become a wallowing casualty of war. Apart from a deluge of cold air pouring through its smashed windscreen, the elevator trimming tabs had been damaged, making the aircraft difficult to control. The rear turret had been hit and the rear compasses no longer worked.

Reid, happy that his crew were still at battle stations, carried on to the target, while saying nothing of his own injuries, which might have affected morale. The idea of returning to England did not cross his mind. Besides, this would present the additional risk of turning head on into the approaching stream of bombers. The icy gale rushing into the aircraft had dried the blood on his face and head and anaesthetised some of the pain. He asked the navigator for a new course and they pressed on, nerves slightly ruffled, but remaining focused and relieved that all four engines were working perfectly.

Night fighters still prowled hungrily among the intruding bombers, eighteen of which would not return to their home bases.

As soon as they had gained height Oboe was attacked even more ferociously by an FW-190 hurtling in off the port beam, intent on not wasting a shell, blasting the entire length of the aeroplane. Both gunners had spotted the fighter at the last moment, but were unable to give their pilot adequate warning to take evasive action. Emmerson replied with a burst from the only Browning still working on the aircraft, but the Lancaster fell out of control. The pilot's body had been peppered with shrapnel, and he received a great blow to his shoulder, which he later described as like being struck by a hammer. He was thrown in a daze over the controls. The wounded Norris helped him pull the bomber out of the dive, then struggled round the aircraft for portable oxygen bottles to help revive his skipper.

This time no reports would filter into the pilot's position that all was well with his crew. Jefferies, the navigator, was dead and slumped across his body was the wireless operator, Jimmy Mann, badly injured, who had been blown off his chair. Jim Norris, the engineer, badly hurt in the arm, instinctively grabbed the control column to help Reid keep them in the land of the living.

Together they slowly brought the Lancaster under control and continued to head for Düsseldorf. The bomber was now more battered and even less functional as a fighting machine. The intercom, hydraulics and compasses had gone, the oxygen system had failed and both turrets were out of action.

Bomb aimer Les Rolton was hit in the hand by shrapnel as the FW-190 raked the port side of the Lancaster. Norris recalls the agonising moment:

'The fighter attacked when I was sitting on the floor filling out my engineer's log. When the cannon shell burst through the windscreen a piece of shrapnel went over the top of me and killed the navigator. Fragments struck my left forearm and some are still embedded in a muscle. My arm becomes stiff in winter. I also had shell splinters in my back and shoulders.'

Baldwin describes how his luck continued to hold:'I had seen the FW-190, but couldn't fire at it because my guns weren't working. Luckily my bullets, contained in two cans all on the port side, were facing outwards. They went up in a great flash, ripping a big hole in the port side of the aircraft. I was untouched. When I climbed down from the turret I could see the moon as plain as anything. It was like looking through a window.

'The engines were still going, but I got down because I couldn't speak to anybody and didn't know what had happened. I didn't want to be sitting there on my own if everybody else had baled out. I went forward and that's when I found the navigator dead, shot in the head and the wireless operator hurt. Jimmy muttered that he had been wounded but didn't say where and although I looked I couldn't see any blood. I could have given him an injection of morphine but he seemed to be content at that moment. I eased him back into his seat, clipped on his parachute and hooked his oxygen mask back on. I didn't know then that we didn't have any oxygen.

'Bill turned round and gave me a thumbs up. The engineer

said he was all right and I told him I would try to help Emmerson. I went back through the fuselage and tapped on his rear turret which he turned a bit and put his thumb up.

'I went back into my turret because there was nothing else I could do. I know it sounds silly but you did feel a little bit safer in the turret. There was no heat in my flying suit and it was bloody cold.Despite my extra clothing and several pairs of gloves I sat on my hands to keep warm.At that time I didn't know if we were going back to England or still heading for the target. I didn't know we'd carried on until we were over Düsseldorf and I saw it burning.'

Reid asked the engineer to get a course from the navigator. Norris came back to say he thought Jeffries was unconscious. One more problem to be added to so many others. Reid put it out of his mind, deciding that as he had memorised the course to the target they could still get there. The bomb aimer, Les Rolton, who had only sustained cuts to a hand,had remained in the nose, unaware of the difficulties above.The engines sounded healthy, he assumed all was well apart from a dead intercom.

Taking rough bearings from the Pole Star Reid, weak from loss of blood and pain, helped by Norris communicating by signals, took over an hour from the encounter with the Bf-110 to reach Düsseldorf. Opening the bomb doors Reid nodded to Norris who caught Rolton's attention to let him know they were approaching the bombing run. Norris says:

'I was leaning down towards the bomb aimer passing hand signals from him to the pilot so he could adjust the run:"left, right, left, a bit to the right" and so on. We bombed at 20,000-odd feet.'

The bombs were released over the target, a ball-bearing factory; the in-board camera took its photograph and would later show a direct hit. Reid was mightily relieved, but only half the job had been done. Now they had to get home.

Steering by the Pole Star and the moon Reid had been steeling himself to get to the target.Concentrating on the return flight was difficult. Because of the loss of hydraulics the bomb doors remained down,making the bomber even more of a beast to control.

The oxygen bottles had run out, the pilot was weak, and shortly after leaving the target he passed out and they went into a steep dive. Norris grabbed the stick and Rolton helped him haul the Lancaster back to an even keel.

There was no question of panic. RAF crews knew about discipline and working competently as a team, but taking over the controls of a big bomber for the first time – and a bomber crippled and many of its instruments u/s – was an experience the flight engineer would have rather been without. He says:

'I tried unsuccessfully to bring Bill round, then Les and I attempted to get him out of his seat but he was too badly hurt and the plane began diving so we didn't try that again. I kept the Pole Star and the moon on my right side all the way home. I had never flown an aeroplane before although I once had a go on the ground in a Link Trainer. I kept poking Reid with my elbow, but there was no response. We kept losing height and the aircraft was very heavy on the controls.'

Norris kept the Lancaster steady as they droned over Germany, easy prey to any inquisitive fighter.

They survived a blizzard of flak over the Dutch coast then halfway across the Channel all four engines cut out. Norris knew immediately what had happened. The fuel tanks needed changing over.

'As we were going down in a strong dive I used hand signs in an attempt to get Les to change the tanks but he couldn't understand. I got him to hold the stick for a few seconds while I went behind to the engineer's compartment and switched fuel cocks and the engines started again. We were now at 8,000 to 10,000 feet.'

He tried to form a plan in his mind about what he should do when they needed to land. As they approached England, Norris knew he was not the best man for this job and his nudging of the unconscious Reid became more agitated.

They crossed the English coast at about 3,000ft and soon saw the lights of an airfield. It was a moment Norris both welcomed and feared.

'We didn't know which airfield it was and I would certainly have had a go to get us down but Bill, after I gave him another hefty thump, suddenly woke up. He saw the lights below and instinctively took over. Distress cartridges were fired and I tried unsuccessfully to pump down the undercarriage then stood beside him in case he passed out again. He made one circuit of the airfield and came in for a belly landing on the concrete runway.'

They touched down with an agonised screech of tearing metal, the impact forcing the hydraulic jacks up through the wings. The bomber did not catch fire. They were at Shipdham, Norfolk, an American airfield. It was 10.01pm. Only now was Reid told that Alan Jeffries was dead.

Jimmy Mann walked with Cyril Baldwin to the waiting ambulance but died from his injuries within twenty-four hours. Baldwin says:

'I think Jimmy had been reaching up to tune his wireless set when he was hit by shrapnel under the armpit. Less than a month after his engagement party Frank and I went north again for his funeral.

'Later that morning we had to go into the plane to get the navigator's bag and secret stuff to take back to Syerston. I saw Alan's helmet on the floor and threw it towards the doorway at the back. Unbeknown to me an officer caught it with his hands and inside there was some of the dead man's head. He played hell with me.'

While Reid and Norris were recovering in hospital from their injuries the other survivors became spare bods, flying with many different crews when required, then 61 Squadron moved to Skellingthorpe. The following January all five survivors of the Düsseldorf raid were taken on a five-day goodwill tour of the Avro factories in the north of England. This included appearing on stage in front of 1,000 aircraft workers, telling their stories. Baldwin, the comedian, was last on the bill, telling jokes. It all went down a treat.

Jim Norris, who had been awarded an immediate Conspicuous Gallantry Medal for bringing O-Oboe back to England, was posted to St Athan as an instructor after completing his first tour, but was not interested in instructing, he wanted to fly. He deliberately failed an instructor's course at Cosford and was sent back to St Athan where he joined 32 Maintenance Unit Test Flight.

Reid invited Baldwin to join him on 617 Squadron at Woodhall Spa, but the gunner refused, saying he had only a few more ops before completing his tour. Besides, his brother-in-law, Frank Bradwell, an engine fitter with 617, had already told him the squadron was full of 'bloody lunatics'.

Bomb aimer Les Rolton joined Reid but was killed with five others when a 12,000lb Tallboy, falling from another Lancaster, ripped through their fuselage. Reid baled out and became a prisoner of war. Frank Emmerson, awarded a DFM after Düsseldorf, was killed on an op shortly after the Avro trip.

Baldwin's plain speaking got him into trouble when flying as rear gunner from Skellingthorpe with New Zealander, Flight Lieutenant 'Pop' Woods. Attacked twice by fighters en route to Berlin, after the gunner sent Woods careering all over the sky in the second series of corkscrews, the pilot gasped: 'I can't keep this up much longer, my arms are aching.'

Baldwin bellowed: "They'll ache a bloody sight more when you're playing your harp, now for God's sake get us out of here.'

Safely back at base the crew were confronted at debriefing by the formidable figure of Group Captain Evan Evans, the station commander who, appalled by Baldwin's wilful insubordination, demanded that he be put on a charge. Luckily the squadron's wing commander intervened and the order was ignored. Instead, at the end of his tour of thirty-five operations, a delighted Cyril Baldwin received a DFM.

CHAPTER THIRTEEN

HELL OVER WARSAW

The morning sun beamed on Polish rear gunner Tadeusz Ruman as he sank wearily to his knees and bent to kiss the ground at Brindisi, astonished to still be alive.

Ruman, a Catholic, had stumbled from the crumpled wreckage of his Liberator on 28 August 1944, determined to give thanks for the safe deliverance of himself and his crew, all Poles, who had come through an extraordinarily gruelling 1,750-mile round trip to Warsaw.

The sun had also shone the previous evening nearly eleven hours before when they had left the Italian airfield, with a precious load of supplies for the Polish Underground army desperately battling with the occupying Germans for repossession of their city. The tragic capital of Poland was ablaze and seen fifty miles away by Ruman's Liberator and four other aircraft from 1586 Special Duties Flight which were carrying guns and ammunition to aid the Warsaw uprising.

The series of courageous but ultimately fruitless operations intended to bring succour to the oppressed Poles is one of the Second World War's forgotten epic stories, yet the courage, skill and determination of those taking part was no less than many others which years afterwards featured in best-selling books and blockbuster movies.

Sixty years later survivors still feel bitter about the meagre recognition they received outside Poland after flying on operations in which so many men were killed. Ruman, who took part in eight of these flights,believes that for sheer heroism, difficulty and audaciousness they should rank alongside the Dambusters raid of 16/17 May 1943.

He says:'I don't want to minimise their effort but any of my comrades would say the dams raid was a picnic in comparison to Warsaw. For instance, the Germans knew we were coming as we had night after night. They could track us a long way out from where we crossed the Tatra Mountains right down to Warsaw. We were also flying very low, as were the dams boys, towards the German guns. But they were a few seconds over the target then off they went. We had to go low through the city which was lit up like day by the fires, and the Germans picked us off with their guns.'

The Poles, misjudging the situation, had begun their uprising on 1 August, believing the Russian army, camped outside the city, would give them supplies to fight the Germans. Stalin ignored their plea, ordering his soldiers to wait until the Germans had left Warsaw before moving in. The Poles appealed to Britain and Winston Churchill sanctioned the supply drops, against the advice of the Air Staff who said the operations would lead to great loss of life and aircraft. The task was given to squadrons based in southern Italy.

Among them were the Polish aircrews of 1586 Special Duties Flight at Brindisi who were motivated by a consuming hatred of the Germans and an appetite for revenge after the destruction of their homeland and the brutal extermination of vast numbers of their people.

Tadeusz Ruman, widely known as Ted, was among thousands of his countrymen who doggedly made their way across Europe to link up with Britain to fight their common enemy.

Ruman, born in Tarnow, near Kraców in 1919, one of seven children of a Post Office clerk, passed a glider pilot's course in 1938 during his summer holidays from college. The following year he learned to fly on the Polish-built RWD 8 monoplane, finishing the course and flying solo nine days before war started.

'My father, Jakub, had refused to sign the form to give permission for me to learn to fly,' says Ruman. 'He told me: "Your mother and I didn't bring you into the world so you could kill yourself." I forged his signature, and I flew. I was determined.'

Poland's military equipment was outdated and their army routed, but they could still fight. Ruman became a courier in the Polish Underground army, passing messages and documents between the Russian-and German-occupied zones. Issued with false identity papers and given the name of Kazimier Zak,he had two years knocked off his age because everyone thought he looked so young.Messages and addresses were written faintly in pencil on the thin paper he used for rolling cigarettes.The work was dangerous but he took it in his stride.

He was arrested on Good Friday, 1940, by a member of the Gestapo but the German, his senses befuddled by drink, unable to find the right key for the cells,glared in irritation at the youth, told him to clear off and not come near him again,otherwise he would really be in trouble.

Ruman's clandestine work ended later that spring when he was caught by the Russians and interrogated by the NKVD secret police. He spent fifteen months on the edge of starvation in overcrowded prisons,including Lwow, in appalling conditions before being told he had been sentenced to fifteen years' hard labour for working against the state, although there had been no trial.

'We were crammed into cells and fed a thin slice of bread early each morning.The rest of the day was spent thinking about when we would get more bread.It didn't matter how old or dry it was. I never expected to survive, but we were released about six weeks after Germany invaded Russia in June 1941.I was skin and bone and for a long time carried bruises from where I had lain on the floor of cells.'

Ruman's hatred of the Germans deepened when he learned how his uncle, Josef Rachlewicz,a member of the Underground army, was hanged on the public square at Skoczow by the Germans. His wife and eleven-year-old daughter, Doroty, were forced to watch. His eyes filling with tears, he says:

'I could never forgive the Germans for that. Doroty never married. Even now, every time she walks across the square she sees her father being hanged. She remembers the exact spot.'

His journey to Britain from Russia was long, arduous and complicated, by trucks, railway wagons and ships, via Tehran, Bombay and Cape Town, arriving in Scotland on 6 June 1942.

'We stayed at a camp near Falkirk in quarantine for a week in case we had some nasty disease before being sent to Blackpool, which was the Polish Air Force depot. None of us could speak English and I never had a lesson.I just picked it up. I was a quick learner and had the benefit of a photographic memory.

'Interviewed by Group Captain Pniewski in Blackpool I told

him I wanted to be a pilot. He said:"We have enough pilots, and you would have to wait six, maybe twelve months." But I wanted to fight and he said the quickest way to get into the war was to be an air gunner. So I went on a course at RAF Evanton, north of Inverness, and that is how I started. I became a rear gunner.'

In the spring of 1943, Sergeant Ted Ruman joined a Polish crew and was posted to Hemswell, north of Lincoln, with 305 (Ziemia Wielkopolska) Squadron, flying Wellingtons. It was here he was nicknamed 'Hawkeye' for his ability to pick out the flitting outline of enemy fighters in the darkest night.

Their first sortie was to Krefeld where he remembers the flak appearing 'like sizzling sausages' ahead of them.

'You didn't realise the danger, not at first. We learned that no flak was even more dangerous because night fighters could be around. Flying in the aircraft was like being in a coffin, but we got used to it.

'Before we went to bomb Wuppertal that summer the intelligence officer said at briefing that the attack would cause numerous fires because most of the houses were made of wood, and that is how it was. Casualties were high in the town and that pleased us. Providing a lot of Germans were killed we were satisfied. We wanted to kill Germans, the more the merrier. After seeing what they had done to Poland this could be considered a part repayment. We went to Wuppertal again, Cologne and Düsseldorf, and twice through the guns guarding Essen.

'The scariest operation was during the Battle of Hamburg when we went low right into the port to drop mines. We came in at less than twenty feet above the water, and were fired on by ships in the harbour. At the same time hundreds of our aircraft above were dropping bombs, we were lucky not to be hit by one. We dropped the mines and got away quickly.'

New runways being laid at Hemswell forced the squadron to move a few miles south to Ingham from where operations continued. In September the squadron was posted to what would become the 2nd Tactical Air Force at Swanton Morley, flying North American Mitchells.

On Sunday 14 November, Ruman woke up late as usual a few minutes before the sergeants' mess was due to stop serving breakfast at 9am. He leaped from the bed, slapped water on his face, did not stop to shave, wound a scarf around where his tie should have been and raced to the mess. Too late, he settled for a mug of milk.Returning thoughtfully to the billet he asked his wireless operator, Marion Andruszkow, to go with him to mass.

Andruszkow, an early riser, who had enjoyed a leisurely breakfast,looked up briefly from the riveting pages of the *Sunday People* and replied, half joking: 'My mother prays for me.' His mother had also prayed for Andruszkow's brother who had died during the Battle of Britain.

'We had a thirty-minute training flight arranged for 3pm. In the crewroom after lunch Henryk Anglik, the skipper, said we would be flying in formations of threes. We got into the garry and set off for the aircraft.We'd taken part in seventeen bombing operations and dozens of air tests, none of which I had missed. Today it was different. The WAAF driving the van had just changed into second gear when I suddenly jumped out. The others shouted: "Where are you going?" And I replied, not knowing why:"I'm going to try and start the car." Three of us had bought a Ford 8 car between us for twenty-eight pounds and it wouldn't start, it may have been the dampness of November. We wanted to drive it that night to a Norwich cinema.

'I don't know to this day what made me leave the garry because I knew nothing about engines and never even went to look at the car that afternoon. Outside the crewroom another gunner, Sergeant Jan Twardowski, a spare bod, said:"Aren't you flying,Tadeusz?" I said:"No, I'm going to the car." He said:"I'll go instead." He took the next van to dispersal.The others were already in the aircraft with the door shut, but when Jan arrived it was opened, the ladder put up and he joined them.

'I was looking straight down the runway from our billet and could see aircraft forming in the air, but our Mitchell, which should have been leading the second trio, was still on the ground running along on one wheel. I couldn't understand this as our skipper was always so careful, never any fooling about. He took off and gained height, but at the same time was turning to starboard.The aircraft disappeared, still turning right, and I laid down on my bed.

'I heard aircraft landing then some fellows came in and told me I'd lost my crew. I said:"Don't be ridiculous. Don't joke like this."Then I realised they were telling the truth.When they said I should be pleased to be alive I felt like a murderer because our crew was a family, always together.

'They had crashed near Fakenham and caught fire. We thought the steering lines might have jammed. All four were killed and burned like chickens. Only the pilot's body was identified.Somehow part of his left trouser pocket had survived, stuck in the mud. It contained a love letter from his girlfriend. After the funeral I returned the blood-stained letter to the girl but, with her permission, kept the envelope.

'No one flew the Mitchells operationally and the squadron went on to Mosquitoes but I was posted to 1586 Polish Special Duties Flight, based with Halifaxes and Liberators at Brindisi, Italy. We flew at night, sleeping on the warm Adriatic beaches during the day. Our job was mainly to supply the Underground in Poland, Yugoslavia, Greece and north Italy, mostly Poland – eleven times we went there – usually dropping during a full moon near a forest,often in the vicinity of Lublin.The Germans knew we'd been but at that time the nights belonged to the Underground. First thing in the morning the Germans arrived, but it was too late. By then everything had been taken away deep into the forest. It was strange flying over our own country at first, but we were proud and glad to be doing it.

'We also dropped agents, including some Italians. One, I remember, began crying at the moment he was supposed to bale out. He was frightened, so we had to bring him back.

'We flew low on all these trips. Over Germany we were at twenty-odd thousand feet.Now we flew at no more than five or six thousand.We were fired at by anti-aircraft guns but often flew so low that fighters – which always came in from below – would not have attacked us.Even so, we always had to watch out in case one tried.'

Polish aircrews whooped for joy when hearing of the initiative to airlift supplies right into the city of Warsaw where the Underground army was setting about the Germans.

'The Warsaw uprising started on 1 August 1944. We were all excited to get started, everyone wanted to go. On 4 August the first supply drops were made and we were among the crews leaving Brindisi that night, packed with guns and ammunition. It was a reasonably quiet operation. We only saw a few bursts of anti-aircraft fire near Kraków and Warsaw was quiet. We had surprised the Germans.But as the drops continued they became more dangerous and once we were caught in an electrical storm and the entire aircraft was covered by millions of tiny flickering stars. We were not frightened by that, it was preferable to being attacked by a fighter.

'Another time, heading towards a church tower in Warsaw, the pilot cried:"Jesus Christ!" and we just scraped over it.'

When Flight Lieutenant Jan Mioduchowski joined Ruman's crew during the supply drops he became skipper because he outranked their regular pilot, Warrant Officer Henryk Jastrzebski, but the commissioned officer was content for the other man, now officially the second pilot, to continue flying into Warsaw because of his greater experience.

'Jan was a very nice chap,' says Ruman, 'but the crew were more comfortable with Henryk at the controls. He was a fine pilot and we had done so many ops together. And it was Henryk who gave the crew their instructions.'

Ruman had completed a first tour of operations and went into a second and third without a break. By 26 August he had flown a total of seventy operations, fifty-three from Brindisi, more than his crewmates, but no one wanted to stop. Poland was relying on them.

On the night of 27 August five crews from 1586 Special Duties Flight were briefed for the latest supply drop to Warsaw, the eighth for Ruman and his crewmates. They had a new wireless operator, Flying Officer Nowicki because their normal radio man was being rested.

It would not have taken many German military brains to deduce that an outburst of fierce activity among the Poles in Warsaw, coinciding with more regular deliveries by RAF aircraft meant that the Allies were endeavouring to assist a major uprising which clearly needed to be suppressed swiftly and decisively. After that first night defensive positions were gradually strengthened, with more anti-aircraft guns being moved into the Polish capital, along the route taken by the British bombers. Every succeeding drop became more hazardous. The Germans only had to wait. The Allied aircraft appeared conveniently, one at a time. It was as easy as shooting sparrows off a branch. More patrolling enemy fighters appeared in the sky near Kraków, Poland's former capital, and towards the end of August these operations had almost reached the status of mission impossible. But they continued.

'Every time it was worse to Warsaw. We had lost so many crews who were replaced by new chaps who didn't come back.

But the worst thing for us as a crew was the waiting during the hours before a flight. Time dragged. We were continually looking at our watches and finding the hands had hardly moved. We knew we were going and had time to think about it, which was not good because we knew anything could happen. Once on the plane we were so busy there was no time to think and worry.'

One distinct advantage the Poles had over the British and South African crews on these flights was that they knew Warsaw. Many had lived or studied here before the war. They knew the streets, the squares, the high buildings, including St John's Cathedral, churches and university, the parks, the river Vistula snaking its way through the city and the bridges which crossed it. Their hearts were here, too and their determination to return night after night did not waver.

The dropping zones were marked each night in different places by hurricane lamps arranged in a cross. It was vitally important that each drop of supply containers was made accurately. Ruman explains:

'The Underground army still held pockets of Warsaw, but in the next street from the lamps the Germans might be in command and if the drop was made a second too early or too late everything would go to the enemy. For greater accuracy we flew very low. Brindisi was in touch with the Underground before we left the airfield, but during the flight we had no radio contact, not even over Warsaw. We knew if the burning cross was not in position the Germans had over-run their position and, consequently, we would not drop. So far we had always seen the cross.'

It was a fine summer's evening as Liberator KG927 GR S-Sugar heaved itself off the runway at Brindisi, its belly full of aid. The pilot set a course that would take them over Yugoslavia, Hungary and Czechoslovakia, before crossing the Vistula to Warsaw. They knew the route by now, together with the main trouble spots, areas to avoid, while aware that the enemy might have sneaked in more guns.

It was a long haul but the night was clear with almost a full moon to enable them to pick out landmarks, and for any watching gunner or fighter, to get a bead on them. They climbed over the Carpathians, slipping cautiously down the familiar grassy slopes of the Tatra Mountains along the Polish and Czechoslovakian border, aware that the Germans would now be following their progress on radar screens with increasing interest.

The first shots were fired from anti-aircraft guns in the Kraków area but they droned on safely, bracing themselves for the inevitable hostile reception over Warsaw as they came down to 300ft at around 140mph over the city, heading for the tiny DZ. Tracer and light flak were zipping past long before they spotted the cross of hurricane lamps, standing in a square across which smoke drifted eerily from buildings set on fire by the Germans. They held their breath as Jastrzebski nudged the aircraft towards it and seconds later the despatcher, Flying Officer Bednarski, pressed the button for the bomb doors to open and deliver the supply containers to the waiting Poles hiding in the shadows. At the same time the intense beam of a searchlight smacked into their faces and anti-aircraft shells were fired at them from all sides. The pilot remained cool although at such low speed it was impossible to manoeuvre at their height of less than 100ft, no higher than a boy would fly a model aeroplane.

On the southern side of the railway, which divided the city from east to west, were several open spaces. More guns opened up from there and the neighbouring airfield, hammering holes into the aircraft.

'We were skimming over roof tops,' says Ruman. 'I saw soldiers on the roofs, only a few feet from our wing tip, firing at us with rifles, revolvers, anything. I opened fire and hoped I hit some of them, but we were going too fast making it impossible to see.'

Had the gunner been issued with a box of grenades he could have inflicted spectacular damage among the roof-top snipers. The pilot dragged the Liberator up to clear some of the higher buildings and found the aircraft obstinately pulling to port, but there was no time to check for damage and he turned into the smoke rising from burning buildings, seeking shelter, however pathetic, but the flak remained intense and constant as they were now the target for about 500 guns yet somehow, they kept going. Some tracer missed the bomber and smashed into the upper storeys of buildings the other side of them. Henryk Jastrzebski desperately tried to gain height but the aircraft's three bellowing engines did not respond. He attempted to feather the port outer engine which was no longer delivering power, but neither feathering system was functioning. As they crept away west of the city, they seemed to be hanging by their finger tips to an invisible 300ft cliff face.

The flight engineer, Flight Sergeant Emil Szczerba, reported the despatcher had been wounded in the arm.The pilot spared a moment to check up on his crew and accounted for everyone except Ruman who did not reply from his rear turret. The former gunner explains:

'I had left the turret because it was useless. The hydraulics feeding the turret had been hit so I couldn't turn it or fire the guns. I came into the fuselage to give first aid to Bednarski.'

Some of the crew had seen the amount of damage the aircraft had sustained and suggested it might be sensible to bale out.One even thought they could try landing in Russia, an idea received with contempt, but the pilot was too busy to make an immediate decision. They were still under heavy bombardment when Szczerba crawled through the fuselage to give a damage report. The bomb doors had stuck open because the hydraulic oil tank had been hit and emptied. One door was eventually closed by hand,the other was too badly damaged to move.The port gauges of manifold pressure and revs and the artificial horizon were all u/s.

They were flying at 2,200 revs for normal cruising and all they could do was to give fine pitch: 2,700 revs,getting another 10mph in speed and this they used for climbing.They crawled to 800ft and the pilot decided to see if they could gain more height to cross the Carpathians.

Four hours from Brindisi,Szczerba reported they had enough fuel for three hours' flying. Jastrzebski said they would continue until reaching Yugoslavia and bale out over partisan territory. They had crossed the Vistula, reached 4,000ft and were flying at 150mph.

The unusually loud noise of the Liberator's three straining engines attracted the attention of a German unit withdrawing from Russia and they quickly calibrated their guns.

Ruman was keeping watch on the port side through one of the big holes which had already been punched in both sides of the fuselage.When two bursts of light flak riddled the rear of the aircraft, Ruman noticed that the second was closer to him than the first and he instinctively jumped away a moment before a third salvo struck where he had been standing.The first burst hit the starboard inner engine, causing a fire, quickly extinguished, the second shot away the flaps close to the fuselage. The third would have killed the rear gunner if he had not been so quick on his feet. They were now flying on two engines, but the Liberator had hoisted itself to 4,500ft and slipped cautiously through a pass in the mountains.

The fuel problem in an aircraft which was difficult to control helped focus the attention of the navigator, Flying Officer Stanislaw Kleybor, a cool fearless man, on keeping them on the shortest track to base and they slowly topped 8,000ft before going over the Dinaric Alps.

The engineer reported regularly on the fuel situation and crossing the Danube he told the skipper that the petrol was only half-an-hour short of base. They began a steady descent, saving fuel, and decided to ditch, if necessary, as close to Brindisi as possible. The wireless had been hit so they could not alert base with their problem, but the IFF was working and they could always switch on emergency.

Approaching the airfield they made emergency contact, warning base to stand by for a crash landing. They came straight in to land at 160mph, too fast but, fearing stalling, the pilot had been unable to reduce speed. The brake pressure had showed the correct 1,050lb, but leads to the gauge had been hit and on landing they realised they had no brakes.

Jastrzebski switched off ignition but it had no effect because the engines were too hot. Without brakes the right-hand rudder was applied otherwise the aircraft would have hurtled to disaster into the sea at the end of the runway. The Liberator tore into soft ground, twisted 160 degrees to the right churning through a stretch of rough stones and wild grape bushes, ripping away the undercarriage and stopped, its hot engines hissing, with enough fuel left for another five minutes' flying.

All the crew who had gathered quietly behind the pilot over the airfield got out unhurt. Their parachutes, which had not been checked for weeks, were found riddled with bullets. The other four aircraft sent to Warsaw from 1586 Flight that night did not return.

By 22 September, as Polish aircrews still struggled to get supplies into Warsaw, it was clear the uprising had failed. Eight days later General Tadeusz Bor-Komorowski, the Polish commander, surrendered to the Germans. Many of the Underground army were executed or thrown into concentration camps.

Ruman wanted to continue flying but was told he had done enough. Four DFCs and two DFMs – including an immediate one to Ruman – were awarded to Henryk Jastrzebski and his crew. Ted Ruman later married, settled in Blackpool and became a civil servant with the Air Ministry.

In 1974 he returned to Poland for the first time since his imprisonment by the Russians. He has since met three British prime ministers and the Queen and, with other supply drop veterans, has been feted by Polish leaders.

CHAPTER FOURTEEN

THE OLD LADY OF SKELLINGTHORPE

In the edgy blackness of night, the snorting N–Nan did not look any different to the Lancasters which had just taken off, or those impatiently shuffling into position behind.

But those watching from the side of the runway at Skellingthorpe knew, as did those manning the control caravan, that this was the legendary ED860 QR N–Nan, which had completed 130 bombing operations, 105 with 61 Squadron.

Built at A. V. Roe's huge Woodford, Manchester, factory in March 1943, she had flown about 250,000 miles on bombing missions in 1,031 hours. In Bomber Command terms battle-scarred Nan was a very old lady, one of only thirty-five Lancasters from over 6,000-odd flown in Bomber Command, which would reach the milestone of 100 sorties.

The bellowing of the Lancaster III's four 1,460hp Packard Merlin engines reached a thundering crescendo as the pilot, Flying Officer Laurie Pearse, ran them up against the brakes, building up the power which would send them surging down the runway, with a full bomb load to drop on the submarine pens at Bergen, Norway. It would be Pearse's third operation, including one as second dickey. For Nan it would be her 131st.

Pearse's wireless operator, Sergeant Bill Perry, well remembers that night of 28 October 1944. They had flown in Nan to Walcheren on a daylight operation five days before and Perry was still wondering why the old girl had been entrusted to such an inexperienced crew, while hoping that the heartening combination of her longevity, experience and luck would help bring them safely home.

'It was our first night trip. We had the green light from the caravan at 10.35pm, the skipper released the brakes, we moved forward and immediately swung off the runway to port. The port wheel crushed one of the runway glim lamps, puncturing the tyre. He got us back on the runway, but the tyre was going down quickly and we swung so violently to port he couldn't correct it with the engines. We were doing about 65mph as she hit a soft spot in the grass and dug in. The port tyre was flat, the undercarriage collapsed and the skipper shouted: "Brace yourselves!" as we swung round.'

N-Nan would never again roar exultantly across the North Sea with a belly full of bombs. Her outstanding bombing career had ended squirming ingloriously in a patch of Lincolnshire mud. The starboard outer engine was ripped off. All the nose and lower part of the Lancaster's fuselage, including the bomb bay, were crushed.

'The flask of coffee under my seat was flattened as I clung to a metal pole and my first thought was: "The bombs! The bombs!" We had a full load of armour-piercing bombs and I was expecting the aircraft to go up at any time. Luckily we didn't have a 4,000lb Cookie which carried three fuses on its nose and was very fragile.

'The skipper remained calm, calling me up to fire a red Very light to warn anyone coming up behind. We were off the runway but they wouldn't know that. He quickly countermanded his order, realising fuel was oozing out of the wing and a Very light scorching into the night might easily cause a fire. But I didn't even hear Laurie's first order. I was halfway through the aircraft to the rear door. I went past the mid-upper gunner who was just getting down, so I knew he was all right, and I saw the rear gunner as I got out. We all left quickly and only the flight engineer was hurt when he bumped an eye stepping off the wing.'

Laurie Pearse was never allowed to forget the ignominious demise of N-Nan. The commander of 61 Squadron was so angry he told the Australian pilot to personally visit each ground section and apologise for the accident.

Next day fuel was pumped into a bowser from the wreck and a crane brought in to lift it so armourers could work on the delicate job of defusing the bombs. By nightfall Nan had been dismantled and removed by huge Queen Mary lorries.

'The official version of the accident,' says Perry, 'is that the pilot disobeyed orders and the aircraft swung to port while going down the runway. In fact,it swung immediately we set off.'

Pearse blamed a senior officer for having issued a new order to use twice the normal boost of the superchargers on takeoff, but no one listened. Forty-eight hours later, Pearse passed a searching air test with an experienced pilot sitting beside him. Next day he flew to Homberg.

The N-Nan incident was not the first time they had faced difficulties on a runway.

'While stationed at 1654 HCU, Wigsley, we landed halfway down the runway in a Stirling. We ran out of runway at 40mph, missed the overshoot area, went through a fence, across a road, through a hedge and into a farmyard, pulling up five feet from the farmhouse door.

'The farmer came out, a bit shocked, and the first thing he said was:"Where am I going to put my beast?" His donkey was in a field which now had a big hole in the hedge. The farmer seemed less concerned that a big Stirling bomber, with bits dropping off it, was standing in his yard.

'The Wigsley commanding officer, an Australian, Kingsford-Smith, who was a bit of a pig, gave our pilot a good dressing-down in front of everybody.'

Only four days before the N-Nan debacle Pearse and his crew were involved in a routine air-to-sea firing exercise which might easily have ended the flying career of them all. They left Skellingthorpe at 2.50pm in Lancaster LL843 QR R-Roger, heading straight for the North Sea.

Laurie Pearse had already told his navigator, fellow-Australian Flight Sergeant Bob Pettigrew, a scrubbed pilot,to take over the controls on some training flights. It was useful to have someone who could handle the aircraft if the skipper was injured or killed.

That afternoon after the smoke floats had been dropped into a designated training area of the sea for the two gunners to fire at, Pettigrew was ushered into the pilot's seat. Perry, who had completed a navigational course, temporarily replaced him.

'We should have gone down to around 1,000ft,' Perry recalls. 'But because Laurie had decided Bob would fly the plane we were up at 10,000ft, useless for the gunners. Bob was banking round and round the floats and the gunners were firing while the skipper, for some unknown reason, went back to the rear gunner and was talking to him. It did not seem a very good idea and when the time came to return to base I told Bob the course he needed.

'By now Bob had forgotten that he was already banking and he turned round at the same time to go back to Skellingthorpe. We flipped right over on our back and began charging towards the sea at a rate of knots.How the skipper got back from the rear turret nobody will ever know. He and Bob were both dragging on the stick but couldn't pull us out of the dive. In the end Laurie turned the trim tabs fully back, they had another go and pulled it out at less than 1,000ft.When we got to the bottom of the dive, G-force really took hold and with the weight that was pressing me in I felt as if I weighed about forty-five stone.

'Almost immediately we began going straight up and they were pushing like mad on the stick to straighten us out. Eventually the plane went over the top and at this point,because of the weightlessness, the desk top in my own compartment opened on its own.The Very cartridges came floating out, and I felt myself being raised off my seat.We were now on an even keel but the aircraft started shaking, vibrating terribly from end to end. We didn't know what was happening and I said to Laurie: "Do you want me to send an 'O' message." This was an emergency message, second only in priority to an SOS.

'He said: "Hang on a bit." Then he realised what had happened.

'When we went over the top all the petrol had gone from the bottom of the tanks to the top and the pumps were pumping air. The propellers were windmilling far faster than they should have been so when the fuel got through to the engines it was like dropping a car into bottom gear at 60mph.

'We were okay then,except for this terrible smell.We couldn't make out what it was until someone found the overturned Elsen which had smothered the back of the aircraft.After landing we had a whip round and gave £1 to the ground crew to clean it up.

'The navigator took the controls on other training exercises but the rest of us laid down the condition that Laurie would not leave his side.We couldn't stand going through all that again.We said nothing to anyone about what had happened.'

The crew were mostly aged around twenty-one except the engineer who, at thirty, was a year older than the pilot. Laurie Pearse had worked in the ambulance service in Sydney before joining Bomber Command. A short man, he needed wooden blocks taped to the rudder pedals so his feet could reach them.

The only thing that was guaranteed to demolish the good humour of Bob Pettigrew, from Melbourne, was when the Englishmen teased him or his skipper by calling them 'Colonials'.

In 1924, Arthur Perry had insisted on his son being christened Arthur Edward after himself. His mother, Sarah, who had not wanted another Arthur Edward in their house in Stirchley, Birmingham, never called the boy anything but William or Bill. He grew up, unruffled by his dogmatic parents, and became a plumber before turning eagerly to the RAF.

Sergeant Dave Baker, a college-educated Londoner, even shorter than his skipper, was the bomb aimer.

Mid-upper gunner Sergeant Alan Barker, from Hall Green, Birmingham, was, in the words of Bill Perry: 'A bit more of a lad than the rest of us, a joker, someone who often stepped in where angels feared to tread.'

Once forced to land at Horham, Suffolk, an American base, they were offered a staggering choice for breakfast. They each settled on bacon and two eggs except Barker who cheekily asked for seven eggs, and got them. The others made sure he cleared his plate.

Sergeant Bob Gillanders, the rear gunner, came from Forfar where his father had a business making bagpipes.

Before joining the squadron Pearse and his crew were stationed at 5 Lancaster Finishing School, Syerston. On a night out in Lincoln, awaiting a posting to a squadron, they got chatting at a pub with two Australian pilots.

'Their advice was: watch your engineer, they tend to panic. Our engineer, Sergeant John "Jock" Murray, from Bradford, but born in Scotland, wasn't with us that night, but we remembered their words.

'On 2 November, during a trip to Düsseldorf, we were coned. It caught us right in the middle. You could almost feel the vibration of the big blue light it was that powerful, and immediately six to eight searchlights came on to us.

'Jock panicked, shouting: "We're coned! We're coned." The skipper said, sharply: "Shut up!" That's how he was. We never heard another word from Jock and he became a good engineer. Laurie dived into the cone towards the light gaining quite a bit of speed before pulling up and getting us out of trouble.'

Aircrew were often reminded by chaps who knew about such things that there was an awful lot of sky, plenty to go round, even on a 1,000-bomber raid. Bill Perry was one of those not entirely convinced by these reassurances.

'Time and time again at night we'd suddenly have a plane flash across in front of us, or just above or below, often missing us by a few feet. I didn't see them from my position, but suddenly felt our plane swing away, catching the blast of the other aircraft's slipstream. Following a set route you were not constantly going along the compass heading. The pilot was correcting it one way or another and aircraft were going along like that all the time. It could be a tightly-packed stream and I imagine there were a lot of collisions.'

They needed a generous measure of good fortune and few crews who might have scorned lucky mascots at the beginning of their tour did not secrete the odd charm or two about them when the going got rough. Anything might bring luck to these young men if their belief in it was strong enough and if it was based on irrefutable evidence of indestructibility which could not be ignored.

When, for instance, they realised Bob Pettigrew alone was wearing flying boots on the night N-Nan bought it, his crewmates banned him from wearing them again.

The pilot had a small stuffed horse, made of tartan material, which hung near his dashboard. He could at odd moments be seen admiring its long woolly tail, fine mane and appealing black eyes. Bill Perry wore a dark green scarf his mother had bought him. At first, it was just a warm scarf. Later, as they continued to survive, it took on remarkably efficacious properties and he would never be seen without it on an op.

'You were actually forbidden to have a collar and tie on ops and the squadron commander came round occasionally, checking that chaps were not wearing them. The idea was that if you came down in the sea the first thing that happened would be the collar and tie shrinking in the water and you struggling to get them off.'

Newspapers, always anxious to get fresh angles on the war and sensational exclusive stories over their rivals, were occasionally given the opportunity to send a man into battle aboard an aeroplane.

'One night we were due to take up Duncan Webb, a *Sunday People* war reporter. We'd gone to Scotland to bring an aircraft back which had been repaired, but couldn't take off because the radio was not working. We returned next day and found that the crew which had taken him instead had been shot down. They all baled out and got back to England, including Duncan, who had quite a write-up in the paper, but he did not tell the complete story.

'The crew, friends of ours in the next billet, said they'd put a parachute on Duncan and he lowered himself out of the escape hatch then froze. There wasn't much time and he wouldn't let go until the navigator got the axe and threatened to chop off his fingers. He told us he would have done it, too. Instead, they kicked his fingers away and Duncan was lucky to escape with a broken arm after hitting the tailplane.

'A week or so later someone wrote to the *People* and said: "We've heard all about Duncan Webb, what about the crew?" Another story appeared saying the crew had also made it back to England. But the newspaper did not report that the same crew on their next operation had been shot down and killed.'

The days were short and murky when, on 4 December 1944, they took off from a damp airfield at 4.45pm to attack Heilbronn in ND896 QR Q-Queenie.

'It was a blitz raid of the town, one of two or three we had been on. The intelligence officer, at briefing, told us why he didn't think much of this raid and said: "Well chaps, it's women and children first tonight."

'We bombed and turned for home. I remember there wasn't a lot of flak and we weren't worried about it too much, but there were plenty of fighters. I was listening in to the W/T, not on intercom, when I felt the aircraft suddenly lurch right over and thought we'd been hit. Our guns started firing, I switched on the intercom and heard Gillie, the rear gunner, shouting: "I've hit him! I've hit him!" He'd hit the starboard engine of a Messerschmitt 410, which had attacked us but was now going down. We didn't see it again, but Gill claimed it as a kill which was confirmed after another crew saw it going down in flames.

'After we'd bombed and were clear of the target the skipper always told me to go aft and check that the photoflash had left its chute near the rear door. On this occasion it had jammed. It had the power of a 250lb bomb when it went off and needed to be dealt with and Dave Baker, the bomb aimer wired the fuse, making it safe.

'When we touched down the photoflash came out and there was a great cloud of sparks on the runway behind us.It didn't go off but we warned control so it could be cleared away before anyone else landed.'

Two nights later they went to Giessen in the new N–Nan, PB759 which was to be their regular aircraft.When they were on leave in February, another crew took it to Politz and were shot down.

Cloud hung bleakly over the target when they reached the Urft dam in the Eifel on 8 December.

'The controller came through ordering everyone to make a clockwise circuit of the target. A single Lancaster went anticlockwise, colliding with another Lanc, one losing about three feet from his wing tip.' The other Lancaster, from 630 Squadron,based at East Kirkby, crashed with the loss of six lives.

'Fog had again closed down Skellingthorpe and we were among several squadrons diverted to Tangmere, a fighter airfield. The controller was bringing them in as if they were fighters,one after the other. Normally you wouldn't have another Lanc in the funnel until the one on the ground was clear of the runway.

'We were coming down to the runway when Gillie saw another Lanc, with a damaged wing tip, charging in after us. It was the plane we'd seen over the Urft dam. He was gaining on us and Gillie was screaming at our pilot to get out of the way. Laurie got to the end of the runway more quickly than usual and turned off as fast as he could. Both Lancasters landed okay.'

They were diverted many times to other airfields when returning from raids.

'A haze sometimes formed about 100ft high, completely obscuring the ground, although you couldn't see it standing on the airfield. It was most peculiar. Sometimes,when the haze was sufficiently high, we landed at Skellingthorpe when two ground staff were standing beside the head of the runway firing white Very lights.The pilot aimed between them to get down.When you broke through the haze you could see the ground, but it was rather frightening.

'Generally, after being diverted we'd stay in the sergeants'mess overnight. Beds were rarely available. If you could find an armchair you were lucky, otherwise you had to sit for the rest of the night in an ordinary hard chair before taking off next morning.

'The best place to be diverted to was Tangmere. They had beds all made up for us. Five cigarettes were on each bed and on every tenth bed there was a box of matches. Razors had also been provided. The second time we landed there it was entirely different. They must have changed COs.

Bill Perry remembers Skellingthorpe, an airfield sited three miles from Lincoln city centre, as basic and freezing in winter.

'We slept in Nissen huts, each containing two crews and a coke-burning stove with the metal pipe going through the roof. Fuel was short, we scrounged it from all over the place, sometimes paying the ground crew to get some for us, usually from the fuel dump. They never let us down. The hut was cold by morning when we got up and we had to walk forty yards to the blooming freezing wash house before breakfast with greatcoats over our pyjamas.'

The emergency hatch blew in during takeoff in LL911 X-X-ray at 6.15pm on 16 January 1945 for the 9hr 40min round trip to Brüx, just inside the Czechoslovakian border. The fierce blast of icy air blew out a big piece of perspex from the cockpit above the pilot.

'The ground staff had loaded all the Window through the hatch but hadn't replaced it properly. It was wedged half in and half out. Laurie told Jock, the engineer: "Can you get rid of it?" He told him to lash himself to a rope in case he fell out while doing it. But Jock, being a Scotsman, didn't want to lose the hatch and tied it with rope to a ring fitted to the escape hatch cover, so after he'd pushed it out he could carefully ease it back inside. But when the slipstream caught the hatch cover it was whipped out and hit the aircraft aft with a resounding bang. When Jock pulled in the rope all that was left was an elongated section of the ring.'

Pearse cried anxiously: 'What's happened, Jock?' There was no reply, so they feared he had been sucked to his death, then the bomb aimer found the engineer so shocked he was speechless.

Perry says: 'We carried on but there was a terrible draught from the hole in the floor and it was affecting the aircraft's performance, acting like an air brake. I chopped the top off the rest bed with the axe. We put that over the hole and piled all the Window on top to hold it in place.'

No one was sorry when they were ordered to abandon the attack on the Dortmund-Ems canal at Ladbergen on 24 February 1945 as the target was enveloped in cloud. Laurie Pearse was at the controls of a brand-new Lancaster, RF123 X-X-ray, which he would fly until the end of the war.

'The German canals were the bane of my life,' explains Perry. 'Every time we went there previous damage had been repaired and the searchlights and guns seemed to have doubled in number. Besides, if you were going to somewhere like Berlin at least you could go into Lincoln the next night and brag about it. No one was interested in the enemy's canals. Civilians probably thought we were just bombing a few barges.

'We got back and joined the circuit over Skellingthorpe, orbiting with maybe 1,000ft between each plane, getting lower as aircraft landed. We got permission to land, calling out "X-X-Ray, funnel", as we turned into the funnel. That area was prohibited to everybody except the aircraft that was landing.

'Suddenly a plane shot across in front of us only feet away. It was nearly curtains. Laurie had to pull up quick. I switched on the intercom and heard him exclaim: "I'll find out who that bleeding bastard was and make him bloody suffer." He was really mad.

'As we touched down the airfield lights were switched off and we heard over the VHF set: "Bandits! Bandits!" German fighters were in the circuit and we presumed it had been a Messerschmitt 210 or 410, a twin-engine plane, that had hurtled across in front of us in a split-second misjudgement. He had probably meant to come in behind when we would have been sitting ducks with flaps and wheels down. We were all off watch at this point and our rear gunner was probably halfway out of his turret. We were home; we were safe. How wrong could we be?

'We saw a couple of German fighters going across the airfield, firing tracers, after we landed. The Germans had taken everyone by surprise and we supposed they had mingled with the bomber stream which was returning to England and were listening in to our calls on the VHF over the airfield. They knew the channels we worked on. After that we always remained on watch until we were on the ground.'

On 5 March, before the ten-hour sortie to attack a synthetic oil factory at Böhlen, near Leipzig, they were issued with useful additions to their survival kit: little silk Union Jacks to be waved at Russian soldiers if forced to bale out behind their lines. Our Russian comrades were believed to be even less friendly than the Germans. The helpful intelligence officer taught them the Russian words for 'I am an Englishman.'

Death was never far from the aircrews during the bomber war. But nothing affected Bill Perry more than the daylight trip to attack military barracks and the town of Nordhausen, east of Göttingen, on 4 April 1945, a month before the end of hostilities.

'We were on the bombing run at 14,000ft and I was watching a Lancaster through the window in my little office. The plane was a quarter to half-a-mile away on the starboard side. His bomb doors were open, although I didn't see his first 500-pounders drop out. I did see the 4,000lb Cookie.

'It seemed to come out and stop, hanging there for a split second, keeping pace with the Lancaster. Then it tipped over and I watched a 500lb hang-up come out and hit it. It must have struck one of the fuses on the big bomb. I saw it explode and the back half of the aeroplane seemed to disappear. I couldn't believe it.

'I watched the wings and the cabin area go down in one piece, like a great leaf, almost to the ground, before it vanished into smoke or haze.

'No one survived. Getting out would have been impossible with G-force, unless somebody had been blown out by the explosion. Other chaps who saw it going down thought it had been hit by bombs falling from another aircraft. Gillie, our rear gunner, said he saw the Lanc burning as it went down, but only I seemed to have seen what really happened.'

Another witness to the end of the Lancaster which bombed itself out of the sky was 61 Squadron pilot Flight Lieutenant D. G. G. Phillips who, in his report said he saw it going down in flames over the target area at 9.21pm: 'Presumably hit by bombs from above. There being no flak or fighters.'

After the war they flew to Italy on Operation Dodge, bringing soldiers home, spending three days over there at a time.

'We took as many cigarettes as we could buy in England because we could sell them and strangely, pepper, in Italy at enormous profits. We went round the mess emptying all the pepper-pots before flying out there and black marketeering on the slopes of Vesuvius. The Italians bought our chocolate rations, even after they'd melted and hardened into oddly-shaped blocks. Alan Barker took off his socks and sold them,because they'd buy any article of clothing, but when he pulled off his shirt we convinced him that was not a good idea.'

CHAPTER FIFTEEN

THE WRONG CODE

David Ward did not have to put on a uniform and fight for King and country. He worked for his father, who farmed 500 acres in the lush Leicestershire countryside around the tiny hamlet of Bescaby, helping put food into British pantries.

But at twenty-three, watching bombers and fighters rip exultantly through the sky as he called cows in for milking or mucked out the pigs, farming seemed to be a job for older men who had lost their appetite for adventure. He recalls:

'In the middle of 1941 chaps who were in reserved occupations were allowed to volunteer for aircrew. That was my chance. I cycled into Leicester, signed up and on the way home called in at the Horseshoes pub in the nearby village of Waltham on the Wolds for a stiff whisky. I'd never drunk Scotch before, but I needed it to face my father, whose forefathers had been farmers in that area for at least 200 years. Then I told him. He made a great fuss, but I joined up the following January.

'Like most chaps I wanted to be a pilot and was disappointed to be among those who failed the course although, with hindsight, I don't think my reflexes were good enough.'

Luck was often on his side. After initial training he was one of twenty men posted to Wigtown, Scotland, for an advanced flying course.

During a gunnery exercise four trainees were in an Anson taking turns to fire at a drogue towed by a Lysander. Ward remembers:

'It was a morning trip and I was detailed to be on it but another fellow asked if he could swap with me as he wanted the afternoon off. The Anson and Lysander collided within a few minutes of takeoff and fell into Wigtown Bay. There were no survivors. Someone's mistake had wiped out eight lives.'

Ward decided to try his luck as a bomb aimer. He completed his training, was commissioned in August 1942 and later, at 22 OTU, Wellesbourne Mountford, near Stratford-on-Avon, joined a Wellington crew skippered by an American, Flight Sergeant Tucker. A former bush pilot, Tucker was in his thirties. Looking for more adventurous flying, but unwilling to wait for the procrastinating USA to join the war, he had signed on in the RAF. Ward describes him as 'quiet, with no great sense of humour and not very likeable. We just didn't click somehow, I don't know why.'

They were based with the Canadian 420 (Snowy Owl) Squadron at Middleton St George, County Durham.

When Ward joined up he nurtured the stirring image of being in the cockpit of a speeding Spitfire with a white silk scarf streaming behind as he dived out of the sun to shoot up an evil coven of German bombers. His eventual job on the aeroplane was rather less dashing. Apart from assisting the pilot at takeoff, holding the throttles forward as they charged down the runway, he spent each trip stretched out on his belly peering down through the nose of a twin-engine Wellington bomber into the murk of a soulless night. But it was more exciting than milking cows twice a day.

'What we didn't realise, because we were never told, was that so many more of our bombers were being shot down by night fighters than ever were by flak. Most of the time at night I couldn't see anything from my position, not even whether we were over sea or land. I was literally very much in the dark until we got near the target, someone was shooting, or searchlights were probing the blackness. We had been told what it was like on ops but my first sight of flak and searchlights didn't seem real. It seemed to be part of another rather mad world.

'Bombing was strictly on Pathfinder markers. It was easy enough to get our aircraft over the markers if we ever got in the right area. I wouldn't guarantee that on one or two raids, where there was a lot of cloud, we actually hit our target. We saw lights below the cloud and bombed a bit vaguely at times. More than likely we were miles away from the target.'

If one bomber went astray others, equally lost, often followed to deliver their load on the bombs they saw exploding, hoping they had found the correct aiming point. It would become a hard task after the war for historians to calculate how many Germans died because the Allies could not find their briefed target. It was equally difficult to estimate how many British bombers had been lost through collision or catching a bomb dropped from another aircraft flying at a higher altitude. So many miserable imponderables are wrapped up in the bleak statistics of war.

By now it was clear that war was even more dangerous than Ward had imagined and the nastiness of combat was brought home abruptly to him when his best friend, Pilot Officer Frank Noon, another bomb aimer, from Ilkley, was lost without trace with his crew on 29 January 1943 during a sortie to Lorient.

'Frank slept in the next bed to me in a Nissen hut at Middleton St George. We trained together and were failed pilots together. He was lost before I'd even been on my first operation. I once went to find his name on the Runnymede memorial which is for airmen with no known grave.'

Their early sorties were with incendiaries against targets at Lorient and Cologne and, on 27 February 1943 they were briefed to drop two mines off one of the Frisians, a chain of low-lying islands which extend off the north-west coasts of Holland and Germany to the west coast of Denmark.

'We did it at low-level, finding the right island and going on a timed run out to sea to drop the mines in what was supposed to be an enemy shipping lane. It was sometimes difficult to find the right island because we flew out as individual aircraft. It was my job to locate it. I had a map and a torch beside me, but mostly you had to remember the shape of the island from our briefing.'

Other gardening trips followed and they also visited the notable German night spots of Duisburg, and Essen, where Ward saw bombers colliding and blowing up over the target.

A series of training exercises followed an operation against Frankfurt before 420 Squadron packed its bags and was posted on 15 May 1943 to the Middle East to help attack German positions in Italy, as the Allies prepared for the invasion of Sicily. Had anyone on the squadron known a few months before that they only had to survive one more ghastly British winter before being given a posting to the sun, three hearty cheers for the War Cabinet would have resounded throughout the station. The reality was somewhat different. Soon after they had landed, it was clear that the eagerly anticipated delights of North Africa were less inviting than visiting a crowded pub serving warm beer on a wet night in Darlington.

'We were among sixty Wellingtons from three Canadian squadrons to fly from England via Morocco and Blida, Algeria, and on to an American air base near Constantine, where we were not expected. To keep us out of their way the Americans pushed our planes into an Arab village. Everyone had to sleep in the aircraft or on the ground beside them. We sat around for ten days playing cards and fending off scrounging Arabs. There was one welcome break when Bob Hope arrived to give a show.

'The airfield we were eventually sent to, south of Tunis, had been bulldozed out of a dried-up lake and the runway was laid-out on the hard mud. It was bloody awful: hot, dusty, sticky, the home for millions of hungry flies, and we lived four to a tent. Airmen had a rougher time with more chaps in their tents, while officers enjoyed the luxury of camp beds. I still have mine.

'Tucker was transferred straightaway to the USAAF and the crew was scattered throughout the squadron. I flew six operations as a spare bod before joining another American pilot, Flying Officer Vic Ardis, who had somehow lost his bomb aimer. Vic, from Santa Monica, California, was totally different to Tucker. He was younger, livelier and full of fun.

'Sorties from Tunisia were quite different to those from England, and, in a way, more rewarding. We bombed at night, just the same, but nights were much lighter and we could identify targets which were never as busily defended. Trips were less scary too. We hardly lost any aircraft and never saw or heard of enemy night fighters operating there. Ops were more interesting for me because map reading came into it a great deal.

'We attacked numerous targets in Italy, including railway stations, railway yards, airfields and steel works. We usually bombed much lower, from 6,000 to 8,000 feet which was out of range of medium flak. We did a lot of stooges up the Straits of Messina when the Germans were evacuating Sicily. We were supposed to drop a couple of bombs every so often to make the Germans keep their heads down.'

David Ward's logbook records two sorties on 9 August 1943 when they pounded beaches north of Messina from two different Wellingtons, HE239 and HE965.

The Germans were in full retreat across the Straits of Messina by the middle of August and by the seventeenth all 100,000 Axis troops were in Italy.

Ward returned to England at the end of his first tour, leaving Vic Ardis the chore of finding another bomb aimer.

The family farm became a peaceful retreat from the frenzy of war but after some welcome leave Ward was posted to Manby, north Lincolnshire, flying Blenheims, training to be an instructor. He was then sent to Mona, Anglesey in February 1944 to pass on his wisdom to bunches of eager sprog bomb aimers packed into Ansons. He quickly loathed instructing and decided to take drastic steps to prevent himself going potty.

'I wrote a letter to the CO in which I carefully explained that my lack of ability for instructing amounted to extreme incompetence while my dislike of it had become a phobia. I wanted to go back to operational flying. Nothing was said but within a week I'd been posted to 298 Squadron which was flying Halifax Vs with Rolls-Royce Merlin 22 engines from Tarrant Rushton, Dorset. Soon after I joined the squadron's B Flight became 644 Squadron.'

His new skipper was the amiable Flying Officer Bob Baird, from Beith, near Glasgow. He had a happy crew, comfortable in each other's company, with a mixed bag of duties which ranged from delivering supplies to the Resistance to towing Horsa and Hamilcar gliders and ops involving the SOE and SAS. Most of these sorties were carried out at night, often at low level.

Baird's navigator was an Australian, Warrant Officer Walter 'Mac' McGeachin. The wireless operator, Flying Officer Jack Goggin, came from Stanford-le-Hope, which stood beside the murky water of the Thames, down river on the Essex coast, a short distance from Tilbury which was heavily battered during the Blitz.

Flight Sergeant Paddy Mescall, the flight engineer, was a big gentle Ulsterman and rear gunner Sergeant John McManus, a Lancashire lad. The 644 Squadron Halifaxes did not have mid-upper gunners.

'We carried arms and ammunition and once, after D-Day, we dropped a Jeep with three SAS people not far behind the Normandy lines. We had a specially-adapted aircraft, with the bomb bay cut out for the Jeep. It was released on several parachutes in a special cradle so it didn't land on its wheels.'

At 8pm on 5 October 1944 they took off from Tarrant Rushton in LL403 G-George for another routine op, carrying nine containers holding sten guns, revolvers, ammunition and cigarettes for the Resistance, and a few more unusual items like sweets and chocolates. It was Ward's twenty-fourth operation of his second tour; his fifty-ninth overall. Their ETA was 10pm over a damp field near Putten, twenty-five miles south of the Zuider Zee.

The field would be frugally marked by four torches in the shape of an 'L' held by courageous members of the Resistance who might be shot dead at any minute if a German patrol arrived, attracted by the low-flying aircraft.

Only a few stars were visible that night as George crossed the English coast at 2,000ft north of Ipswich, dropping as low as the pilot dared, fifty feet, to slip furtively over the North Sea. Their hopes were high for a satisfactory trip without a lot of interference from the enemy, for around 750 Lancasters and Mosquitoes were hitting Wilhelmshaven and Saarbrücken that night. With luck, German radar technicians would be too busy dealing with them to notice a solitary blip drifting with feigned innocence towards Holland after George began climbing.

'Fifteen miles before the Dutch coast we began climbing to 2,000ft to avoid the guns, although we rarely saw flak during these ops,' says Ward. 'Then, as we crossed over land north of Amsterdam, Bob put the stick into a flat-out dive until the altimeter showed less than 100ft. The moon had risen so we could map read. We found our turning point to come down for the dropping zone, just south of the Zuider Zee.

'Approaching the DZ area we climbed to 500ft, but could not see any lights from our reception committee and after circling a couple of times Bob decided to fly away for twenty minutes in order not to attract too much attention.'

On their return to the DZ they saw torches but the important one at the bottom of the 'L' was flashing the wrong letter, which meant something had gone wrong and they could not drop the supplies. A moment later the anxiety and confusion over the signal from the ground was compounded when a dazzling light floated down just behind the Halifax.

'We thought it was a German parachute flare to show fighters where we were and I began looking around to see if I could spot one. I believe the others were doing the same, including the pilot which meant he wasn't really looking at what he was doing. He may also have been temporarily blinded by the flare. This caused him either to push the stick forward or side-slip on the turn. Seconds later the wireless operator, who only had this little perspex window on the port side he could peer out of, suddenly said in a very restrained voice: "Aren't we getting a bit low, Bob?" Jack Goggin had spotted the dim outline of trees as the Halifax roared past them at 180mph. His warning came too late.'

Suddenly the starboard wing smashed tumultuously into a tree. The pilot immediately throttled back on the port engines in an attempt to cut down the speed and keep the aircraft straight and level. His action triggered the bellow of the undercarriage warning klaxon as both starboard engines hit the ground and tore themselves to pieces, and the ripped-off wing erupted into flames behind them. The pilot struggled at the controls as four of his crew scrambled to the crash positions behind the main spar while rear gunner John McManus hung on inside his turret.

The aircraft smashed into the ground on its belly but remained defiantly upright as, with a clear run, it slithered and gouged through a grass field, the frightful sound of tearing and screeching metal penetrating the quiet Dutch countryside. As it slowly crunched to a stop David Ward reached up to release the astrodome.

'When the astrodome flew off the others climbed over me to get out. There was a bit of panic, but I couldn't see any point in fighting them. There was a fear of the fuselage catching fire and an explosion. But the port wing was burning separately some distance away and the rest of the plane, which was intact, didn't catch fire. That's when we heard John McManus, who was trapped inside his turret, shouting: "Lemme out!" From that point John's nickname was Lemme. We pushed the guns, turning his turret to release him, then talked about where we should go. Happily, we didn't have a scratch or a bruise between us.'

Flames from the mangled wing were soaring high in the air, an invitation to any German soldiers in the vicinity, so they decided quickly to go south.

'We were making for the dropping zone armed with a small compass, taking a bearing from the stars. After walking about three miles through rough country Lemme spotted three men standing silently 100 yards away near a wood, watching us. One approached carrying a sten gun.

'As soon as we said the code word "Maquis" the Dutchmen relaxed and began treating us like long-lost brothers. They said they'd been looking for us after hearing our plane crash. They led us away into the darkness and within two hours of crashing we were eating sugarless porridge in a farmhouse, home of the Kamphuis family on the outskirts of Voorthuizen village, six miles south of Putten. The farmer was a Resistance leader.

'We learned that two days before our scheduled drop the Resistance had ambushed a German staff car. The Germans responded by rounding up 600 men in Putten, aged from sixteen to sixty, and sending them to labour camps. Only 140 returned after the war. Among the men taken were those who had been expected to be waiting for us in the field, but their replacements had got the wrong code letter.

'After crashing we hadn't done our job. We should have removed all the maps and set fire to the plane but we panicked. We had expected the Germans to be there within minutes but they didn't arrive until next morning.'

The Resistance went carefully through the Halifax, taking away maps and anything they thought might be important to the Germans. They also removed and buried some Browning machine guns which would have been no use to them. The supplies carried by the aircraft had been crushed in the crash.

The airmen remained in the farmhouse for seven days through several scares because members of the Dutch SS lived in the village, German soldiers were billeted at farms, and an intensive hunt with tracker dogs was launched after a patrol found the Halifax but no bodies.

'A few days after we had been moved from the farmhouse to another safe house outside Barneveld, Mr Kamphuis was given away by a German deserter he had sheltered and was arrested. The farmer was shot on 16 November outside the schoolhouse in Voorthuizen. His body lay there as a warning for three days before the Germans allowed it to be moved.'

The crew of G-George was split up and Ward and McGeachin, the navigator, spent ten days together in a hay loft. They had a scare while cycling along a main road with two Dutch guides when a German soldier held up his hand for them to stop.

'He only wanted a light for his cigarette which one of the Dutchmen gave him in the friendliest manner while we looked on with forced smiles. We had an uncomfortable three weeks sleeping under a floor in a twelve-foot by one-and-a-half foot space, creeping about during the day, speaking in whispers because only four of the twelve people in the house knew we were there.'

On 18 November the entire Halifax crew were reunited, joining several British and American paratroopers who had escaped the debacle of the Arnhem landings. The group gradually expanded until 130 evaders waited in a large unused poultry hut twelve miles from the Rhine. However, the plan to get them across the river and into the Allied lines went badly wrong. Ward recalls leaving the hut in pouring rain at four in the morning led by two guides to a small wood nearer the river.

'Everyone was soon soaked to the skin. We waited until dusk before starting out on the last lap. By 2am we were within three miles of the river when suddenly, a German shouted: "Halt!" Some stopped, others scattered. The sentry didn't shoot but he must have raised the alarm.

'Many who had been in front of me disappeared and I found myself in a small group in a wood led by Major John Coke, of the King's Own Scottish Borderers. Another German stepped from behind a tree and also shouted: "Halt!" Coke, just in front of me, said: "Freund!" Within seconds the German fired his automatic weapon and Coke was killed instantly.

'What followed is not very clear. I remember seeing the flames as the German opened up, and me diving for the deck and being hit at the same time.

'I was struck by two bullets, one between my shoulder blade and spine, which lodged against my right hip. The other went through my left heel. I lay for two hours on the wet ground, the shoulder wound giving me hell, until an RAMC lieutenant from our party who had been captured gave me a double shot of morphine and put me out for twelve hours. I came to next morning with a couple of Germans carrying me into a military hospital, a requisitioned castle.

'The next two weeks passed pleasantly enough with my treatment and the food leaving nothing to be desired. The German doctor, however, refused my request to be allowed to listen to the BBC Radio news. He said it would not be good for me.'

After being transferred to a hospital manned by British

doctors in the town of Apeldoorn, Ward and two Army officers captured at Arnhem had, by Christmas, almost completed their plans for escape.

On 18 January 1945 the prisoners at the hospital were told they were to be moved next day to Germany and the three plotters knew it was time to leave. One man was not well enough to go so Ward and Major Gordon Sherriff, a Scot, whose right elbow had been shattered by a bullet, teamed up with an American, Sergeant Bob Delange, who had been shot in the chest while parachuting into Arnhem.

After Ward had been shot his battledress was cut off by the RAMC lieutenant to get at his wound. At the same time his dog tags were accidentally snipped off and not returned. He needed some form of identification otherwise, if caught, he could be shot as a spy. His eyes fell on the medical chart which hung from the end of his bed. He shrugged. His name was on it and would have to do. He slipped the chart into his pocket.

'It went like clockwork. We took everything we could lay our hands on: food, medical supplies, clothes, blankets and a map.'

British doctor Major Rigby Jones helped them build up their supplies and turn traction bars into a useful ladder.

At 10pm, wearing their uniforms, Sherriff with his crippled arm in a sling, they slipped through one of the few windows without bars, crept along a balcony, climbed six feet to another, across a corner to a third, dropped ten feet on to a narrow ledge then six feet on to an air-raid shelter at the back of the hospital, jumped on to crunching gravel and away.

They were heading for the village of Wapenveld fifteen miles to the north, the home of a Protestant parson who would put them in touch with the Resistance. It was bitterly cold with a biting wind. Walking across fields and tracks they had to endure ice, slush, floods and dykes until reaching a road and following a canal. They were young and had been fit, but were still recovering from bullet wounds.

At 3.30am, with three miles to go, they were exhausted and lost. David Ward was tortured by severe cramp in his thighs and the American's feet were torn and bleeding from the ill-fitting boots he had stolen.

They spent the rest of the night uncomfortably on top of a stack of corn in an open-ended barn at an isolated farm. Later that morning, unable to face another freezing night in the open they spoke to the farmer who gave them food and hot drinks and allowed them the luxury of sleeping in the shelter of an unoccupied pig sty.

The men remained here four days before walking north, leaving a blanket in thanks for the farmer's kindness. They found the parson who moved them further north to another safe house but hopes of an early return to England were dashed when people who might have helped were arrested by the Gestapo. They stayed at two houses whose resourceful owners used electricity tapped from lines serving the Germans.

The three men, now in civilian clothes, holding forged papers, were riding bicycles with two guides towards Barneveld where they hoped to make contact with British forces, when they were stopped by German soldiers. They gave them the slip and headed to Apeldoorn and another safe house after negotiating a road teeming with German troops. The American was taken into the safe hands of American agents when they left Apeldoorn. Ward recalls:

'By 15 April we had been hearing the rumble of artillery and next day saw tired and dirty enemy soldiers retreating past the house Gordon and I were in. We were no more than two miles from where the Halifax had crashed. By 18 April all the Germans seemed to have gone. We were standing outside the house wondering if we should leave in an attempt to contact our own forces when we saw two men approaching. We were delighted to find that they were British SAS officers who had been told of our whereabouts and had come to collect us. Two days later we were flown in a Dakota back to England.'

In February 1945 David Ward's Distinguished Flying Cross was announced in the *London Gazette*. He had also been mentioned in despatches. He says simply:

'I'd done a lot of flying and the DFC was just for outliving my contemporaries.'

G–George's pilot Bob Baird and navigator Walter McGeachin were both captured on 19 November 1944 and became prisoners of war. Flight engineer Paddy Mescall eluded capture on the night of 18 November and crossed the Rhine two days later, one of only three of the 130 men to make it. Wireless operator Jack Goggin escaped to England in February 1945.

Despite numerous inquiries over many years Ward has been

unable to find out what happened to rear gunner John 'Lemme' McManus.

David Ward has been back to Holland many times with his wife, Dulcie, tracing all but two of the families who sheltered him during the war.

One of his wartime souvenirs is the German bullet which ripped into his back.

CHAPTER SIXTEEN

A GROCER'S BOY GOES TO WAR

The first German bombs Norman Mason remembers falling on Southend struck the town's new high school for boys in the spring of 1940. A fifteen-year-old errand boy with the International Tea Company in The Broadway, he was appalled by the devastation which included nearby houses and the assembly hall.

He wheeled his bicycle among stunned pedestrians staring at the wrecked school buildings in Prittlewell Chase and knew his life would never be the same again. A few days previously the boys had been evacuated to Mansfield but the horror of what might have been occupied many people's minds for a long time.

Before the war Southend-on-Sea had been one of the more popular holiday resorts in England, with a casino, a yachting centre, and the longest pier in the country, an unlikely target for German bombs. But the long narrow county borough of Southend, which stretched from Shoeburyness in the east to Hadleigh in the west, hugging ten miles of the sand, shingle and muddy north shore of the busy Thames estuary, was a clear signpost to London. Some enemy bomber crews were tempted to rough up the first British town they saw after crossing the North Sea, and the last British town to which they could deliver hang-ups following a raid upon the capital.

The dread of enemy attack arrived early in Southend. On the night of 3 September 1939, a few hours after war had been declared, Southend was plunged into terror when anti-aircraft guns stationed along the foreshore and the end of the pier suddenly began booming, to be joined by the thunder of guns from ships in the estuary, together with whatever Shoeburyness garrison could point skywards.

'I have never heard a barrage like it since,' says Mason.'It was real panic, there were no German aircraft, but when the all-clear siren sounded scores of ARP wardens went round ringing their hand bells,indicating that the area was clear of gas.Many people, confused, then thought they had missed the whirr of the wardens'rattles which warned of gas being present and fought to put on their gas masks.'

One day in late autumn, 1940, during the Battle of Britain, a Heinkel III bomber, pursued by a Hurricane fighter, crashed in Southchurch. There were no survivors. Mason's father, Fred, a baker's clerk and part-time leading fireman, was quickly on the scene with a fire appliance.

When German bombs did fall on Southend, scores of people were killed and injured. Unexploded bombs, too, became a problem.At first the area in which they had fallen was closed to traffic and no one was allowed to pass until the bomb had been removed.

'As the number of these bombs became so great regulations seemed to fade away. I recall looking into a hole marked by an "Unexploded bomb" notice and seeing the fins of a 250-pounder which had been there several days. Trestling had been put round it but anyone could go up to have a look and many people did.'

An oil storage depot,bombed on Canvey Island and Coryton, burned for days;the prevailing wind sent a foul blanket of smoke over Southend and rain draped a sooty mantle over cabbages growing in the Masons'back garden on the Sutton Road council estate.

A Polish pilot got his first glimpse of Southend one morning when he baled out of a crippled fighter and landed on the glass roof of the London Co-op's milk bottling station in West Road. Mason, who saw the RAF pilot drift down, the sun glinting on his white parachute, says:

'Little did I know that four years later I too would take to a parachute to save my life.'

Norman, a founder-member of the town's 1115 ATC Squadron, waited impatiently for his eighteenth birthday on 16 January 1943 before applying to enlist in the RAF and train as a flight engineer. Keen to join the war effort he also wanted to help pay back the Germans for their cowardly attacks on innocent civilians.

He left his three-year apprenticeship in the grocery and provision trade, and on 14 March went by bus to Cardington, Bedfordshire, for an aircrew selection board. A poor traveller, he arrived with an upset stomach made even more fragile by his first RAF meal.

'At the servery I was handed a dinner plate upon which rested two pilchards in tomato sauce, a dollop of raspberry jam and a piece of fruit cake. The cake was soaking up the tomato sauce, and raspberry jam was seasoning one of the pilchards. I later learned that this was not the usual presentation, they were simply short of crockery.'

Young men easily adapted to the RAF's way of doing things and Mason, a positive and cheerful type, was soon whisked off to the Aircrew Reception Centre at Lord's Cricket Ground.

'I was billeted in luxury flats at St James' Court, St John's Wood. The interior of the building had been protected from us lot by an inner lining of wood panelling. The cookhouse was at London Zoo restaurant, which was massively infested by cockroaches.'

At some British RAF training bases the war had occasionally seemed remote, almost part of someone else's life, but not on the south coast, where intruder raids were an ever-present threat While he was at 3 ITW, Torquay, impressively polished and creased, learning to march at an impeccable 140 paces to the minute, the conflict became agonisingly more personal when a single FW-190 bombed a Sunday school in the Devon resort, killing several children.

There was a severe setback to his training when, in the grip of pneumonia and pleurisy, Mason spent six weeks recovering in hospital while his fellow trainees finished their course and fled the vast chilly expanse of St Athan, Glamorgan in search of a bomber crew.

So weak he had to learn to walk again, Mason joined another course, passed his examinations, earning his brevet and sergeant's stripes. But he never forgot the last words of advice from a warrant officer examiner:

'If you pass, don't think you know it all. You have no experience, that is still to come.'

The words struck home. Mason was the only Englishman in

a Halifax crew of Canadians at 1664 HCU, Dishforth, Yorkshire.
He was aware that his flying experience was lacking. To date he
had clocked up ten minutes in a De Haviland Rapide, a twin-
engine biplane, which had visited Southend airport to give the
air cadets a treat.

The skipper was Flight Lieutenant Tom Callaghan a slightly-
built man in his mid-twenties, from Sudbury, Ontario, who had
spent a considerable time instructing in Canada before being
posted to Britain.

Twenty-four-year-old Canadian navigator Flying Officer Jack
Shrapnel-Ward, was a descendant of Colonel Henry Shrapnel
who, in 1784, put numerous bullets into a shell, confirming his
expectations when it exploded that the number of casualties
increased satisfactorily. Shrapnel-Ward had good reason not to
cherish the memory of his distinguished ancestor during many
hours spent flying through flak over Germany.

The tall studious navigator was the only officer in the crew to
socialise with the four senior NCOs, visiting their billet
occasionally for a hand or two of bridge, at which he excelled.
A fine pianist, he often got feet tapping in the officers' mess.

Wireless operator Flight Sergeant Ray Colquhoun, twenty-
two, came from Kingston, Ontario.

Flying Officer Alec Stadnyk, from Calgary, the shortest man in
the crew at 5ft 5in, was twenty-three.

Nineteen-year-old Flight Sergeant Bill Cooper, the chubby-
faced mid-upper gunner, from Alberta, was believed to have put
up his age to become an airman. A keen sportsman, he played for
the RCAF's premier ice hockey team.

Flight Sergeant Adam Cragg, twenty-three, had already lived a
full life as a cowboy and lumberjack in British Columbia, before
turning to the war for more adventure. Mason recalls his
crewmate as 'a rounded character having a winning way with
women'.

Training at Dishforth ended on 22 April 1944 and Mason had
now totted up a more respectable 43hr 30min flying time.

'No squadron required replacement crews at this time and we
were posted briefly as a crew to a battle school at Dalton, north
Yorkshire. The school was managed by dour British soldiers,
most from the Twelfth Army which had retreated from Burma.
They were not happy men.

'On this course we assumed the rank of Army privates. Our

uniform was PT shorts and singlets, no socks, Army boots and fatigues. Officers were allowed to wear their cheese-cutter hats. Every move was at the double and the days were spent on battle training, mostly in fields, occasionally in the classroom.'

Outside they endured the torment of wearying obstacle courses, with much squirming through drain pipes half-filled with water, useful training for men flying aeroplanes.

No tears were shed after a signal arrived for them to be posted to 77 Squadron at Elvington, near York. Soon afterwards the squadron was packed off to a brand-new airfield at Full Sutton ten miles away.

'During May we were not overworked as a crew. We completed four ops, none lasting more than four hours. June was little better after our pilot fell and injured himself while cycling back to camp one night.'

Norman Mason went on his first daylight sortie over France as a spare bod with Flight Lieutenant Bill Walker on 25 June 1944 to attack a flying bomb site. Walker, an announcer for the Canadian Broadcasting Company before joining the RCAF, was popular in the mess where he and Shrapnel-Ward, together with other talented officers, helped deflect minds from war for an hour or two of fun.

The engineer had heard harrowing tales of Allied bombers being bombed by their own aircraft, described euphemistically as 'friendly fire' but until his one op with Walker, he had never experienced the horror of seeing it happen.

'We were over the target when I saw bombs fall from one Halifax and hit another directly below it. The bomber blew up and disintegrated before our eyes. We then had the incongruous and eerie sight of the stricken aircraft's dinghy, instantaneously released from its housing inboard of the port inner engine, automatically inflated by a carbon dioxide bottle, floating majestically down to earth, bright orange in colour, vivid in the brilliant morning sunshine.'

With Tom Callaghan back in the driver's seat they completed eight operations in July, including the close support of the land forces at Caen and a long haul to Stuttgart. Another eleven operations were reeled off in August, one of which was a daylight attack in MZ321 N-Nan on the twenty-seventh against a synthetic oil refinery at Homberg.

'The sun was shining in a cloudless sky a few minutes after

two in the afternoon. We had just left the target at 18,500ft, happy to be on our way home, when the aircraft was hit and a splinter of flak burst through the starboard cabin window at an angle, severing an artery in my left wrist. I was standing beside the pilot with my left hand on the undercarriage and bomb door control quadrant.

'Arterial bleeding at 20,000ft has to be experienced to be believed. There was no pressurised cabin in those days and the density of the air was much reduced causing, on every heartbeat, a column of blood to spout up to the canopy of the cabin, then stream down the windscreen.

'The smell of blood in such a rarefied atmosphere is remarkably pungent. Tom was aware of the situation and, over the intercom, called for our bomb aimer, Alec Stadnyk, to come to my assistance.

'Alec staunched the bleeding, applied a shell dressing, administered morphine and, under my direction, ably carried out my duties as engineer until we reached base two hours later.

'It had been the skipper's original intention to land at the emergency airfield at Manston, Kent. Radio silence was broken to advise our flight commander, Squadron Leader Harry Bridges, of the situation. He was flying his aircraft in close formation with us on our starboard beam.

'Later, no doubt due to the feeling of wellbeing created by the morphine, I suggested that we should return to base. I had the absurd idea that I could be treated at the station's sick quarters and return to duty without too long a delay.

'I was taken to York military hospital, surgically repaired and later transferred to Carlton Towers auxiliary military hospital, a converted stately home north of Goole, where I was kept until mid-October. Tom Callaghan came to see me and presented me with the piece of 88mm shell splinter which had been the cause of my problem.'

It was in the grounds of Carlton Towers, where Mason, stoically recuperating, discovered a mass of four-leaf clovers, long regarded as reliable symbols of great good fortune. He was a man in a job which largely depended on luck and he harvested a sheaf of clovers that he believed should carry himself and his crewmates safely through the rest of the war. To make sure of the invincibility of their magical properties he kept seven or eight for himself pressed carefully inside the folded card which had to be signed when he was issued with his flying kit.

Mason flew again on 28 October, as second engineer on a short cross-country exercise, successfully passing his assessment by Flight Lieutenant Tom Kilpatrick, and he returned to operational flying on 4 November, when Callaghan's Halifax was one of 749 aircraft sent to attack Bochum.

'My crew had only done one operation while I had been away. The rest of the time they spent transporting vitally-needed motor fuel to Brussels airport.'

On 16 November his crew were not on the battle order and Mason was relaxed in the engineers' section playing cribbage, when he was approached by the engineer leader and asked to fly with Flight Lieutenant Clive Beadle, whose own man was indisposed.

'I agreed and was ordered to report directly to the briefing room where briefing was in progress. Beadle's crew were senior to mine on the squadron, but apart from knowing them by sight I knew little else about them. I was amazed to find that the crew complement was already eight and I made the total nine. Categories were hidden beneath flying clothing and it was not until we positioned ourselves in the aircraft that I knew my crewmates' functions.'

One was Flying Officer Owen McAlinden, flying second dickey on his first operation. Another was mid-under gunner, Flying Officer L.L.Davis, an Australian, armed with a single .5in Browning machine gun in the uncomfortable ventral blister.

'We were lead aircraft. This practise was introduced soon after Bomber Command reopened its daylight offensive against the enemy. The leading aeroplane carried an above-average navigator. Ours was Flying Officer Bill Williams. It was his responsibility to navigate to the target with the squadron formating on us in tactical pairs strung out behind.'

The 77 Squadron Halifaxes were to be part of a massive onslaught that afternoon by 1,188 aircraft of Bomber Command against three towns:Düren, Heinsburg and Jülich. Their aim was to cut communications behind German lines in order for American troops to press forward.

Beadle's aircraft, MZ750 KN J-Jig, was among 413 Halifaxes, seventy-eight Lancasters and seventeen Mosquitoes sent to attack Jülich where a high concentration of German troops had been reported, including the Hermann Goering Division of

Armour. Over 1,200 aircraft from the Americans' 8th Air Force had already pummelled the town that morning.'The object was to destroy everything standing,to stun,confuse, daze and kill the enemy.'

Later, after the dust had settled from over 9,400 tons of bombs exploding on the targets it was clear that each town had been virtually wiped out at minimal loss to the attacking forces.

To identify itself as the lead aircraft, Beadle's Halifax was dragging a white drogue, similar in size to a wind sock flying at airfields.The long line for the drogue was attached by ground personnel to the tail wheel assembly at the takeoff point on the runway.The drogue was usually solemnly unfurled by the station commander.

At every turning point the navigator asked Norman Mason to fire the prearranged two-colour Very signal.

'The weather was perfect. Approaching the target we were subjected to very accurate anti-aircraft fire. I believe the drogue trailing behind made us particularly interesting to enemy gunners.

'I realised the aircraft had been damaged when I became aware of the smell of cordite. It was said by the old lags that if you see the flak,that's okay, if you can hear it,it's close. But if you can smell it, you've probably had it.

'After our bombs had been released the weight was considerably reduced and the centre of gravity changes. Immediately the nose of the aircraft goes up and it must be re-trimmed.The first thing a pilot must do is rotate his elevator trim forward to get the nose down and the tail up to avoid climbing unnecessarily. When the skipper operated the trim tab it didn't work.

'He said: "Elevator trim tab's u/s, Engineer." I was a bit stumped at that point.I could see he was rotating the wheel and nothing was happening.Then he pushed the stick forward and said:"The elevator's u/s, Engineer."

'By this time I thought he needed a bit of encouragement. I looked at the fuel gauges and everything seemed to be all right, so I said:"Fuel's okay, Skipper."Which was of no help to him at all.

'He then said: "Put on parachutes." At this point it became apparent that the intercom was unserviceable aft of my position. All three gunners were out of communication.The skipper told me to pass on his instructions to the gunners and find out if they were all right. None had been injured and on my return to the cockpit Beadle gave the order: "Jump! Jump!"'

McAlinden was scrambling through the forward escape hatch when he realised his parachute had opened and was trailing yards of silk inside the aircraft. Trapped outside in the ferocious slipstream, terror gave him phenomenal strength clinging desperately by his fingers to the edge of the hatch. Pilot Officer Danny Nimmo, the wireless operator, swiftly gathered the mass of silk, stamped on McAlinden's fingers and as he dropped out with an anguished cry, thrust the parachute after him. Nimmo said afterwards he believed he had sent McAlinden to his death.

McAlinden survived. He with Williams, Nimmo and bomb aimer Flight Lieutenant Peter Sinclair landed in Germany and became POWs.

Meanwhile Beadle was still in control of the aircraft. Mason says:

'The skipper had brought the nose down by reducing power on the engines. He didn't want to lose height excessively so he pushed the throttles up again, causing the engines to take over and come up, regaining a bit of height. We were porpoising along and I thought he was doing extremely well.

'The slipstream through the open forward escape hatch was playing havoc with the navigator's abandoned charts. The pilot and I had removed our flying helmets prior to baling out which made conversation between us difficult. The aircraft was gradually losing height and Beadle suggested that we might try to make the Allied lines. I agreed and managed to grab one of Bill Williams' maps for him.

'The pilot then said: "If the gunners have not yet left the aircraft fetch them up front, I'd like to see them leave."

'I was just in time to prevent the rear gunner, Flight Sergeant Frank Robertson, leaving via the rear door. The mid-upper, Cliff Marsden, and Davis were waiting ready to follow him out. All three followed me back up the fuselage and at 6,500ft the pilot considered we should resume abandoning the aircraft. I was ordered out next, leaving by the forward hatch facing aft.'

The others followed Mason out although Davis, a good friend of the pilot, refused to leave until Beadle had left his seat and was down by the front exit.

The Halifax droned on without its crew, slipping steadily

lower until it ran out of sky, finally to crash on a Belgian farmhouse. Fortunately, the building was empty, the family were out working in the fields.

Mason landed without difficulty or injury in a wood near the village of Maarheeze, Holland.

'I was not certain that I was clear of enemy territory and had set about the mammoth task of burying my parachute when I heard voices and, turning, saw two male civilians approaching, both trundling bicycles. Then came shouts and through the trees appeared a British Army officer of the Duke of Wellington Regiment, followed by a party of soldiers.

'The two civilians were ordered to carry my parachute and I was taken to company headquarters in Maarheeze.

'I spent that night as a guest of the officers'mess,having been welcomed late that afternoon by most of the inhabitants of the village. According to the commanding officer of the Ar my unit, they had expressed the wish to shake the hand of the "gallant airman of the Royal Air Force" now in their midst.They had been aware many times of Bomber Command's activities, but never before had they actually seen an airman. The gratitude shown to me was almost overwhelming bearing in mind I was still a teenager.'

Still carrying his parachute, he was taken next day by Jeep to Weert for interrogation,then on to Eindhoven,headquarters for 83 Group Tactical Air Force. Another day passed before the engineer was put on an RAF Dakota for Northolt where he met Beadle, Davis and Robertson. They were driven to St John's Wood and interrogated at 6 Hall Road, the British reception centre for RAF evaders, where they learned that Flight Sergeant Marsden had broken an ankle on landing and was recovering at a Belgian hospital.

Mason was able to scrounge a few hours to get a train to Southend where his parents were still coming to terms with the contents of a telegram which told them he was missing.

Back at Full Sutton he was welcomed by his regular crew who gave him the cherished nickname of 'Golden Bollocks' in celebration of his good fortune at avoiding death or serious injury and the Germans.

'It was usual practise for returning aircrew to give a gift to the packer of their parachute and Frank Robertson and I went to the parachute section next day and asked to see "JS",the initials on the flaps of our 'chutes. She was a very pretty WAAF and I gave her some jewellery.

'The sergeant in charge of the section said hopefully: "I suppose you haven't got your parachute with you?" I said I had not, which was true, because it was back in the billet.

'The parachute was just the right size to go into my back pack and I took it home on my seven days of survivor's leave. I still have it.

'I received a letter in Southend from the RAF instructing me to report to a personnel holding unit at Morecambe. But my crew were in Full Sutton and, feeling a little rebellious, I thought:"Bugger Morecambe".'

He ignored the order, intending to help his crewmates finish their tour, although he had completed his. Few aircrew returned doggedly to their squadron to fly gratuitous sorties after negotiating two lots of survivor's leave.

It was business as usual for Tom Callaghan and his full crew when they resumed operations on 5 December 1944, attacking railway installations at Soest, near Dortmund.

'On our return,' says Mason,'we discovered we were unable to operate the undercarriage and flaps and were diverted to Carnaby, the emergency airfield near Bridlington. Over Carnaby the undercart was successfully lowered and locked down by means of the emergency system – introducing pneumatic pressure into the hydraulic system. The pilot made a flapless landing.'

Norman Mason was unaware his non-appearance at Morecambe had caused some grinding of teeth after RAF clerks had discovered that their implicit orders to the engineer had apparently been wilfully disregarded. Official memos were passed to admin officers whose brows furrowed,and a more threatening telegram was sent to him at his parents' home in Chestnut Grove, Southend.

On 18 December the crew bombed Duisburg which was uneventful but a day or so later Mason received a letter from his father, enclosing a telegram which clearly stated that any further delay of his appearance at Morecambe would lead to his arrest for being absent without leave. He says:

'It occurred to me that I should advise the squadron adjutant immediately of the content of the telegram. I explained to him I had received the telegram that day. His reaction was also immediate. He said:"You realise that you are not on the strength of this squadron?" No, I did not.'

The flight lieutenant stared again at the telegram and said: 'You will not fly until this matter has been sorted out.' He hesitated, fixing the young engineer with a worried frown:'You haven't flown since you returned from survivors' leave?'

Mason watched a red glow appear in the officer's face after he admitted flying to Soest and Duisburg.

'I cannot recall his exact words but it certainly contained a few expletives. It amounted to me not flying again until he had dealt with the situation.

'Later that day I was summoned by Tannoy to report back to the adjutant who told me I was now screened. My first tour of ops was complete and so was my crew's.'

Norman Mason had completed thirty-two sorties. Prior to leaving the squadron on Christmas Eve 1944, Flight Lieutenant John Ninian, the engineer leader, told Mason that he had been recommended for the DFM. It was the first he had heard of it and the engineer went home a little elated, but telling no one his news. He learned later that Tom Callaghan, Jack Shrapnel-Ward and Alec Stadnyk had been awarded DFCs.

Confirmation of Norman Mason's award came from an unexpected source.

'While on leave at home in April 1945 I was awakened by my mother holding a copy of the *Southend Standard*, published that day. Our neighbour, Mrs Edna Sharpe, had apparently banged on the party wall of our terraced house and brought my mother's attention to a story inside with the headline:"Grocer's assistant wins DFM".

'I was, of course, excited and proud and later that day went to the *Standard*'s office in Clifftown Road and was shown the Ministry of Information communiqué in which I had been described as "...a valiant member of an aircraft crew".'

His citation, which mentions the severe wound sustained during one operation and the baling out after another, says: he "...resumed his operational duties with undiminished enthusiasm."

'After visiting the *Standard* I popped down to Cecil Raven's, a gentleman's outfitter and military tailor in town, to buy a piece of DFM medal ribbon, went home and sewed it on my uniform jacket.'

CHAPTER SEVENTEEN

THE KILLING SKIES

Bob Guthrie joined the RAF in 1942 for excitement, but it was two years before he got a real taste of it and then, in less than a week,his war was over and the hardships began,as he languished in a POW camp.

A piece of First World War shrapnel had taken over fifteen years to work insidiously through the head of his father, Belgium-born Robert Guthrie, before it killed him in 1933. A man of conspicuous intelligence, speaking seven languages, he had been an interpreter.

Bob, his elder son, was ten years old, the second boy, Charlie, eleven months younger. Bob Guthrie had his father's capacity for study, his brother was more interested in engineering. The elder boy vowed that one day he would achieve the sort of success which, had he lived, would have made his father proud. His mother, too, of course, for Mabel Guthrie, a buyer for a departmental store in their home town of Reading, made sure that life continued as normally as possible for her sons.

Neither boy, at first, regarded going to a Surrey boarding school as normal, but it provided them with an excellent education which laid a good foundation for their lives,and it was entirely free, paid for by an association within the group of companies for whom their mother worked.

Bob Guthrie left Russell School,Addington,aged sixteen,and patiently marked time for two years in a dull job as a clerk with Post Office Telephones until joining the RAF on 19 February 1942.Always keen on mathematics,he wanted to be a navigator and was accepted for training.

Guthrie spent much of this in England at seaside resorts,

billeted in top hotels, with good food, and while there was little time for exploring beaches and cliff tops these were postings which offered pure and bracing air to benefit clear receptive minds.

In Torquay, where he did his initial training, the town also provided less welcome recreation, like diving under beds when German aircraft came roaring over the English Channel. He recalls:

'We could actually look over the harbour from our hotel and three times saw fighters coming in.As they flew in over the sea an old wreck of a ship which was moored across the front of the harbour to prevent enemy vessels coming in was scuppered, hoping this would prevent it being bombed and losing its usefulness.The water was soon pumped out and the ship back in position. We were in our bedroom when a fighter machine-gunned the upper floors of the hotel. No one was hurt, but it was a bit unexpected.'

Guthrie's passion for long-distance cycling and lawn tennis gave him an advantage over less-fit trainees when they were sent on ten-mile cross-country marches,carrying full packs and rifles, which he enjoyed. He learned how to take a gas-operated Vickers gun to pieces while blindfolded, became proficient at clay pigeon shooting, and was acquainted with the under-rated exhilaration of square-bashing.

But by the time they were posted to Eastbourne two months later and settled in comfortably at The Grand Hotel, he was ready for his first glimpse of a navigation chart.

'There were about thirty of us on the navigation course. I loved maths so navigation was a subject which really appealed to me: getting from A to B with all the possible complications in between. Obviously the main problem was wind and you needed to get the speed right because it was no good getting to where you wanted to be five minutes late, or even five minutes early.

'But it was the wind which was so important. Some of it could be ferocious as on our trip to Nuremburg much later when it was over 100mph, pushing so many aircraft off course. If you were going due north, for instance, and had a wind pushing in from the east you would actually set off in a north-easterly direction.

'From Eastbourne we were taken by train to Trafford,

Manchester, a holding point where we were given the sort of hot-weather kit which suggested we were going to South Africa. Another train took us to the Clyde where we got on the former Cunard liner, *Queen Elizabeth*, now a troop ship. They took our kit back and gave us some different stuff before we set sail for Canada. I think it was done quite deliberately so we wouldn't know where we were going.'

Guthrie arrived at Rivers, Manitoba, in September 1942 and was based there until the following February. His first impressions were not good: squinting into a storm of dust being whipped wickedly across the prewar airfield by lively gusts of wind,and being bedded down in huge hangars with hundreds of other trainees struggling to come to terms with their unusual surroundings.There was no room here for young men whose first concern was their dignity. After six years sleeping in a school dormitory Guthrie quickly adapted to the conditions, settling down to enjoy learning more about navigation and getting out of the classroom into the air.

'I enjoyed flying in Avro Ansons although it was not the ideal place for training, particularly for navigators. You knew you would be unable to see anything at night when you got back to England because of the blackout. But here, as soon as you got airborne you could see the lights of Winnipeg 150 miles away. They specialised in astro-navigation and I became pretty good at that. It was a busy life, because when you weren't actually flying you were in the classroom.

'Rivers was called a town but was no bigger than an English village. It had only one brick building, a bank. Everything else was made of wood. We went by bus to dances at Brandon, a town forty miles away. Occasionally we got a lift in an Anson when around twenty of us piled into the aircraft which managed to get off the ground with us sitting on the floor in our best blues.

'On our forty-eight-hour passes every third week we went into Winnipeg where there were always loads of people happy to welcome you into their homes.'

Experienced pilots got bored flying sprog navigators backwards and forwards every day at 8,000ft,the equivalent of a truck driver grinding for mindless hours across featureless Canadian plains. Guthrie, who was navigating, remembers one Canadian flying officer sighing bleakly and saying:'Okay chaps we'll do a bit of low-level now.' He eased the twin-engine Anson down, smiling wearily, pleased to be doing something that was not in a steady straight line, and they saw the ground rushing past a few feet below.

Suddenly they felt an odd thump and a sudden intake of breath preceded the aircraft swiftly gaining height before the pilot reported hoarsely:'Oh Christ! We've hit a horse.' No one dared risk swivelling to take a look. The truth was sometimes best left to take care of itself. They rapidly left the area, Guthrie continued his good work, the pilot stopped complaining about the tedium of his job and for the next few weeks, unlike the horse, they kept their heads down. If an angry farmer, waving a hefty bill from a vet or knacker's yard, complained to the Air Force about an irresponsible pilot maiming or killing his thoroughbred horse, they did not hear about it. Life sank back into the pleasantly cosseted routine of preparing for war.

At the end of the course the navigators took an intensive fourteen-subject examination and heard nothing more about it until one morning in early February 1943, they were slumped in the sergeants' mess at the holding camp in Monckton, New Brunswick, on the east coast, after a three-day train ride, heading back to England. A corporal suddenly appeared brandishing a list.

'He called out six chaps' names, including mine, then cried: "Get your kit together, you've just been made officers." That was it, nothing official, just the corporal and his list. So, a bit surprised, we moved into the officers' mess. I discovered later that I had come third out of the forty in the course exam and they commissioned the first six. That was their way.'

Back in England, after fourteen days' leave, the navigators encountered one of several blockages in training and Guthrie was sent on a gentle two-week diversion with the Grenadier Guards on the Yorkshire Moors. He learned to drive a Churchill tank, on his first driving lesson.

The earthbound Guardsmen were intrigued to have a fully-qualified RAF navigation officer in their midst and one evening decided to make use of the quietly-spoken and confident young man whose wide experience should get him from a Lincolnshire bomber airfield to Berlin without too much inconvenience. They put him in charge of navigating a three-ton Bedford truck across the moors to a farm twenty miles away.

'We ended up in a farmyard, but it was the wrong farm. I had to admit I was lost and the soldiers laughed, but it was all good humoured even though I did blush with embarrassment. It was certainly true that every sign in Britain had been taken down early in the war, but I had no excuses, they had given me a map.'

As Air Ministry clerks struggled to unclog an over-stretched system which funnelled graduates from flying schools all over the world through operational units in Britain to the killing skies above Europe, Guthrie again found himself at another large pleasant seaside hotel. This time in Sidmouth, Devon.

'They had nothing else for us to do during the six weeks we were there apart from a lot of navigation practise, including astro-navigation and dead reckoning stuff, all in the classroom.'

He was eventually crewed up at 14 OTU, Market Harborough, Leicestershire, in September 1943, becoming part of a five-man crew who all, like him, were eager to become operational. Here they flew twin-engine Vickers Wellingtons, and learned to depend on each other, gradually turning into a team.

Bob Guthrie had met Sybil Lewington, a pretty fair-haired girl at a dance in Reading after returning from Canada. Guthrie was twenty when they were married in their home town on 18 November.

The crew's training was put on hold for several weeks when Guthrie twice succumbed to severe bouts of tonsillitis and another time when John Langlands, the pilot, fell off the back of a truck taking them to dispersal.

'We were given a holding posting to Scampton for a few days, just before and after Christmas 1943, when I was grounded by tonsillitis. I got the job of signing everybody's Christmas railway warrants. I signed hundreds, including my own.'

Leaving here they were converted on to heavy aircraft with Stirlings during their month at 1661 HCU, Winthorpe, Nottinghamshire, where they picked up a flight engineer and a mid-upper gunner.

'I was not alone in disliking the Stirling. It was a dodgy sort of aircraft. You couldn't get much over 15,000ft in them and it was bad for icing. We had to land in a hurry once after getting iced up, touching down with only two engines going, which was nasty. And yet for some jobs, low-level stuff, dropping agents and supplies over France, for instance, they were very good.

'At the same time I was converted to Gee, which was

interesting, something we didn't have on the Wellingtons. Once you got used to it you could use Gee to bring your aircraft in to the end of the runway.

'From there we went on to four better engines at 5 Lancaster Finishing School, Syerston, Nottinghamshire, where I also learned about H2S, quite different to Gee. With H2S the aircraft sends its signal down and you get this picture of the terrain below. We had special maps which contained the outline pictures of towns and could do some very good reckoning from those. You were not supposed to use Gee or H2S when you were over enemy territory – although some navigators did – because the Germans could home in on them. We found our targets by dead reckoning, although by now the Pathfinders were operating.'

In March 1944, as ready as they could be to go into battle, thirty-one-year-old Flying Officer John Langlands and his crew were posted to 630 Squadron at East Kirkby, set on the gentle southern edge of the Lincolnshire Wolds, within a few miles of the North Sea.

Calm, well disciplined, the tall and slim Langlands, Jock to his crew, had been a policeman, based in Edinburgh, before satisfying his itch to fly.

His navigator, Flying Officer Bob Guthrie, scraped together twenty-five pounds to buy a Singer car soon after arriving at East Kirkby.

'The whole thing was made of fabric stretched over a wooden frame. Five of us could squeeze into it and we often went to Boston for a drink.'

The wireless operator, Sergeant Geoff Jeffery, a twenty-two-year-old, came from Kent. Pilot Officer Benny Bryans, the bomb aimer, used to nip home to nearby Leicester when stationed at Market Harborough.

Flight engineer Sergeant Norman Goring, twenty-three, from Hull, did not mind being called 'Hermann' by everyone, not even displaying mild irritation when bods shiftily compared his slender frame to pictures they had seen of the bloated chief of the Luftwaffe. Satisfied the two men could not possibly be even remotely related they cheerfully accepted the former motor mechanic as one of their own. Lacking self-confidence, Goring quietly enjoyed his notoriety.

The twenty-one-year-old mid-upper gunner, Sergeant Bud Coffey, a boisterous and wisecracking Canadian, kept his more reserved crewmates chuckling at times when it was not easy to find anything to laugh about.

Flight Sergeant Alan Drake, a Lancastrian, already in the RAF ten years and married, had been an armourer before re-mustering to aircrew. He was now a rear gunner.

A step nearer to their first operation they plunged into a series of training exercises and long cross-country flights, at least one at night beyond the north of Scotland, which took over seven hours.

On the afternoon of 26 March 1944, the day after Guthrie's twenty-first birthday, he received a dubious belated present when they were briefed for an operation against Essen. It was difficult to imagine a worse target for a sprog aircrew's first sortie. The Ruhr town, situated near vast iron and coal deposits, was ringed with anti-aircraft guns defending the giant Krupps arms and munition works.

Enemy controllers were taken by surprise that night by Bomber Command's change of tactics. After a long fierce onslaught lasting over four months against Berlin and other distant targets, 705 bombers were sent to strike Essen, only a few miles from the border with Holland. Consequently, fewer Allied aircraft were lost: six Lancasters and three Halifaxes, 1.3 per cent of the attacking force. The raid was considered a success, with 1,756 houses destroyed, forty-eight industrial buildings seriously damaged, at least 550 people killed and over 1,500 injured.

Jock Langlands and his crew, having encountered no fighters and little flak, wondered why Essen had been described as such a terrifying hell hole. Guthrie says:

'After training for two years I had been excited by the thought of going to Essen, our first op, but we weren't shaken by what we saw. I saw nothing of the attack, of course, shut away in my little curtained-off office, but I can't remember Jock calling out anything about flak and no one saw any fighters. Back at East Kirkby the seven of us had a brief chat about the op and we thought if our other trips were no worse than this we shouldn't have much to worry about.'

A heavy snowfall brought airfields to a standstill later that week and everybody not required for urgent work was handed a shovel and set to work on the clogged runway.

'We were all out there from the wing commander downwards shovelling snow off the runway, piling it along the sides. We cleared it then, on the morning of 30 March, everybody did an air test.'

Langlands had been given the squadron commander's Lancaster, ME664 LE-T for that night's attack on Nuremburg. The aircraft had only recently arrived at the airfield and stepping inside they could smell new paint and marvel at its crisp freshness. The CO was Wing Commander Bill Deas, holder of a DSO and two DFCs, who had bagged the aircraft after it had arrived on the squadron.

'We were briefed at tea time and the intelligence officer stressed it would be a long trip, but although it was a moonlit night we would be flying roughly between two layers of cloud. When we got up, of course, there was not a cloud in the sky. The met side of it was chronic. We found out later that some of the wind directions were almost the reverse of what we'd been given. I was working in the navigators' room for an hour or more before going out to the aircraft, planning our courses with all the winds we'd been given.

'Waiting for takeoff we were quietly confident. We knew we had a good skipper. Jock had proved himself by putting down a sick Stirling and we'd had an emergency landing in a Wellington at OTU, landing at a small airfield which normally only dealt with Tiger Moths. We got down all right, carrying our practise bomb; it was a different matter taking off on the short runway, but he did it without a fuss. This time we had high-explosive bombs on board.'

They took off at 10.16pm and soon realised that the promised cloud cover was non-existent. Crossing the enemy coast with the moonlight obligingly illuminating every aircraft in the invading force for any prowling night fighter was extremely daunting. Sure enough, they were targeted. The first successful attack by a German fighter was near Charleroi, Belgium. Its victim was the first of ninety-five bombers which would be shot down on the most disastrous night of the war for Bomber Command.

The unexpected soft touch of Essen had not prepared the Langlands crew for what followed. Nor could anyone in the main stream have imagined the ghastly wholesale slaughter which was about to rip through them. Most of the helpless victims were shot down along and either side of a straight line which ran from the west in Charleroi and Namur to the east through Wetzlar and Fulda and on for another few miles before dropping down almost due south towards Nuremburg, a leg which accounted for another nineteen British aircraft. Three more were shot down on their return home.

German pilots could hardly believe their good fortune as the British bombers seemed to be lining up willingly to be attacked, like targets moving with predictable restraint across the back of a fairground shooting booth.

'There were so many problems. Instead of us being given dog legs to confuse the Germans we had long stretches of 150 miles of straight flying to negotiate, terrible planning. The fighters were waiting, picking us off like rabbits on these long runs. We were nearly all off course because of the changing winds. We were given another wind by radio fairly soon after getting over enemy territory, but that was wrong, too, and we didn't stand much of a chance. My crewmates reported up to a dozen of our bombers going down on all sides and I wrote them into my log.'

Langlands' Lancaster had been blown between ten and fifteen miles north of the briefed course, near Eisenach, when they were attacked by a fighter.

'We were running late and about to turn south for the run into Nuremburg when I heard this terrifyingly loud clatter, obviously cannon shells hitting the aircraft. Some of the shrapnel went between the pilot and myself and I received a thump on the leg from either a bit of shell or it might have been some metal from the damaged aircraft. My leg didn't hurt terribly, nor did it bleed, but over sixty years later I still have the bruise.

'We were hit by twenty or thirty cannon shells. Immediately there was a scramble among the crew because part of the starboard wing was on fire. The pilot gave orders for us to abandon the aircraft and Benny Bryans, the bomb aimer, went to pull open the escape hatch in the nose.

'I left my position and noticed chaps moving about in a hurry at the front. Benny couldn't get the hatch open, so Hermann, the engineer, went down and dragged it up. He pushed out Benny who became unconscious as he dropped into the sky. He came to when he was going down, then passed out again. We were at 20,000ft, perhaps it was the lack of oxygen.

'One of the starboard engines was on fire, but the port motors were working normally. Jock was waiting for us all to leave, keeping the aircraft level. The engineer dropped out and I followed.

'I don't know exactly what happened next. Jock Langlands baled out safely, but no one escaped from the back. The wireless operator and both gunners went down with the aircraft. Their normal exit was through the rear door. No one who survived had seen them moving towards the back and although the pilot would have tried to make contact with them if they were off intercom he wouldn't have much to go by. I have often speculated that as it was a new aircraft the rear door may have been so stiff they couldn't get it open.

'We had been told to count to ten before opening our parachutes, but I counted more than that. There was a fierce gale blowing and although I couldn't see them I could hear the noise of a lot of other aircraft and didn't want to get tangled up with one. I didn't see our aeroplane after I'd jumped out and don't think the bombs had been jettisoned. I was frightened and remember pulling the ripcord at about 15,000ft, the parachute opening and having the handle left in my hand. I thought there was no point in having that and threw it away.

'As I came down the sound of aeroplane engines receded. It was a bright moon but I couldn't see anything until I got near the ground and saw a forest coming up to meet me. I tried to aim for a clearing and fortunately missed it. I discovered later that the trees had been sawn down and only two-foot-high stumps were left. I could have been killed if I'd dropped on them. Instead I landed on a fir tree, unhitched my parachute and climbed down.

'My flying boots had been blown off because, foolishly, I always left them unzipped on the aircraft. Then I saw that the parachute had streamed some distance down the tree and I climbed a little way back up, cut off some of the silk and bound it round my stockinged feet. I must have looked a bit odd but it was fairly comfortable.

'I found a fairly wide track running through the forest and set off down it at about 1am. I walked until around 9am and saw an older man coming towards me. He was holding a revolver and he gestured with it for me to put up my hands. He took me to a house and half-an-hour later soldiers or police turned up in a Volkswagen car and took me to the nearest airfield. The others were there: Hermann, Benny and Jock. We were taken to the officers' mess where we pretended not to recognise each other. We were given a meal and the Germans couldn't have been kinder.'

They endured the ritual of most prisoners of war: solitary confinement for a week on bread and water at Dulag Luft, the interrogation centre near Frankfurt, before being herded into railway trucks. Guthrie remembers the sign in German painted on the sides: '40 men or 4 horses.' The men rested on tiers of wooden shelves around each truck.

'We were shunted about quite violently in the sidings of Berlin. There was a raid on the city or the outskirts and they liked to leave prisoners in the sidings so there was a chance of them being wiped out by their own bombs. When the engine driver jammed on the brakes Benny was thrown from a top shelf, falling on my legs, hurting the one damaged in the aircraft. By the time we got to Stalag Luft I, Barth, on the Baltic coast I couldn't walk and was hauled along in a horse-drawn cart, but I was better in a week or two.'

When news that Langlands and his crew had bought it reached him, Wing Commander Deas shrugged philosophically at the loss of his aircraft. That could easily be replaced, but three crews from 630 Squadron had been lost that night, and he had twenty-one difficult letters of condolence to write to their families.

Deas himself and his crew were shot down on the night of 7/8 July during the raid on St-Leu-d'Esserent with Deas himself and five of his crew being killed.

'I was moved into Room 24 of Block 5 at Barth. We weren't badly treated and in conditions like that we all had to muck in, taking turns to cook, for instance. The winter was bad so we couldn't get any water and had to boil down snow. Most of the day was spent walking round the wire fence, talking.

'The SS came in occasionally, brought us out on parade and searched the whole camp. We might stand up for ten hours, sometimes through the night. You would have problems if you moved more than a few inches.

'Among the prisoners were enough Football League footballers for a full team, a member of the London Philharmonic Orchestra and two American medal winners from the 1936 Berlin Olympic Games.

'Early in May two of our chaps went out to meet the Russians before they arrived at the camp. They were good to us. Cattle were driven into the compounds, slaughtered by vets – American POWs – and dished up as plates of beef to the hungry prisoners.

Everybody was told not to eat too much after being used to small meals for a long time. Even so, two Americans died from overeating.

'The Russians laid on entertainment, a complete two hour show with singing and dancing. Thousands of us watched it.

'Some of us went out of the camp for a walk round and found a German family lying dead on the grass. It was terribly sad. The father had shot his wife and two children, then killed himself. I believe they were afraid of the Russians.

'On 15 May the Americans arrived at the nearby airfield with Flying Fortresses to take us back to England. Three days later I was home in Reading.'

A teacher for over thirty years, Bob Guthrie was a deputy head at a secondary school in Stamford, Lincolnshire, when he retired in 1985.

CHAPTER EIGHTEEN

THE FATEFUL SWAP

Sergeant Ted Mercer peered bleakly out through the flaps of his tent at the teeming rain beating down on the soggy grass. This scene of desolation, misery and inactivity had not been part of his grand vision of fighting the war. Shivering pitifully beneath the unseasonable summer downpour were lines of khaki tents in a large field, beyond which stood the expanse of RAF Padgate where chaps could move about normally and were not being treated like wretched outcasts.

Nineteen-year-old Mercer was among 300 disgruntled newly-qualified pilots who had arrived in England in high spirits after training at Clewiston, Florida. They docked at Liverpool in July 1942 aboard an American troop ship which had successfully avoided the attention of German U-boats in the North Atlantic. And now they were marooned under canvas because one of the 5,000 American soldiers who had travelled with them aboard the SS *Maloja* had gone down with suspected smallpox.

'We were stuck there in quarantine for two weeks,' says Mercer. 'In charge of us was an ex-Guards officer who had transferred to the RAF with the rank of wing commander. A right sod he was. Some of the lads were detailed to patrol the boundaries of the field to stop us getting out. He carried out inspections, particularly at night when he found one chap asleep who was supposed to be on guard. He soon had him running round the field doing pack drill. When the rain stopped he organised games, sports, housey-housey and quiz sessions, which helped pass the time. Food was delivered by van and cooks were brought in, producing our meals in a kitchen tent. It could have been worse, but for us, the war was at a standstill. And we never

did find out if that Yank really had smallpox.' The scare passed
and the sprog pilots were dispersed all over the country.

Mercer came from Great Harwood, near Blackburn, where his
father, George, ran his own pharmacy. Ted Mercer and his older
brother, Richard, had been fascinated by aeroplanes since their
uncle, Jack Withington, took them to Croydon airport and they
peered excitedly inside the cramped cockpit of Handley Page's
four-engine biplane airliner, HP42. Some time later they
watched a display by Sir Alan Cobham's air circus at Whalley,
Lancashire, but their father refused to give them 10s (50p) each
to pay for a flight with the great man.

Richard, the first of the Mercer brothers to join the RAF,
failed his pilot's course and so became a navigator, flying
Armstrong Whitworth Whitleys, then, from the same company,
twin-engine Albemarles, towing gliders from Tunisia for the
invasion of Sicily. He later returned to England.

Before becoming an airman in August 1941 Ted Mercer had
what he regarded as a lucky escape when plans for him to study
architecture with another uncle foundered. In the meantime he
had to earn a living and was offered a job as a clerk in the
expense accounts department of the civil service with the
Admiralty at Sheerness, many miles away from his home.

'I could not imagine a more boring job, working at a desk all
day with figures, but when they started up the Local Defence
Volunteers I joined it and life became more interesting, at night
anyway. We patrolled the dockyard armed with Royal Navy
rifles. We never saw anything suspicious, although one of our
chaps was killed after a patrol. We used to doss down in one of
the cellars below the offices and a fellow was carelessly operating
the bolt while unloading his Lee Enfield. He rammed one round
up against another round in the breech and the bullet went
flying around the cellar, finishing up smashing sideways into
somebody's chest.'

Mercer got acquainted with Airspeed Oxfords at 12 (P)AFU,
Grantham (Spitalgate) before moving to 14 OTU, Cottesmore,
Rutland, in October, picking up his first crew and flying the
Wellington IC.

'This early Wimpey had Pegasus engines and was not very
good. If you had an engine stop you were in dead trouble. The
prop would not feather, it just used to windmill, causing a lot of
drag. We lost two Wellingtons and chaps died in crashes while I

was there. Later on I flew the Wellington III with the Hercules engines, which was a much better job altogether.

'At the end of my heavy conversion training on Lancasters at Swinderby I was taken aback to be called into the Wingco's office. He told me I was being posted to 83 Pathfinders Squadron at Wyton, Cambridgeshire, but my navigator was to be replaced by a flight lieutenant who had been instructing at a navigation school in Canada and he would be made captain of the aircraft. My original navigator would replace my bomb aimer who was to be given to another crew. I was right pissed off by all of this but as I was only a lowly sergeant, what could I say? When a wing commander starts laying down the law you tend to go along with him. I learned later that a pilot friend of mine who had been approached in the same way refused point-blank to agree to any of it. It had never occurred to me to do that.

'I flew a few second dickey trips from Wyton then, on the way back from attacking Stettin, I was taken ill with pain in my lower gut and went into RAF Hospital Ely where my appendix was whipped out. I was off flying for a month and by the time I came back my crew were well established with another pilot. A short time after that they all went missing. So I pieced together a scratch crew from odds and sods around the airfield. You could describe them as lost souls who had all been with other crews but now, for different reasons, no longer had one.'

La Spezia on the north-east coast of Italy was the target for Mercer's first bombing operation on 13 April 1943.

'I was flying from Wyton on the first of three trips as second dickey with Flying Officer Tommy Wilmott. In a sense it was fantastic to see the flares and bombs and anti-aircraft shells banging away; weird too because I had never seen anything like it in my life, and you could not hear it above the noise of our Rolls-Royce Merlin engines.'

'On 15 August we were on the far side of the Alps at 20,000ft when an engine failed due to some mechanical fault. All we could do was carry on and drop our bombs on Milan, but on the way back we had to divert to a more southerly route, going down at first to about 12,000ft, then 8,000ft over southern France. We were lucky, having a very uneventful return. Normally you might expect to be shot at all the way. My gunners were especially vigilant. I had reminded them not to fall asleep, but I was joking because they were always on the ball.'

On 6 September 1943 they were briefed to bomb Munich. Mercer had completed nine trips and was now a pilot officer, but for this sortie he was given a sprog navigator who had not even been to an operational training unit.

'I understood it was some sort of an experiment, but if so it was a failure. He got lost between Wyton and the south coast of England. He told me in some agitation over the intercom that the Dalton computer he used for working out our course when you put the wind and direction speed on it was missing. He reckoned someone had pinched it and he had no idea where he was. There was only one thing to be done. I said: "This is bloody hopeless, we're never going to get anywhere." So I jettisoned the bombs in the Channel and returned to base.

'I received a bollocking from my commanding officer, Wing Commander John Searby, who was not interested in hearing about my navigator's inability to navigate. He was only concerned that I had not somehow carried on to Munich instead of dumping our bombs. He felt my decision was something which had to be discouraged on the squadron. I said I couldn't trust a navigator who could not find his way out of England and Searby ended up by threatening to kick me out of his office. No disciplinary action was taken but my crew was split up and scattered and in September I was posted to 44 (Rhodesia) Squadron at Dunholme Lodge, Lincolnshire.'

Having been given an undeserved rough ride by his two previous squadron commanders who refused to listen to him, Mercer's unease deepened slightly at Dunholme where he was told he had been given a crew who had refused to fly with their pilot.

'Any apprehension I had soon disappeared because I got on very well with my new crew. They were a good bunch of lads. Their previous pilot, a sergeant, had been taken off flying altogether because he kept turning back for no good reason. They'd been with him for three months. When he saw the target in the distance lighting up and things going on he turned round and came back. He was probably getting more and more scared of his job every time he went up. He just wasn't cut out for it. I had no ill feelings against him. I just thought: "Poor sod".'

The frightened pilot was said to be LMF – lacking moral fibre – which involved him being reduced to the lowest rank of AC2 and sending him without delay to a highly-disciplined camp in

Sheffield which specialised in dealing with men whose nerve had snapped. He would spend the rest of the war doing the dirtiest jobs that could be found for him. Little sympathy was spared on such men except quietly by other aircrews who knew the immense stresses involved in bombing operations, while being extremely relieved that they had so far managed to cope.

Mercer's crew at Dunholme were all sergeants, although Vic Purvis, the quietly-efficient navigator, and the more extrovert Bert Baker, the wireless operator were later commissioned.

Most men kept their thoughts to themselves about bombing operations, or underplayed the awfulness of a raid by making light of it. A veteran pilot at the same airfield, who had been on several rough trips frequently woke up screaming, plagued by repetitive nightmares, but insisted that he carried on flying. Many had cosy little bolt holes they created for themselves when they were not flying, seeking refuge in a favourite pub, or a cinema, or a rendezvous with a regular girlfriend. Ted Mercer went ballroom dancing.

'I enjoyed flying, but there was always a feeling of apprehension when you were on ops and I used to wonder how long I would last. I told myself I'd be all right, but I could not be sure. I used to nip into Lincoln to a dance hall when I had time. The music and moving across the dance floor with a girl in my arms helped push the bombing to the back of my mind for a couple of hours. I didn't have a girlfriend but the dancing was so wonderfully relaxing and did me a lot of good.'

On the night of 3/4 December 1943, Mercer came in at 20,500ft over the target three times at Leipzig in Lancaster DV331 before he was satisfied they would hit it.

'Leipzig was a hairy area, fairly busy, heavily defended, and a lot of flak was coming up at us but Bill Barker, my bomb aimer, twice told me we weren't approaching the target indicator on the right heading. Over the years I've looked back at this and thought I must have been out of my tiny mind. It was dark with 10/10ths cloud, and I twice had to rejoin the main stream, not the safest manoeuvre. But we were instructed to bomb on a certain heading on one of the TIs. If you weren't on the right heading at the right speed then your bombs would not hit the target. We always wanted to feel that we'd hit the target. You went to do a job and do it properly or your efforts were wasted.'

On the morning of 6 December Mercer's brother was killed

while practising formation flying.

'Richard, a flying officer, was with 296 Squadron based at Hurn, near Bournemouth. He was on a training flight when their Albemarle had engine trouble and finished up in an untidy heap near the airfield. He was twenty-three. I was given a forty-eight-hour pass to attend his funeral.'

A lack of oil pressure in the starboard engine had forced the Albemarle pilot to break away and attempt a landing. He missed the runway at the first attempt and next time the engine stopped. The pilot was unable to prevent the port engine, at full power, pulling the aircraft over on to its back.

On 7 January 1944 Ted Mercer and his crew set off at 3.45pm for a routine air firing exercise off the Lincolnshire coast in Lancaster ME574 KM W-Willie. The weather was cold, but clear and dry and they would be in the air for forty-five minutes.

Before takeoff both gunners had talked about swapping positions for this flight. Bill Welch, the mid-upper gunner had eagerly expressed a wish to experience a flight in the rear turret which he knew would be totally different to being perched on top of the aeroplane.

'I've never been in the tail before, I just want to see what it's like,' he told Mercer, who had no objection to the two men exchanging positions. Sergeant W. J. Manley climbed into the mid-upper turret as his crewmate enjoyed a different view from the tail.

There was a new face in the cockpit that afternoon. Bert Capps had been replaced by Flight Lieutenant 'Chunky' Burrows, the short, stocky flight engineer leader who told Mercer he wanted to keep his hand in. It was a decision he later regretted.

Returning to the airfield Burrows reported overheating in the port outer engine which was shut down. Ted Mercer recalls how an ordinary training exercise unexpectedly turned into disaster.

'We got back to Dunholme Lodge but I made a bad approach, knew I wasn't going to make it and went round again.

'Something I didn't know a lot about at the time was the pitfalls of asymmetric flying. If you have an engine stopped – particularly an outboard one – there is a speed below which you will not keep straight. I was below that speed when I came to open up the power. It's all right if you're on low power, but not at full power. This is why I couldn't keep it straight. The trim of the whole aircraft had been affected by the loss of that engine and the two starboard engines were trying to pull us to the left, so I had to put right rudder on, but it wasn't enough because of the low speed. I was only maintaining the height we had. If we'd been able to get a clear run we might have got a bit of height.

'No one was terribly worried at this stage. The crew were all at their stations except the bomb aimer who was sitting near the wireless operator. That was standard practice. I had told control that I was going round again and no other aircraft were in the circuit. As I came over the runway at full power, I was already turning because I couldn't keep it straight.'

The Lancaster was flying roughly at 90mph at a height of between fifty and 100 feet, the pilot still struggling to gain altitude and keep the bomber straight after he had passed over the airfield. It was then he noticed the line of pylons stepping out arrogantly in front of him, hanging dull, but deadly, necklaces of electrical cables beyond the airfield. Normally pilots took little notice of them, except registering the vague thought that they were not ideally positioned for someone in a sick aircraft anxiously looking for a painless touchdown. Which is what Ted Mercer thought now.

As he was not gaining height and it was too risky to try flying under the cables he decided to do a safe wheels-up crash landing. His crew, who could do nothing to help, trusted him to get them down in one piece.

Here was a pilot who had brought his Lancaster safely back from the other side of the Alps on three engines and had survived the unpleasantness of Berlin more times than he could remember and now a piddling little training flight was getting the better of him. He would probably get his leg pulled later in the mess.

Fields unfurled beneath them, some more attractive and inviting than others, but there was no time to be selective as the pylons were getting worryingly closer. A long hedge, with a tall tree looming out of it, briefly registered as he wrestled with the controls.

He watched the ground, rougher than he would have liked, come up rather too quickly to meet them. The Lancaster struck it on her belly with a tortured kerumph and swivelled round in a complete crunching circle, the rear turret smashing into the tree. Flames flickered balefully from three hot engines,spreading quickly. Fire is a great motivator inside an aircraft and six men scrambled out within seconds.The seventh, Bill Welch, trapped in the crushed rear turret, had come to the end of his joy ride. Although the others saw his initial futile struggles to escape, his legs were held fast inside the turret, and their frantic efforts to release him were hopeless. The gunner, who had sustained multiple .injuries, slipped into unconsciousness from which he would not recover. He was dead before he could be pulled from the wreckage.

Appalled by the savage moment it took to reduce one healthy young man to a lump of torn and battered flesh his crewmates were, at first, ashamed that their relief at being alive had overwhelmed their shock and sorrow at their comrade's sudden death. Their sense of shame soon passed. It had to in war otherwise those who were left to fight would be continually blaming themselves for the death and injury of others. RAF discipline had taught these young men that they did not have enough time to mourn everyone who did not survive.

'First on the scene were some officers from control, and the station commander, Group Captain Butler, was also there. We were ushered away from the crash site before anything was done with the rear turret.They never told me what they did with the turret, or Bill.And I didn't want to ask.They were trying to get him out when we left. The engines had caught fire initially, spreading to the fuel tanks.The aircraft was burned out.

'There was, of course, an inquiry into the crash and it was decided that I had not flown the aircraft properly. If you were adjudged to have been at least partly responsible for an accident, a red endorsement was put into your logbook. My station commander put one in mine, but it was attached to it so inadequately it was clear that he had not intended for it to be in there permanently and I removed it.'

For a long time afterwards Mercer re-ran the seconds leading up to the crash through his mind, asking himself if he could somehow have made a better job of the landing.

'We would all have been all right if that damned tree had not been there,' he says quietly. 'Looking back it was partly bad luck and partly inexperience and ignorance. My total flying hours were 700, less than half on Lancs.These days you wouldn't get a licence as a copilot with those hours.But we coped as well as we could.In 1940,some of the fighter boys had a lot less experience than we had on bombers.'

Comparing the staggering similarity of his crash to his brother's, Ted Mercer says: 'They were both examples of the problem when applying full power with one engine stopped – and in Richard's case, fifty per cent of the power.

No one could ever be sure how a crash involving loss of life and an aircraft could affect a pilot emotionally. Mercer endured a short period of testing his nerve and ability following the crash, in the middle of which came an unexpected surprise.

On 9 January Mercer went up with his flight commander, Squadron Leader Shorthouse, to practise landings and three-engine overshoots.On 13 January he took off again on an air test and formation flying.Six days later he carried out a night-flying test and more formation flying.

It was during this period that Mercer learned that he had been awarded an immediate DFC. The citation, signed by Group Captain Butler, dated 15 January 1944, reads:

'Flying Officer Mercer has now completed twenty-three successful operational sorties including six against Berlin, two against Munich and three to Italy. This record has provided much evidence of his high courage and his determination.As,for example, the attack on Leipzig on 3 December 1943 when he made three bombing runs because he was not satisfied with the heading and speed of his aircraft at the release point.

'This officer has recently been involved in a crash in which his rear gunner died in the aircraft in spite of the efforts of his comrades to extricate him. Coming on top of the strain of an operational tour nearly completed it required courage and character to decide, as Flying Officer Mercer quickly did, that it was his duty to resume and complete his operational tour as quickly as possible.

'His conduct in the incident described above comes as no surprise to his colleagues of crew and squadron to whom his selfless devotion to duty and high personal courage have been an inspiration throughout his association with them. I strongly recommend Flying Officer Mercer for an immediate award of the Distinguished Flying Cross.'

On 20 January, having satisfied senior officers that he was a good pilot despite that one mistake, he was back on ops: to Berlin,his seventh trip to the Big City. He had two new gunners,

Flight Sergeant E. D. Pratt and Warrant Officer C. A. Wilkie. They came from a crew in which the others had finished their tour. Manley joined a crew short of one gunner.

Berlin was a stiff test for a young pilot who had just been through a traumatic experience. Ted Mercer says:

'Operations against Berlin were always hectic. It was very heavily defended. So was the Ruhr but you got there and back a little bit more quickly, if you survived, and you weren't over enemy territory as long as when you were going to Berlin, Munich, Stuttgart or Leipzig. There were also places en route to Berlin which were protected by large numbers of anti-aircraft guns. We were attacked by fighters on ops to Berlin but we had practised the corkscrew a good deal during training. I was quite a hot operator on the corkscrew.

'The rear gunner on two different occasions had detected a fighter on our tail and yelled: "Dive port!" I went down port, changing, up port, rolling, up starboard, changing, down starboard, rolling, down port. We'd completed a sequence of corkscrewing and escaped, losing between 500ft and 1,000ft. This manoeuvre was also used if you were caught in a cone of searchlights.'

Mercer aborted the sortie to Berlin after the starboard inner engine of Lancaster DV384 lost power, began misfiring and created considerable vibration. The engine was feathered, bombs jettisoned, and they returned safely to base on three engines.

He was promoted to flight lieutenant at the beginning of February.

They set off for Berlin again on 15 February in ME634, attacking the city satisfactorily from 21,000ft in 10/10ths cloud. When he was debriefed back at Dunholme Lodge, Mercer told the intelligence officer:

'The route was good and the Pathfinders were quite good. The target was identified by Gee and we bombed in the centre of three Wanganui flares. The cloud was too thick for anything to be seen of fires or definite results, but the bombing appeared to be quite well concentrated.'

Mercer's last sortie, his twenty-ninth, was in ND574 to Augsburg on 25 February 1944 after which he reported they could see the fires taking hold when they were still fifty miles short of the target.

The pilot had done more sorties than his crew who carried

on flying with other pilots. Navigator Vic Purvis was later awarded a DFC, but he was killed with all his crew on the attack on St-Leu-d'Esserent on 7 July 1944. Three 44 Squadron aircraft came down that night and ten men were killed. Bomb aimer Bill Barker, who received a DFM, survived his first tour. Wireless operator Bert Baker was later awarded a DFC.

The following month Mercer went on a course at 1660 HCU, Swinderby, to instruct on Stirling IIIs. In May 1944 he was at 1654 HCU, Wigsley, Nottinghamshire, again as an instructor.

'All aircraft, because of the torque factor from the propellers, had a tendency to swing. With the Stirling, the swing was to port. You had to correct this on the rudders and by opening up on the port engines ahead of the starboard motors. Some pupils didn't always manage this very well and a swing on a Stirling very easily got out of control and you'd get a collapsed undercarriage. At one stage I remember counting five Stirlings in silly-looking positions around the airfield.

'On one occasion a chap swung on takeoff and began heading right towards the control tower. There was some rough ground in front of the tower, the port undercarriage collapsed and the wing tip dug into the ground. There was no fire and no one was hurt but the crash fractured a fuel tank. My flight commander, who had been sitting in his office watching this all happen, grabbed a bucket and came running out with it to hold under the dripping petrol saying that it was doing no one any good draining into the ground. He filled the bucket and promptly syphoned it into his car. I can't imagine what effect high-octane fuel had on an ordinary car in those days. This was at a time when I didn't even own a bicycle. When I wasn't flying and wanted to go somewhere I just caught a bus or walked.'

Ted Mercer was demobbed from the RAF in July 1946, but carried on flying, joining BOAC. He retired with Monarch Airlines at the end of September 1982, a month before his sixtieth birthday. After forty-one years as the pilot of many different aeroplanes, he had logged 22,350 flying hours.

CHAPTER NINETEEN

COLLISION

A shadowy figure moved furtively through the billet of two dozen sleeping young men, bare feet padding slowly but purposefully across the polished linoleum floor. Ignoring the medley of grunts, belches, farts, and whinnying nightmares, which had been coarsely tuned by that night's merry intake of beer at the sergeants' mess, he paused by a bed.

Reaching down to clutch the metal frame, he heaved. As his gasping flailing victim slid to the floor the airman ran back to his own bed, stifling a triumphant chortle, and assumed the curled-up posture of deep and contented sleep.

Twenty-year-old Les Duggan, struggling miserably on the cold linoleum in a tangle of sheets and blankets, dragged the rattling bed upright, sorted out the mattress, drew the bedding up to his ears and lay there, heart thumping, angrily plotting revenge. This was the third time he had been tipped out of bed while fast asleep and he was fed up with it. A shy, sensitive lad he had hoped in vain that his crewmates would get bored with this silly and upsetting nightly ritual. He knew they were testing him and knew also that he had to do something about it.

Next night, after lights out, before his tormentors were due to get started, he moved swiftly through the Nissen hut and catapulted three Canadians out of their beds.

Duggan says: 'They left me alone after that. It had all started because I was so shy about getting undressed in front of so many chaps, sliding out of my underpants and into pyjamas at the side of the bed. That night I grew up a little, for in their eyes I had become one of them.'

His shyness among strangers was an unexpected anxiety because he was used to having a lot of people around him. He was brought up in a small two-bedroom terraced house in Droitwich, Worcestershire, where six children shared two beds in one room, while a seventh squeezed into the cramped boxroom. Duggan's father, Tommy, was a shunter on the railway and money was tight. Dripping was more often spread on bread than jam, apples and oranges were rare luxuries, and the children wore hand-me-downs. Les Duggan's first pair of long trousers had been worn by a waiter.

A bright boy, he should have gone to grammar school, but his parents could not afford the uniform and they needed him to start earning money. He was a roundsman for the Co-op, before joining the RAF in October 1941. An athletic six-footer, he qualified as a wireless operator/air gunner, and joined Bill Cameron's crew at 23 OTU, Stratford (Atherstone). In the summer of 1943 they were posted to 419 (Moose) Squadron at Middleton St George, County Durham. Duggan remembers his skipper with affection:

'Bill was an only child born to middle-aged parents in Sarnia, Ontario. He didn't smoke, and didn't drink until he started flying bombers, then he learned how to enjoy a beer with a whisky chaser. He was a little dour, but had a sense of humour; not wicked, but you could get a laugh out of him. He was about twenty-one, a broad strong silent man. We were all sergeants, about the same age, except the rear gunner, and we got on together absolutely fine.'

Navigator Ernie Birtch, from Ottawa, a diminutive figure, was a quiet, private individual. The bomb aimer, Victor 'Windy' Wintzer, tall and slender, was brought up in Ontario. Paddy Mullany, the only other non-Canadian in the crew, an Irishman, was the flight engineer.

Mid-upper gunner Beverly Scharf, a smart brash good-looking six-footer, was believed to have added a year to his age before being accepted into the Royal Canadian Air Force. Like Cameron, he hailed from Sarnia, Ontario. Unlike Cameron he occasionally had to be taken by his crewmates to their aeroplane and connected to the oxygen supply which was admirable for dealing with hangovers.

Bert Boos – pronounced 'Bows' – the swarthy rear gunner, from Calgary, was ten years older than the others. He was small and thin, but his charm and the mischievous glint in his eye made him irresistible to women. On their days off the crew went to the spa town of Harrogate, known for its refinement and culture. The gunner came as rather a shock to the genteel middle classes for he had no compunction in making passionate love during the day to his girlfriend in the town's public gardens.

Their first really testing operation came on the night of 28/29 June when the target was Cologne and they were briefly attacked by a fighter and struck by a blast of flak. Duggan, methodically feeding Window through the flare chute astern, knew nothing about either incident, until glancing down he saw a hole in the floor about two inches from his feet. He looked up and saw a matching cavity in the roof. As horror merged belatedly with instinct for self-preservation he pressed his thighs together and covered his manhood. Even today he chuckles at the memory.

The rear gunner saw off a Ju-88 and a Messerschmitt Bf-110 during a six-hour trip to Aachen on 13/14 July, but their war became even more lively the following month. Duggan says:

'We had just got back off leave when we were sent to Hamburg on 2 August. We ran into a storm with violent lightning and had to jettison our bombs. It was a horrible night and came at the end of the period when Hamburg was virtually obliterated.'

Les Duggan cannot remember the target they were approaching when his pilot was taken short, only the ghastly effect it had on him personally.

'Bill was desperate to go to the toilet but was not going to ask someone to take over the controls so he could hurry aft to the Elsen. I took the batteries out of my torch and handed it to him, thinking that would be sufficient. It wasn't. The overflow, which was quite considerable, squirted over my face and leather helmet. I yelled: "Bloody hell Bill, you've pissed all over me."' On subsequent trips the wireless operator appreciated Cameron's thoughtfulness in providing himself with a more reliable emergency receptacle.

Ops to Mannheim and Nuremburg followed and on 12 August they went to Milan where he was awed by the snow-capped peaks of the Alps, often towering above them, seeming close enough to flick off a wing.

Les Duggan celebrated his twenty-first birthday in a low-key manner by flying to Peenemünde on 17 August, when they were part of a force of 596 aircraft briefed to attack the target on the

Baltic coast where the Germans were developing the secret V2 rockets.

'We normally liked to get up to 20,000ft to bomb but tonight we had to drop the bombs from 4,000ft. We'd been told that if we did not wipe out the site then we would have to go back the next night, and every succeeding night until it was destroyed, so we were keyed up for this one.

'I saw four aircraft coned by searchlights on the way to Peenemünde. The flak came sweeping up and all four bombers exploded. They just disappeared. I remember thinking that if we were hurt or damaged the neutral Sweden was not that far away and we might have put down there. Shortly afterwards, near Flensburg, Germany, just below the Danish border, we were coned.'

The searchlights stuck doggedly to their prey as the gunners below moved quickly to calculate the bomber's position, begin the chase and deliver the aircraft and its crew to a Baltic graveyard. The Halifax hurtled into an almost suicidal dive, down a smooth cliff face of sky, chased by the lights and clawed at by flak which never quite managed to turn its plunge into crash, but there were compensations for the ack-ack batteries in the long stream of other aircraft coming over to be shot at. Forty bombers were lost that night, but the raid was considered a great success, setting back the Germans' work on the V2.

Cameron's crew dropped their bombs and Duggan remembers his amazement at seeing dust and debris from the destruction below being flung above their aircraft.

The sorties piled up: Leverkusen, Berlin, Nuremburg and Mönchengladbach. They were working satisfactorily through their tour, having notched up over a dozen bombing operations, when an announcement came over the Tannoy ordering Cameron, Birtch, Wintzer, Duggan and Boos to report immediately to their squadron commander's office. Duggan remembers their curiosity at this unexpected invitation.

'We were one of the senior crews at a time when chaps were averaging three operations if they were lucky. We thought that because of the number of ops we'd completed the skipper was, perhaps, being recommended for a gong. Or maybe we were all going to get a nice pat on the back.'

It did not occur to them that because Wing Commander Fleming had not wanted to see Paddy Mullany or Bev Scharf, whom they had picked up at 1664 Heavy Conversion Unit, Croft, they should search farther back in their memory for a possible explanation.

Fleming glared at the five men as they filed into his office, not sure if they should stand at attention or throw him friendly grins. Some squadron commanders were known for their unsettling habit of initially disguising good news with a scowl, so they were relaxed, unprepared for Fleming's wrath.

The wing commander took up a piece of official-looking paper which he flourished before his darkened face and he launched into them fiercely as if they were a bunch of unruly schoolboys, and a late night escapade some weeks earlier filtered uneasily into their minds.

'While at OTU we had one particularly memorable night on the booze in Stratford-on-Avon,' says Duggan. 'The pubs were closed, everyone was staggering home and we got on our bicycles to ride back to base. We didn't have lights but we were, after all, regularly going off to bomb Germany to save Britain. What did it matter that we didn't carry lights on our bikes? We were laughing, singing and wobbling about then suddenly met a zealous policeman standing in the road waving us down. I suppose we were all drunk but managed to give him our names and service numbers which he wrote down in his notebook. We all thought that was that, but no. British justice prevailed and we were to be summoned. We couldn't believe it but Fleming read us the riot act for being stupid and upsetting the policeman. We didn't go to court and the squadron paid our fines.'

On 31 August, Bill Cameron was at the controls of Halifax JD270-VR P-Peter which heaved itself off the runway from Middleton St George at 7.58pm. It was their sixteenth operation. The target: the big city, Berlin. Still frozen in their mind was the visit to the German capital on 23 August which Duggan, remembering the blitz of flak awaiting them, describes as 'frightening'. Berlin and the Ruhr were always synonymous with heavy flak and considerable fighter activity, which all added up to a ferocious defence of the German capital.

The flak was heavy this night too as they began their bombing run at 20,000ft over the city where fires were already burning fiercely. Cameron held the Halifax steady as his bomb aimer began directing him gradually towards Pathfinder markers which had been dropped south of the centre of the target after difficulties with their H2S equipment. Duggan recalls the tumultuous moment which led to the deaths of four crewmates and a prolonged spell in prisoner of war camps for the others.

'We released our bombs and had just left the target area, preparing to turn for home when there was a hell of a crash and I was knocked off my feet.'

It was an explosive sound of tearing and disintegration, accompanied by the dull debilitating fear of terminal damage. At first some thought they had received a direct hit from a shell. But there had been the briefest flicker of rapid movement as a dark shape passed extremely close to the Halifax and veered off. They had collided with a German fighter. Had the fighter been a few feet nearer they would have gone straight down.

'The outer tip of the port wing had been sliced away and our port outer engine was on fire. The engineer put the fire out and tried to feather the propeller, but it continued to cartwheel round. The aircraft was still going straight and reasonably level, heading for home. There was no tension aboard at this point. Certainly, I was not frightened to death about what had happened. I knew if anything happened to us it would be over in an instant and we'd know nothing about it. We don't know what happened to the fighter, it went off into the clouds.'

They had the typical black sense of humour which attached itself to most bomber aircrews, but none considered that they would claim the German aircraft as a 'possible' when they returned to base. There was too much to think about and they were hoping their luck would hold and they could make it back to England. It was soon clear that they would be lucky to clear Germany for as they headed towards home they could see pieces falling off the port wing which, before their eyes, was disconcertingly getting shorter.

The damage to the wing spread as if it had been infected with a particularly virulent form of dry rot. Bill Cameron complained of the controls sticking and asked Les Duggan and Bev Scharf to see if any big packages of Window had slipped during the collision and were jamming any vital equipment, but they found nothing unusual.

The crew heard the clipped exchanges between the skipper and flight engineer as hope turned quickly to anxiety before plummeting to despair as more chunks of wing, severely weakened by the collision and increasingly enfeebled by the vibration of the engines, were whipped away in the slipstream.

'Not much more than two minutes passed between the collision and the moment when the port outer engine literally fell off the plane and we now had less than half our port wing remaining. The aircraft became unstable, tipped to one side, and went into a dive. The skipper told us to prepare for baling out. At the rear, Boos, Scharf and myself had our 'chutes on and we listened patiently for Bill's instructions over the intercom.'

The trio assumed that bomb aimer Windy Wintzer and navigator Ernie Birtch, who would leave by the forward escape hatch in the nose, had also clipped on their parachutes. They waited while Cameron and Mullany struggled to drag up the nose of their crippled aircraft, praying they would succeed, while knowing it was unlikely. Duggan, gripped by a persistent worry, suddenly switched on his intercom.

'What height are we, Bill? There was a pause, then the reply came: "Less than 5,000ft, Doug. Time to bale out, boys." Boos, Scharf and myself went quickly to the rear escape hatch.'

Many aircrew given the order to jump hesitated. It was surely, after all, not the act of a totally sober individual to launch himself into space from a disabled aeroplane without having the benefit of any proper training to do so. Such vacillation cost many men their lives during the bomber war. At the rear of the doomed Halifax three men looked fearfully into the void which had the additional disconcerting intimidation of Germany being spread out beneath it. A red carpet would not be waiting for them. What would be?

'You would hardly believe it,' says Duggan, 'but we had a discussion about who was going out first. One said: "You go first." And the one who was pointed at said: "No, you go."'

It was as if time had been suspended while they carried out a hurried but well-mannered consideration of who deserved to be the first man out. Should it be the oldest? The youngest? The one with longest service, or whoever had most commitments at home? The bomber plunged below 4,000ft towards eternity as Duggan brought the tense debate to an end. At least now the aircraft was going down at a less precipitous angle.

'I went out first, in a hurry, but quite easily. Some time later Bert told me: "Your bloody parachute was practically open before you left the plane." I was lucky because obviously it could have caught the tail plane, wrapped around it, and that would have been the end of me.

'I was scared coming down. It was dark, but I noticed the outline of woods as I drew near to the ground. I landed in a field near two haystacks, not far from the town of Halle. I crept into one of the haystacks and lit a fag to calm my nerves.'

Forty-seven aircraft were lost on this raid, including two other Halifaxes from 419 Squadron. A total of 237 men died, three were fatally injured, 101 became POWs, and three were evaders.

No one knows why Birtch and Wintzer were unable to bale out of P-Peter. Duggan believes they may have failed to open the escape hatch. Cameron and Mullany also died in the wreck.

Stubbing out the cigarette Duggan's nostrils were pleasantly assailed by the smell of hay. A summer's night in Germany seemed much the same as in England and with a little imagination he could almost imagine that he had slipped out of the camp at Middleton St George to walk across a field. But he was a lucky man, still alive after a midair collision.

'I was understandably nervous. We'd heard that there were men unlucky to be shot down over Berlin after bombing the city who had actually been thrown alive into the flames of burning buildings. I was some distance south of Berlin but the thought still troubled me.

'I spent a while in the haystack then got to my feet. I'd hidden my parachute in nearby woods. I had a little compass and knew which way to walk. West. I can't remember hearing anything. It was a quiet night.

'I was wearing my flying boots which were not made for walking and it was hard going over the fields. I somehow got on to a road when it was gradually getting lighter. A single-deck bus suddenly passed me on an empty road, well out of town. It had some sort of gas propulsion, and a big contraption was carried on the trailer it was towing. I remember saying to myself: "You really are damned lucky," when there was a screech of brakes. The coach began emptying, there was a loud pattering of feet and I was surrounded by thirty to forty people, men and women, young and old who were on their way to work. They didn't treat me too badly, but directed me towards the bus and I got in.

'I went to sit down and was angrily hollered at. I don't know what they were saying but they were satisfied when I remained standing. They wanted to keep their eyes on me.

'I was taken into Halle and locked in a police cell. Shortly afterwards angry people began pouring into the police station, it was obvious they were after my hide. Shouting and pointing at me, no more than ten feet away, they looked pretty ferocious and unpleasant. From the noise they were making and the expressions on their faces I knew they wanted to take me outside and string me up. I was petrified. There was only one policeman on duty and it is due to him that I'm here today. He could easily have handed me over, or they could have overpowered him and grabbed me. But he pulled a gun out and seemed to be warning them not to make any moves towards me. They gradually dispersed and it quietened down.'

Eventually two armed Luftwaffe airmen came to take him to Kothen aerodrome. But the airman's ordeal continued.

'We went outside and I was made to stand in the middle of the road while the two Germans were on either side of me on the pavements. Then we walked. It was pretty frightening. I was in full view of everybody who knew who and what I was, then we got into a truck.

'I was treated well at the aerodrome although they gave me a good rollicking when I refused to eat the meal put in front of me. It looked like soup but was horrible. They gave me an apple instead.'

At Dulag Luft Duggan was told he was being sent to a punishment camp following the Allies' indiscreet bombing of Munich where Adolf Hitler had been addressing a meeting or rally.

After three days crammed in a railway truck, unable to sit down, he entered the gates of Stalag IVb, Mühlberg, south of Dresden.

'We had to wait outside while Russian prisoners were moved out. The big hut we were moved into was filthy in every possible way, with faeces and urine on the floor and rats running about the rafters. We cleared up the huts which were crowded with three-tier bunks.

'We were told the Germans had made the mistake of letting three Alsatians into the compound to keep the Russians under control. But the Russians, who were starving, killed and ate the dogs. When we got organised, which wasn't often, we gave some of our food to the Russians who did not receive the equivalent to our Red Cross parcels, and we didn't get many at Mühlberg.

'We became so weak through lack of food that when we walked to the bog in the hut if two of us met one didn't step aside. We slid or sidled past each other. Bert Boos was in the same hut. He was a good man and helped me overcome the difficulty of being a POW. He was small, as thin as a rake, and seemed able to live on nothing. He shared his food with me. For instance, if we had two slices of bread he always gave me his crusts.'

Boos was also enterprising and fearless. In winter temperatures plummeted, fuel was in short supply, there never being enough to feed the one big stove in the hut. Morale was at a low ebb and the Canadian had a plan to do something about it.

'Somehow Bert made a key which would open the door to the fuel store. The building was fenced off from the rest of the camp and one night he and I crept out of the hut, ducking down to avoid the searchlights from the watchtowers. We cut a way through the wire fence surrounding our compound and slid into a sort of channel between two more wire barriers. I was quite scared.'

Duggan's fear might have been prompted by remembering the POW at Mühlberg who was shot for reaching through the wire to pick a wild strawberry.

It was not a straightforward route to the store and it took some time but the false key worked and they filled sacks with coal briquettes and dragged them back to the hut. Eventually working details for plundering fuel were organised all round the camp until the Germans changed the locks. Duggan does not remember any reprisals being taken against prisoners.

'One man I will never forget at Muhlberg was a feldwebel, a small man, but a bastard. He would line us up and if one man's face was not to his liking he bashed him cruelly with his rifle. After we had been liberated by the Russian Cossacks the feldwebel was found hanging from a tree.'

Life became curiously unpredictable after the Germans had fled the camp. The Russians ordered the POWs to remain until official orders came through for them to be moved out, but the men were starving and ranged through the countryside looking for food, until they walked so far they decided not to return.

Duggan lost contact with Bert Boos, learning months later that his crewmate was lucky to escape serious injury riding in a Jeep which had collided head-on with a Tiger tank manned by inebriated Germans.

'I was with Fred Taylor, an Australian pilot who had been shot down on his first op,' says Duggan. 'We met a German, a decent lad, who was also scrounging food. He'd been with a tank regiment and lost an arm on the Russian front. His name was Leufman and he invited us to his home in Bismarckstrasse, Riesa, for a meal.

'At his apartment he introduced us to his charming wife and their son and she cooked a good corned beef hash which we washed down with a drop of whisky. He later took us to a shed where he had hidden a Luger pistol, explaining that if the Russians came and turned nasty one bullet was for his wife, another for his son, and a third for himself.

'We met a young English-speaking German woman who had a horse and cart and asked us to go as her protectors to Hamburg. We said no, realising if the Russians found us together they would have raped her and shot us. We heard of many German women being raped by Russian soldiers.

'We walked across the ruins of a bridge over the Elbe where the Americans were based. Passing several houses who should I see at one but Bev Scharf. When I shouted for him to come with us he pointed to a pretty Polish girl and shook his head, grinning. He was happy to stay.'

A few weeks later Les Duggan got off a bus in Droitwich and began walking through the dark streets. For many months he had longed for the end of the war, fantasising about meeting friends and going to The Swan pub in Ombersley Street, and Salters Hall cinema. But he had changed. He had not only lost over five of his thirteen stones in Germany, the rigours of being a POW had eroded his self-confidence and dignity until he had become frightened of people.

'I was painfully thin, not good to look at. I hadn't had a breakdown, but something had happened to me and I hid myself as much as I could in the town. I didn't want to meet people. I could not handle what I had been through and didn't want to be asked questions about my experiences. I slipped into Nine Foot Alley which led to my home in St Nicholas Street. Outside the house was a big "Welcome home, Les" sign with bunting and flags, but I didn't see them until I was taken out next day.

'My nerves had been shot to pieces, I had trouble eating, and occasionally frightened my family by dancing on my bed brandishing a German bayonet. Eventually I quietened down and followed my dad and grandfather by getting a job on the railway.'

CHAPTER TWENTY

A FUTURE BEYOND TOMORROW

The Lancaster skimmed sedately over the sleeping Leicestershire countryside, its four engines purring sweetly, wheels down, flaps fully extended. At the end of a series of circuits and landings the eyes of the skipper, Pilot Officer John McCarthy, were riveted on the Bottesford runway no more than 300ft ahead when, suddenly, both starboard engines stopped.

Sergeant John Banfield had been sitting comfortably at his wireless set, when disaster loomed. He recalls the next excruciating seconds.

'The aircraft veered to starboard, I thought Mac was trying to put us down on the perimeter track which ran virtually parallel with the public road, but we kept turning towards a farmhouse in the small village of Normanton. We hit several heavy trees in the garden, which severed the undercarriage from the fuselage and were skidding along at 100mph when the two port motors wrapped themselves around a huge willow at the side of the road. The starboard wing struck a chimneystack at Normanton Lodge, removed a corner of a bedroom, hit the deck and caught fire.'

The farmer's daughter stood trembling at the window of her shattered bedroom, staring at wreckage engulfed by flames beyond her home, unable to imagine anyone getting out alive.

'We were lucky,' says Banfield. 'All four of us escaped through the starboard sliding window without injury.'

It was just after 1.30am when McCarthy and his three crewmates emerged from a ditch beyond the burning aircraft and looked back at Lancaster R5498 Z–Zebra burning itself out.

'A careful search of the wreckage revealed the cause of the crash was a faulty fuel pump. The same thing had happened that night to another Lancaster on the same exercise, but it managed to recover at 2,000ft and landed on two engines at Waddington. Another faulty fuel pump.'

Possible sabotage was ruled out as the cause of engine failure in both aircraft on the early morning of 8 April 1942. But Z-Zebra's crash demonstrated how quickly a comfortable flight could turn into tragedy; and how an aircrew relaxing for a second could quickly become a dead aircrew.

Although perturbed by their narrow escape John Banfield was not a stranger to drama.

'While I was at 14 OTU, Cottesmore, Rutland, in June 1941, we flew Hampdens and Ansons, mostly cast-offs from operational squadrons and serviced by green ground crews. There were a lot of flying accidents. I was called out for pall-bearing duty three times after three different accidents.

'A German aircraft came over one night, describing a smoke ring directly over the airfield, marking the target. Half-a-dozen German bombers then went through the ring and released their bombs, luckily hitting nothing apart from the ground. The following night we were sitting in the mess when Lord Haw-Haw came on the wireless and said RAF Cottesmore had been razed to the ground.'

The longer a man served in the RAF, the more often his attention was drawn to the difficulty of planning a future beyond tomorrow. The thirty men on a gunnery course at 10 Bomber and Gunnery School, Dumfries, with Banfield the previous month were given an early chance to put their future on to a more secure footing.

'The station warrant officer told us: "Anybody who wants to pull out from becoming aircrew can do so now without disgrace. All that will happen is you'll be discharged from the RAF and called up later in the normal way."'

'Nobody dropped out of the course and we carried on flying Whitleys up and down the Solway Firth, shooting at drogues towed by Fairey Battle light bombers. One day a Battle managed to collide with a Whitley. Luckily they were at a fair height, the Whitley pilot skilfully aimed at the Dumfries runway and put down successfully. The Battle made a forced landing on a sandy beach. Although the gunner in the Whitley's rear turret was flung back into the fuselage by the impact of the collision no one was hurt. Lucky devils.'

John Banfield, brought up in Hayes, Kent, was an apprentice printer on a weekly wage of 7s 6d (37½p) when he joined the RAF on 3 September 1940, exactly 12 months after war had been declared. He was twenty.

'I was a bit naive, I thought our targets would all be military and,of course, they weren't,it was total war. But total war didn't become evident until the Germans started bombing London and then it didn't bother me.'

In September 1941 he was posted to 207 Squadron at Waddington and promptly laid low by paratyphoid which, he said, caused a mild panic within 5 Group during his five-week isolation in Lincoln City Hospital.Time dragged as he listened gloomily to bombers droning almost constantly overhead, on training exercises by day, and at night, heading to and from enemy targets. Discharged from hospital the second wireless operator/front air gunner languished further weeks in station sick quarters at Waddington before being returned to 207 Squadron in December.

By now 207 Squadron had moved to Bottesford with twin-engine Manchesters and Banfield, now a spare bod, was pleased to take over from a sick front gunner on 22 January 1942 for his first sortie. The skipper was the sumptuously-moustached Flying Officer Jack Wooldridge DFM,known affectionately as 'Dim'. A composer, having studied with Sibelius,he often excused himself from the mess to work on his symphony. Flying second dickey in R5796 on the attack against Münster was John McCarthy, a burly former New Zealand policeman, whose crew Banfield would join the following month.

'We had a steady run in, soon locating the target by the horseshoe shape of the Dortmund-Ems canal around the town. Dim was a wizard pilot because as he went in he throttled back, then accelerated, and each time a cone of searchlights came up, either at the front or behind us. He seemed to read what the searchlights would do. That could be one of the reasons why he made it to the end of the war.

'Six 1,000lb bombs went down from 15,000ft and we turned on a course for home. I saw two lights moving below and reported this to Dim who said: "Let's have a look." We went down to 500ft and saw a train pulling away from Münster. Dim aimed the aircraft towards the lights, I lined up my guns and fired a burst into them.'

They passed over the train, turned to follow it, the crew groaning with disappointment to see it disappearing into the safety of a tunnel.

Still a spare bod, Banfield was in the front turret of Flying Officer J. H. 'Prune' Leland's Manchester for the attack against Brest on 25 January.

'I actually saw a German fighter going in front and underneath us and was about to open up when Leland said: "Don't fire at him. Don't attract his attention." So I didn't, but I could have got the damned thing. The trip was spoiled when the navigator got lost coming back. We went all over the place before landing at Bottesford at least two hours late.'

It was his last trip on a Manchester and a third flight was formed at Bottesford to begin converting crews to Lancasters.

There was little to entertain young men at RAF Bottesford, a wartime airfield, opened in September 1941, with its facilities spread over a wide area. It stood in the attractive Vale of Belvoir, but there was nothing appealing about the airfield in the harsh grip of winter. Mud, snow, bitter winds, fog, wet feet, and draughty leaking Nissen huts combined to make this a miserable posting for youngsters trying to fight a war. Resented by some villagers afraid of the sudden influx of 2,000 strangers on their doorsteps, mainly young men with earthy desires, other families took pity on the new arrivals, welcoming them into the cheerful warmth of their homes. Banfield particularly remembers the Doubledays who were frequent hosts to the whole crew.

'Occasionally we had meals with them, but mostly it was general chit-chatting over cups of tea. They were delightful people. Mr Doubleday was the village builder and undertaker. They emigrated to Canada after the war.'

Some crews regarded gardening – laying mines – as easier, less stressful trips. Others treated them with greater respect. Banfield explains:

'When we were mine-laying our instructions were not to fly above 1,200ft. If you released them from a greater height the mines hit the water and exploded even though they came down on parachutes. On 29 May 1942 we dropped five 2,000lb mines from 800ft in the Kattegat, off Copenhagen.

'I was in the front turret as we stooged back along over

Denmark after dropping the mines when a searchlight came up, followed by light flak straight at us. I fired a burst into the searchlight which went out and McCarthy threw the aircraft out of the line of fire, but as we levelled out and passed over the gunsite they opened up again and one shell exploded in the tail unit. A piece of shrapnel went through the arm of our rear gunner, Sergeant Arthur Roddam, a former jockey. Roddy came off flying for a bit, then joined a fresh crew but was killed on an op in August.'

McCarthy and his crew went on all three 1,000-bomber raids which did so much for the morale of Bomber Command and Britain.

'The actual bombing of Cologne on 30/31 May was scheduled to take ninety minutes. It was quite a simple job for us. We were due over the target in the last twenty minutes, but before crossing the Dutch coast we saw what looked like a fiery moon on the horizon. Getting nearer we realised it was Cologne burning. The city was a mass of flames, a horrific scene, when we dropped our bombs into it. I cannot believe how everyone managed to miss the cathedral.'

The crew encountered rather more trouble after attacking Bremen on 29 June 1942.

'We had been briefed not to go out to the north-east of the target after bombing because heavy anti-aircraft guns were known to be in that area. McCarthy, nevertheless, chose to go out that way and, at first, there was no flak. Then we were caught by a box barrage. The first shells exploded together about fifty feet below us. A bit higher and we'd have been blasted out of the sky. We got free of it but the whole of the fuselage was like a colander from shrapnel when we landed at Bottesford.

'The crews on the Manchester and Lancaster bombers would later be changed by replacing the copilot and front gunner/second wireless operator with a flight engineer and bomb aimer. When asked if I would like to re-muster as a bomb aimer, I had said: "Not likely, I don't want to go away for more training." Told I would remain on 207 Squadron during my training, I agreed. It was a decision that saved my life.'

He did one more trip, his fourteenth with John McCarthy, on 19 July, to attack the U-boat construction yards at Vegesack, a few miles down river from Bremen, before leaving his crew on 21 July.

Three days later twenty-seven-year-old McCarthy and his crew were killed on the attack against Duisburg, shot down on the Dutch-German border. The dead included Banfield's replacement, Flight Sergeant Ron Edmonds, and the other two men who had survived the crash at Normanton, Flight Sergeant Leo Da Salle, the Canadian second pilot, and one of the two observers, Flight Sergeant Jack Leahy.

Familiar faces vanished with grim regularity from 207 Squadron and, with equal grimness mixed with dogged determination, those who remained carried on with the war. There was nothing else they could do. Except drink in the mess and local pubs or slip away for an evening enjoying the simple pleasure of village dances at Bottesford and nearby Long Bennington. Enduring attachments were made at these dances. Inevitably, others fizzled out, including John Banfield's friendship with Sedgebrook girl Joan May, after 207 Squadron was posted to Langar on 21 September because the runway at Bottesford was breaking up and needed urgent repairs.

Banfield's new skipper was Flight Sergeant Barry Chaster, a cheerful twenty-one-year-old Canadian of Duncan, Vancouver Island, who had a wide dazzling smile. His crew were all sergeants.

'We didn't talk much about where we'd come from or what we had done before joining the RAF,' says Banfield.'We were so intent on the job in hand.'

Gordon Marwood, twenty-two, from Barking, Essex, was the navigator, Banfield the newly-qualified bomb aimer. The wireless operator was thirty-year-old Ken Pugh. Bill Moger, the only regular airman aboard, was flight engineer, Ivan Lineker, twenty-one, the mid-upper gunner, and twenty-year-old Wally Harris, rear gunner.

Following weeks of low-level formation flying, they were among ninety-four Lancasters from nine 5 Group squadrons sent on a daring daylight attack on 17 October 1942, without fighter escorts, against Le Creusot, where a large Schneider armament factory was said to be the equivalent to Krupps.

'The attacking force was all in a loose box formation. The lead crews were at 500ft, with the others stepped down by 100ft to our squadron's fifteen aircraft in the rear at 200ft. The objective was that we should appear on German radar, then disappear on descending to the lower-level flight for Le Creusot, which was 300 miles inside France.

'The next time we could be detected on German radar was fifty miles from the target, having climbed to 5,000ft to avoid the blast from the 4,000lb bombs, by which time we had been airborne for just over six hours.

'The only loss was one aircraft from 61 Squadron, among six crews detailed to bomb the transformer station supplying the factory with electricity, which went in too low and blew itself up. They were all killed. Apart from that there was just one casualty and he was on our squadron in L7583 A-Apple. His pilot, Sergeant R. S. Wilson, had turned back after the failure of the engine which supplied power to the mid-upper turret. The drill was, if you lost an engine during a daylight op you returned to base. But they were attacked by three Arado floatplanes twenty miles off Brest. The Arados had a fixed forward-firing cannon which meant that although the pilot had a ring sight, he was virtually lining up his aircraft at the target, like a fighter. The floatplanes also had a flexible machine gun at the back.

'Despite the loss of the one turret, two of the German aircraft were shot down and the third turned tail and disappeared. Tragically, the only cannon shell to enter the Lancaster killed the flight engineer, Sergeant Kenneth Chalmers. He was the first chap from 207 Squadron to be killed flying from Langar. They landed safely at St Mawgan, Cornwall.'

There was minimum flak over the target and no enemy fighters attacked the Lancasters, but flying at treetop level across France, birds damaged four aircraft and injured two men.

Barry Chaster was at the controls of Lancaster W4134 EM U-Uncle when they took off from Langar at 5.05pm on 3 January 1943 to take part in an early experimental blind bombing raid. This one, against Essen, with an attacking force of three Pathfinder Mosquitoes and nineteen Lancasters from 5 Group, was Banfield's twenty-fifth sortie.

'The met forecast was 8/10ths cloud over Essen. When we got there it was only about 2/10ths, the searchlights came through easily and we were buffeted about. Flying above 18,000ft, my task was to aim at a flare laid at that height by an Oboe-marking Pathfinder Mosquito at a given time on a given course over the target.

'We overshot the first flare by thirty seconds and I said to Barry: "Go round and I'll catch the second one." The rear gunner had been panicking a bit. I heard him shouting: "For

God's sake, drop the bombs, John." I yelled back: "Hell, no."
Both gunners were scared as we circled round, weaving a little to
line up on the second flare. It was fairly hectic and we were
harassed by searchlights, but I released the bombs successfully.

'We were coned over Essen but managed a tight turn and got
out of it, dodging other cones. We had been briefed to lose
height going home by at least 5,000ft at a time in order to slide
off the German ground control radar screens which would have
to be reset to catch us.

'Ten minutes or so later, flying through the German night
fighter belt between Roermond and Venlo, Holland, I had no
sooner suggested to Barry that we start descending when we
were attacked from astern and below by a Messerschmidt Bf-
110.I was in the front turret and saw tracer come up beneath us.
I lowered the gun and tried unsuccessfully to get the fighter
which had come in from the rear.

'The fighter cannon shell hit just aft of the main spar. It shot
straight through the oxygen cylinders and the main
accumulators – causing the intercom to go dead – and into the
starboard inboard petrol tank which immediately burst into
flames. A petrol line running through forward of the main spar
in the fuselage was severed and blazing away. I felt something pull
on my trouser leg as I got out of the front turret. It was the
navigator, Gordon Marwood, saying: "Bale out!" I thought:
"Fair enough," and clipped the 'chute to my harness. Gordon
had, in fact, misinterpreted Barry's instruction which was:
"Prepare to bale out." But his mistake probably saved our lives.

'I tried to open the escape hatch in the nose, but it wouldn't
budge, probably hit by a shell and jammed.I said to the nav:"Out
through the back door." We'd be singed going through the
blazing petrol line, but might have got away with it and it was
our only chance.

'I followed Gordon up into the fuselage and saw him
disappearing out the starboard side at the point where there was
a sliding window and a perspex blister for looking along the side
of the aircraft. You could get out there although it would be
difficult with a parachute. Then I saw there was a damned great
hole where the window had been.'

An additional obstacle was the starboard inner propeller
which whirled within a foot of the blister and would make
instant mincemeat of any blundering navigator. Before grabbing

Marwood by the heels to drag him back,Banfield saw the engine had been feathered by the engineer and the mainplane was awash with flames.The navigator disappeared,striking his left leg on the tail unit.

'I saw him go and thought:"Hell!"As I got out through the shell hole the slipstream caught me. We were going at around 160mph at the time so it was quite vicious. I was outside, clinging on and my 'chute, still attached to my harness, was still inside the plane.The slipstream had somehow twisted me round and was yanking on me fiercely. If I hadn't the energy to draw the 'chute from inside the aircraft to my chest outside I could have been in trouble. I managed to drag it out, manoeuvred myself into position, let go, fell safely under the mainplane and escaped.

'The last thing I remember was seeing the aircraft go away from me in a ball of flame. I had no recollection of pulling the ripcord, and similarly, nor could a lot of other chaps I've met since.

'I came to hanging from my parachute which had fallen across the top of an elm tree.There was a twenty feet drop between me and the ground. To release yourself from the parachute harness there was a disc on your chest to be pushed and turned.A five-year-old child could do it.But I had run out of energy and hung there helplessly, shouting, for three-quarters of an hour before I saw a row of torches coming towards me. There were some Dutchmen and two Germans. One of the Germans went off, coming back with a ladder and coil of rope. He put crampons on his boots, climbed the tree, neatly transferred me from my parachute to the rope and lowered me down.I couldn't stand up and was lashed to the ladder semi-conscious and taken to a farmhouse.

'My face was cut and bruised, my nose pushed in, my thumb split open and my shoulder hurt. Watched by the family I was cleaned up by Grandma.

'It was about 1am when I was taken to Venlo airfield and examined by a medical officer who spoke good English.He told me I had a badly-wrenched shoulder and concussion.

'Taken fromVenlo, I couldn't walk and rested on the shoulders of two guards.They helped me on to a railway station platform where I saw somebody on a stretcher and the guards took me towards him.Suddenly:"Is that you,Johnny?"Bloody hell,it was

Gordon Marwood. He had a badly cut leg. We were both admitted to Queen Wilhelmina Hospital, the Luftwaffe hospital in Amsterdam, remaining there for four weeks, receiving good medical treatment. We were parted at Dulag Luft, Frankfurt. He was later sent to several different POW camps.'

After Banfield and Marwood had escaped, despite corkscrewing to 15,000ft, the Lancaster was attacked again. The port inner engine cut and the pilot shouted at Bill Moger, his engineer, to pass the word to abandon the aircraft. Moger handed the pilot his parachute and moved resolutely towards the rear of the aircraft. Chaster recalls:

'The aircraft was in a steep dive, but I managed to level out at 5,000ft when the fighter attacked for a third time. His fire went right up the middle of the aircraft, smashing the cockpit, shattering instruments and windscreen and cutting my face. Then the other engines cut and the kite began rolling out of control.

'I decided to get out, trying to push my way through the window on my port side but found it was extremely difficult. So I opened my parachute inside the aircraft and fed it out through the window. I was suddenly pulled out of the kite like a cork from a bottle. On the way down I saw two other parachutes floating below.'

U–Uncle crashed at 8.15pm near Roermond. Chaster landed heavily in a ploughed field. There was no sign of the other men he had seen parachuting down.

He slept that night in a barn, next morning cautiously approaching the Dutch farmer who was not pleased to see him, understandably concerned about the Gestapo billeted next door. He nevertheless gave the pilot milk, black bread and an old coat.

Chaster began walking west, escaping the attention of Germans guarding a bridge, pretending to be deaf and dumb. The cold ate into his limbs and unable to sleep in a barn that night, he continued his long walk until dusk next day when a farmer let him sleep in a shed, warmed by a fire and a meal, consoled by a decent cigar.

The pilot was swiftly passed into the Cométe escape line's many courageous helpers, who guided him through Belgium and France to the Spanish border. He joined a group near Bayeux and crossed the Pyrénees. After a forgettable sojourn in a Spanish jail he was taken to Madrid, then Gibraltar, sailing to

England in a ship which was lucky to avoid being torpedoed.

Barry Chaster returned to 207 Squadron in March 1943, dismayed that a rapid turnover of personnel meant he hardly knew anyone, but eager to be back on operations. He was told this was impossible. If he was again forced to bale out, then captured, the Germans might persuade him to spill the beans about his contacts in the Resistance. Disappointed, Chaster was posted back to Canada.

Both gunners, the wireless operator and flight engineer aboard U-Uncle all died. Banfield believes Ken Pugh, the wireless operator, was probably killed or badly wounded in the first attack because the petrol fire was blazing beside him. He thinks the others died in the later attacks.

The remains of Pugh, Bill Moger, Ivan Lineker and Wally Harris are buried in Jonkerbos war cemetery at Nijmegen, Holland.

U-Uncle was shot down by the persistent Oberleutnant Manfred Meurer, the commanding officer of his squadron at Venlo. Meurer continued shooting down Allied bombers until January 1944 when his fighter collided with a Lancaster near Magdeburg. Meurer, with a total of sixty-five kills, and his wireless operator, Oberfeldwebel Gerhard Scheibe, were both killed.

John Banfield had been a POW for almost two years at Stalag VIIIb, Lansdorf, Silesia when, after weeks of rumours of advancing Russians, the prisoners were ordered to march out of the camp on 22 January 1945.

'It was bitterly cold, the ground deep in snow as we started marching with no idea of our destination. At 2am, after sixteen miles, we were herded into a barn at Frankenau, utterly exhausted. Next morning I was among those discarding kit to lighten the load I was carrying.

'Trudging through miles of open treeless country on rough frozen roads we were afraid of being strafed by machine guns whenever we heard the sound of aircraft. I marched seven days, three without food and drink, apart from handfuls of snow, dragging my kit, unable to keep up with the column, before feigning sickness and falling out with twenty other chaps at Peterwitz. Here we were left at a farm with an elderly Volksturm guard who obtained a horse and cart and took us to the local hospital, but it had been abandoned.

'Back at the farm the Polish family were short of food but gave us some dehydrated vegetables to boil up for soup in a copper in our room.'

The guard disappeared then, on 30 January a column of haggard POWs arrived from Stalag Luft VII, Bankau. They had an RAMC medical officer who tended the feet of the men at the farm suffering from frostbite. Two short marches got them to Goldberg where they were crammed so tightly into cattle trucks they could not all lie down at the same time. In a nightmare journey of three days, the men were only once allowed off the train to relieve themselves.

Arriving at Stalag IIIA, Luckenwalde, thirty miles south of Berlin, they were bedded down on the bare concrete floors of barracks for a month before bunk beds were installed. Food was scarce.

In the middle of April a spearhead of Russian tanks arrived at Luckenwalde on their way to Berlin. Two days after the end of the war, 100 American lorries came to collect the prisoners but were sent away by the Russians. They had to wait as hostages until 28 May when they were taken to Wittenberg and exchanged for Russian POWs from western Germany.

John Banfield was flown back to England via Halle and Brussels, with plenty of time to plan a future beyond tomorrow.

GLOSSARY

AC2	Aircraftman second class
Ack-ack	Anti-aircraft fire
AFU	Advanced Flying Unit
ARP	Air-raid precaution
ATC	Air Training Corps
AVM	Air vice-marshal
Bf-109/110	Messerschmitt 109 or 110
Coning	An aircraft is trapped in a cone of light from several searchlights
Cookie	4,000lb high-explosive bomb
Drogue	Aircraft-towed targets, used in gunnery practise
Dulag Luft	Interrogation centre at Oberursel, near Frankfurt
DZ	Dropping zone
Elsen	Portable chemical toilet
Emmets	Ants
ETA	Estimated time of arrival
Feldwebel	Sergeant
Funnel	Lights on tapered posts leading aircraft on the runway
FW-190	Focke-Wulf 190
Gardening	Mine-laying from aircraft
Garry	15cwt truck

Gee	Navigational aid from ground transmitters
Gee-H	Pulse radio navigational device for blind bombing
H2S	A radar device reading through darkness and thick cloud, giving a picture of the terrain and places below
HCU	Heavy Conversion Unit
IFF	Identification Friend or Foe radar
ITW	Initial Training Wing
Ju-88	Junkers 88
LAC	Leading aircraftman
LMF	Lack of moral fibre
Maquis	A member of an underground resistance group
MT	Motor transport
Oboe marking	A precise radio bombing system using transmissions from two ground stations
OTU	Operational Training Unit
(P)AFU	(Pilot) Advanced Flying Unit
Perry	The perimeter track around an airfield
Photoflash	Hanging in a flare chute, it was released automatically, timed to go off with the bombs, pinpointing where they struck for the on-board camera.
POW	Prisoner of war
PTI	Physical training instructor
Quisling	A traitor who aids an occupying force. Vidkun Quisling (1887-1945), the pro-Nazi Norwegian leader
RAMC	Royal Army Medical Corps
Red Caps	Military police
R/T	Radio telephone

St Elmo's Fire	Blueish harmless electrical discharge seen on aircraft in stormy weather
SAS	Special Air Services
Scrubbed pilot	He has failed his pilot training course
Second dickey	A pilot on his first operation, flying as second pilot
SOE	Special Operations Executive
Spare bod	Man without a regular crew
Sprog	Anyone lacking experience
TI	Target indicator
Volksturm	German Home Guard
Wanganui flares	Sky marking by pathfinders
Wimpey	Wellington
Window	Bundles of metallic strips dropped to confuse German radar
Wingco	Wing commander
W/T	Wireless transmitter

BIBLIOGRAPHY

Barker, Ralph, *Strike Hard, Strike Sure* (Chatto & Windus, 1963)

Barrymore Halpenny, Bruce, *Action Stations 2. Military airfields of Lincolnshire and the East Midlands* (Patrick Stephens, 1981); *Action Stations 4.Military airfields of Yorkshire* (Patrick Stephens, 1982)

Bowyer, Chaz, *Tales From The Bombers* (William Kimber, 1985)

Bowyer, Michael J. F., *Action Stations. 1 Wartime military airfields of East Anglia 1939-1945* (Patrick Stephens,1979)

Brammer, Derek A., *Thundering Through The Clear Air* (Self-published, 1997)

Chorley, W. R., *RAF Bomber Command Losses of the Second World War, 1943; RAF Bomber Command Losses of the Second World War, 1944; RAF Bomber Command Losses of the Second World War, 1945; Bomber Command Losses, Operational Training Units 1940-1947* (Midland Counties Publications, 1996, 1997, 1998, 2002)

Colville, John, *The Fringes Of Power, Downing Street Diaries 1939-1955* (Hodder and Stoughton, 1985)

Goodwin, Barry and Glynne-Owen, Raymond, *207 Squadron RAF Langar 1942-1943* (The Langar Airfield 207 Squadron Memorial Committee, 1994)

Gunby, David, *Sweeping The Skies, a history of No 40 Squadron, RFC and RAF, 1916 to 1956* (Pentland Press, 1995)

Hammerton, Sir J. A., editor of *The Modern Encyclopedia* (The Amalgamated Press, 1930s)

Holmes, Harry, *Avro Lancaster the Definitive Record*, (Airlife, 1997)

Holyoak,Vincent, *On the Wings of the Morning, RAF Bottesford 1941-1945* (Vincent Holyoak, 1945)

Jane's Fighting Aircraft of World War II (Studio Editions Ltd,1992)

Keegan, John, editor of *The Times Atlas of the Second World War*

(Times Books, 1999 reprint)

Middlebrook, Martin and Everitt, Chris, *The Bomber Command War Diaries* (Viking, 1987 reprint)

Morris, Richard, *Guy Gibson* (Viking, 1994)

Orpen, Neil, *Airlift To Warsaw, The Rising of 1944* (W. Foulsham, 1984)

Otter, Patrick, *Lincolnshire Airfields In The Second World War* (Countryside Books, 1996)

Smith, Graham, *Norfolk Airfields In The Second World War* (Countryside Books, 1999 reprint)

Weal, Elke C., Weal, John A. and Barker, Richard F., *Combat Aircraft of World War Two* (Arms and Armour Press, 1977)

INDEX